# Sobering Wisdom

# Sobering Wisdom

**PHILOSOPHICAL EXPLORATIONS
OF TWELVE STEP SPIRITUALITY**

EDITED BY JEROME A. MILLER
AND NICHOLAS PLANTS

UNIVERSITY OF VIRGINIA PRESS | CHARLOTTESVILLE AND LONDON

University of Virginia Press
© 2014 by the Rector and Visitors of the University of Virginia
All rights reserved
Printed in the United States of America on acid-free paper
*First published 2014*

9 8 7 6 5 4 3 2 1

Library of Congress Cataloging-in-Publication Data
Sobering wisdom : philosophical explorations of twelve step
spirituality / edited by Jerome A. Miller and Nicholas Plants.
    pages cm
  Includes bibliographical references and index.
  ISBN 978-0-8139-3652-9 (cloth : alk. paper)
  ISBN 978-0-8139-3653-6 (pbk. : alk. paper)
  ISBN 978-0-8139-3654-3 (ebook)
  1. Religion — Philosophy. 2. Twelve-step programs — Religious
aspects. I. Miller, Jerome A., 1946–  editor.
  BL51.S6145 2014
  204'.42 — dc23                    2014024549

# Contents

# Preface

The publication of *Sobering Wisdom* happily brings to completion what has been a lengthy but engaging process of development.

Some years ago, our fascination with Twelve Step spirituality prompted us to explore the work done on it by our fellow philosophers. We were surprised to discover that there was very little of it. Convinced that it was important to address this lacuna, we widely distributed a "call for abstracts" inviting philosophers to address any aspect of Twelve Step spirituality that they found to be of interest, and to do so from any philosophical point of view that they found helpful. As we emphasized when issuing this "call," our hope was to publish an anthology of essays that would be both philosophically compelling and accessible to a wide readership.

Philosophers of many different persuasions from a wide array of countries responded to this call. From the plethora of abstracts we received, we chose contributors whose exploration of Twelve Step spirituality promised to be fresh, provocative, and illuminating. The contributors we chose proved to be especially patient and generous collaborators. While their essays testify to a remarkable diversity of viewpoint, each of them, in its own distinctive way, has helped us to realize our original purpose of fostering conversation between philosophy and Twelve Step spirituality. We hope that both professional and lay readers of this book will be drawn to continue this important conversation.

# Thanks Giving

We would like to thank our contributors for their commitment to the project and the painstaking work they have done to bring it to such a fruitful completion. Collaborating with them has been a privilege and a joy.

We are deeply grateful to Cathie Brettschneider, Humanities Editor, University of Virginia Press, whose vision, judgment, and kindness helped to sustain us. Her receptivity to innovative work is invaluable—and rare. We also thank Ellen Satrom, Mark Mones, Raennah Mitchell, and the staff of the Press; Colleen Romick Clark, our copyeditor; and Tina Melczarek from the Philosophy Department at Salisbury University. All of them helped remedy our inadequacies.

In this, as in all matters, we've been blessed by the graceful, abiding love of our spouses, Cathy Miller and Larissa Plants; their patience has been unfailing. We give very special thanks to Zoe Plants, who has been a daily source of brightness.

We dedicate this book to all those participating in Twelve Step programs, in gratitude for their inspiration, and to all those struggling to find a way beyond addiction, in gratitude for their courage.

Jerome A. Miller
Nicholas Plants

# Sobering Wisdom

1. We admitted we were powerless over alcohol—that our lives had become unmanageable.

2. Came to believe that a Power greater than ourselves could restore us to sanity.

3. Made a decision to turn our will and our lives over to the care of God *as we understood Him.*

4. Made a searching and fearless moral inventory of ourselves.

5. Admitted to God, to ourselves, and to another human being the exact nature of our wrongs.

6. Were entirely ready to have God remove all these defects of character.

7. Humbly asked Him to remove our shortcomings.

8. Made a list of all persons we had harmed, and became willing to make amends to them all.

9. Made direct amends to such people wherever possible, except when to do so would injure them or others.

10. Continued to take personal inventory and when we were wrong promptly admitted it.

11. Sought through prayer and meditation to improve our conscious contact with God *as we understood Him,* praying only for knowledge of His will for us and the power to carry that out.

12. Having had a spiritual awakening as the result of these steps, we tried to carry this message to alcoholics and to practice these principles in all our affairs.

Source: *Alcoholics Anonymous,* 59

# A Meeting Place for Philosophy and Twelve Step Spirituality

All real living is meeting.
—Martin Buber, *I and Thou*

Imagine a meeting scheduled for seven o'clock on a wintry Wednesday evening in a small Kansas town. Although some urgent political or economic cause might motivate potential attendees to brave cold weather and bad roads, this meeting has a very different purpose. Those present will be invited to admit their powerlessness, to address deeply personal, painful issues, and to acknowledge their need to be transformed. Given such an agenda, it wouldn't be surprising if no one came. But, in all likelihood, some people *will* come—and not just to this meeting in the American heartland. They'll show up at similar meetings in Tokyo and Paris, Moscow and Calgary, Buenos Aires and Cape Town, even though no celebrity spokespersons publicize them and no newspaper or television station reports on them. People have been showing up at such meetings for over seventy-five years now. This is a documentable historical fact. It is also an unprecedented historical phenomenon.

Bill Wilson and Dr. Bob Smith founded the first Alcoholics Anonymous fellowship in Akron, Ohio, in 1935. As AA has grown in size and geographical breadth, the Twelve Step spirituality on which it is based has been adopted by a wide array of kindred fellowships, including Narcotics Anonymous, Al-Anon (for relatives and friends of alcoholics), Overeaters Anonymous, Codependents Anonymous, Adult Children of Alcoholics, Gamblers Anonymous, and Sex and Love Addicts Anonymous. Although there is no elaborate institutional structure that sustains these fellowships, the spirituality they practice has profoundly affected millions of people throughout the world. So it is not surprising that a variety of academic disciplines, including psychology, sociology, and the health sciences, have studied the Twelve Step program of recovery.[1] Philosophers, however, have not as yet paid much attention to it. In fact, we know of no work other than the one you now have in your hands that is primarily devoted to examining this spirituality philosophically.[2] This lack of dialogue is, we believe, unfortunate. For in a number of crucial respects that we will now try to explain, philosophy and Twelve Step spirituality have a profound affinity for each other, even though professional philosophers have been slow to recognize it.

Begin with the fact that both philosophy and Twelve Step spirituality address fundamental questions about the meaning and purpose of our lives. Both focus intently on existential issues that profoundly impact our being as a whole. Indeed, they challenge us to engage in rigorous self-examination—to question deeply ingrained assumptions on which we habitually rely and deeply ingrained habits that we assume cannot be broken. Each can radically enhance our self-awareness and profoundly broaden the horizon of meaning within which we operate. The process of philosophizing and the process of practicing Twelve Step spirituality do not just have the potential to change some part of ourselves or some part of our lives. They have the potential to change how we experience and think about *everything*.

The issues that philosophy and Twelve Step spirituality address—issues relating to freedom, God, authenticity, morality—cannot be addressed by sciences that use empirical methods and depend on quantitative data. Existential meaning and moral value are not factual matters like the chemistry of alcohol or the diagnosis of liver diseases, and for this reason it is sometimes thought that reason cannot be used to explore questions relating to them. Some would say that we should rely on religious faith and defer to religious authority when considering these matters. But philosophy and Twelve Step spirituality alike insist that human intelligence itself can give us insight into them. Philosophy, unlike theology, does not presuppose acceptance of any religious belief or operate inside the doctrinal framework of any religious tradition. The claims it makes are supposed to be accessible to intelligence and plausible to reason.[3] As for Twelve Step spirituality, the founding members of AA who developed it were careful not to wed it to any particular creed, religious institution, or theological system, even though some of them were affiliated with Christian groups. They did not hesitate to draw upon the stories, insights, and linguistic resources of the great religious traditions but did not identify Twelve Step spirituality with any of them. As Twelve Step fellowships have grown and diversified, this independence from religious affiliation has been vigilantly maintained.

In fact, nothing testifies more eloquently to the profound influence that the Twelve Step movement has had on our culture than the now widespread acceptance of the distinction it makes between spirituality and religion. The cultivation of spirituality independent of religion is, of course, not entirely new in the history of American culture. To cite one important example, the Transcendentalism of Emerson and Thoreau was saturated with spiritual import even though it was nondenominational and not bound to any traditional doctrinal framework. But the emergence and sustained existence of fellowships committed to practicing spirituality independently of religious institutions is historically unprecedented. Nothing quite like it has happened before. Moreover, the distinction the Twelve Step program makes between spirituality and religion isn't merely conceptual. It directly informs and shapes the lived experience of the Twelve Step process.[4]

Precisely because it distinguishes spirituality from religion, the Twelve Step enterprise has resonated with the pluralistic, largely secular society in which it has developed. As secularity and pluralism became ascendant in twentieth-century America, culture as a whole became less dependent on, and less deferential to, religious traditions, particularly Christianity. The genius of Twelve Step spirituality lay in its ability to provide those living in this secularized culture a way to address their longing for meaning without having to adhere to a particular religious faith or defined theology. The process of profound personal transformation that the Twelve Steps set in motion suggests that spirituality is a distinctive human capacity with its own unique logic, its own compelling exigencies, its own evolutionary process of growth and maturation.

Participation in this evolutionary process can and sometimes does lead Twelve Step participants to engage in philosophical reflection. We do *not* infer from this that the practice of the Twelve Steps *requires* philosophizing. This spirituality itself and the guidance provided by its official literature can be profoundly efficacious without the help of philosophy. But while Twelve Step practice is distinct from and different from philosophical thinking, it does require one to engage in rigorous, often painfully honest self-reflection. It encourages one to become thoughtfully exploratory, to carefully consider basic questions about how one ought to live, and to make a judgment about which values and convictions one should embrace. As performed by the Twelve Step participant, this process of self-reflection is not just deeply personal. It's vigorously practical. Nevertheless, it has the potential to provoke questions that are relevant not only to oneself but to *everyone*—a kind of questioning that has *universal* import. This shift from the particular to the general, from the concrete to the abstract, from the practical to the intellectual is the shift to philosophizing.[5] Some Twelve Step practitioners find themselves making it.

However, in the official literature of Twelve Step spirituality, one does not find much evidence of a shift to philosophical theorizing. This literature does not typically employ philosophical concepts or terms. It relies on common-sense meanings, not theoretical abstractions. It uses ordinary language and avoids intellectual discourse. The history of other spiritual traditions suggests that this is not at all unusual: when it comes to spirituality, the theoretical exercise of intelligence is usually, if not always, a latecomer. When it first emerges, spirituality typically relies on story, proverb, poetry, myth. The great, paradigmatic texts of the wisdom traditions speak in paradox and parable, and never venture far from the concrete particularities of lived experience. So it has been with the Twelve Step enterprise. Its stories and "slogans" have direct, existential resonance. They make its insights accessible without compromising their profundity. Both the uneducated and the academically trained can find these insights transformative. Twelve Step spirituality is a great leveler, like the addictions to which it responds. "Keep it simple, Stupid" is now one of its well-established imperatives. Those who have followed it have been led by it to the same inexhaustible simplicities: a recognition of our powerlessness and an openness to what is beyond us.

But precisely because stories, proverbs, and parables are powerful catalysts of spiritual awakening, they can provoke one to ask the kind of question that story, proverb, and parable cannot answer. Intelligence is part of the whole person that Twelve Step spirituality is meant to engage. And there is always latent in intelligence a longing for deeper understanding, richer insight, more profound illumination. In every spiritual tradition, this intellectual exigence sooner or later becomes implacable.[6] Neither Buddha nor Jesus was an intellectual. But thinkers trying to cultivate Buddhist and Christian wisdom were led to ask intellectual questions, search for intellectual insight, and develop a language for intellectual exchange. "Keep it simple" is profoundly wise counsel. But the great simplicities of the spirit are not simplistic. All the logical, interpretative, and rhetorical skills of intellect and reason are needed to appreciate and articulate their meaning. For this reason, intellectual exploration can itself become a spiritual exigence. *The actual practice of Twelve Step spirituality can spur one to engage in a philosophical exploration of it.*

Philosophically exploring Twelve Step spirituality differs fundamentally from other ways of intellectually examining issues related to addiction and recovery. Biochemistry can, of course, help us understand the neurological conditions that may predispose one to addiction. Psychological research, especially by clinicians, can provide insight into the therapeutic usefulness of Twelve Step programs and can help to assess its strengths and weaknesses as a treatment strategy. Sociologists can investigate how social forces lead to addiction and condition recovery. Historians of Twelve Step programs can provide insight into their origins, evolution, and relationship to other spiritual movements.[7] But these disciplines aren't equipped to examine the *meaning* of the Twelve Steps themselves. They can't explore the intelligibility and rationality of Twelve Step principles or clarify the connections between its various claims. These are tasks that philosophy is uniquely qualified to undertake. By virtue of its capacity to reflect on our lived experience, it can illuminate the meaning the Twelve Steps have for those who perform them. It can unearth the import latent in the commonsense descriptions of the Steps and try to plumb the uncanny paradoxes that lie at the heart of it. It may be able to uncover profundities in it that customary interpretations of it fail to appreciate.

A concern for profundities of meaning is primal to both philosophy and Twelve Step spirituality and gives them a family resemblance. Philosophy tries to rupture our commonsense conceits; Twelve Step spirituality tries to free us from our enslavements. Philosophy encourages us to let go of our presumptions; Twelve Step spirituality encourages us to "hit bottom" and acknowledge our powerlessness. But both deflate us in order to spring a liberating irony on us: they try to throw us open to the possibility that there is *more* to reality than our assumptions and addictions allow us to access. The profound affinity between them derives from the conviction, implicit in the practice of both, that our reach for deeper meaning and higher purpose isn't foolish. It's the beginning of wisdom.

Given this profound affinity, one can't help but wonder why Twelve Step spirituality and philosophy have been slow, perhaps even reluctant, to develop a relationship.

From the point of view of Twelve Step spirituality, the pivot from the particular to the universal, the practical to the intellectual, that philosophizing involves can pose a real danger. For as Kierkegaard, himself both a philosopher and a practitioner of spirituality, repeatedly and pointedly reminds us, one may be tempted to make this shift for the purpose of *escaping* one's own torturous interiority.[8] Unlike the kind of self-reflection required by the Twelve Steps, philosophical theorizing can be a subtle—hence an extremely effective—way to *disassociate from* one's self. Such disassociation aborts spirituality instead of adding an intellectual dimension to it. To be real, spirituality has to be lived in the first person singular. It has to start with *me*. One can't do the Steps in one's head. One has to allow one's being as a whole to be moved by them.

The danger that philosophizing might subvert the deeply personal, profoundly existential practice of Twelve Step spirituality is exacerbated by the fact that, today, philosophy is typically practiced as a highly professionalized academic discipline. Written in a technical idiom by and often exclusively for the professorate, academic philosophy tends to be a highly abstract cognitive enterprise. Moreover, spirituality is rarely included in its syllabus of concerns. This is understandable, given the fact that spirituality has long been identified with religious traditions from which philosophy, in its quest for autonomy, had to distance itself. The fact that contemporary culture, under the influence of Twelve Step programs, *distinguishes* spirituality from religion has not as yet moved many philosophers to alter their conception of it.

Philosophers *have,* however, become quite attentive to the phenomenon of addiction over the course of the last twenty-five years. This has required them to grapple with the paradoxes of "weak will" that Aristotle[9] was the first to consider. The weak-willed individual seems to be both responsible for his or her appetitive habits and helpless in the face of them. Contemporary philosophers tend to pose the issue this way: Is addiction a disease or a moral deficiency? In developing their response to this dilemma, philosophers have adverted—sometimes sympathetically, sometimes critically—to the Twelve Step approach to the issue.[10] But as Ernst Kurtz, the distinguished historian of Alcoholics Anonymous, has documented, the Twelve Step view has always been that if alcoholism—and, by implication, addiction more generally—*is* a disease, the disease is *spiritual* in nature.[11] Not surprisingly, philosophers such as Francis Seeburger and Kent Dunnington who recognize the impact that addiction has on the *whole* person[12] have a perspicacious appreciation of this Twelve Step conception of it. Their studies imply that because addiction is a spiritual phenomenon, philosophers will have to develop a philosophy of spirituality to understand it.

Acclimated as we are to thinking of it as an academic discipline, we might find the conjunction of "philosophy" with "spirituality" problematic, perhaps even oxymoronic. But philosophy has not always been identified with a scholastic specialty, and there is no reason to assume that philosophizing must have an exclusively academic purpose. Pierre Hadot's studies[13] of the ancients have shown that, for them, philosophy was *a way of living,* a way of being and acting—in short, a kind of spirituality. Philosophical exploration engaged the whole person and opened one to the possibility of living in the world mindfully. Much of what Hadot says of the ancients can also be said of the American Transcendentalists. As Stanley Cavell has explained,[14] the fact that they did not write as academicians does not mean they weren't philosophers. It means that, for them, philosophy was not merely an academic exercise; it was a way of living in attunement with what ultimately matters. It may be that, if philosophy is to develop an understanding of spirituality, it must reawaken to its own spiritual import.

It seems, then, that a meeting of philosophy and Twelve Step spirituality has the potential to be mutually enriching. Philosophizing can illuminate the profundities of Twelve Step practice by addressing the questions it provokes, exploring the insights on which it is based, and sorting out the confusions it sometimes engenders. It can help us unpack the meaning hidden in Twelve Step paradoxes and latent in Twelve Step stories. It can make more patient and thoughtful the debates we have with ourselves and each other about how best to respond to our impotence and fallibilities, our regrets and despairs, our inescapable griefs and undeniable longings. We don't mean to imply that philosophy can solve the mysteries of the spirit. But it can lead us deeper into them.

For its part, Twelve Step spirituality can reinvigorate philosophy by encouraging it to return to the kind of deeply personal process of self-examination that Socratic questioning was meant to provoke. The Twelve Step practitioner provides us a model of interiority. When she asks whether there exists a power greater than her compulsions, whether there is a meaning that can fill the void left by her addictions, whether being true to herself requires succumbing to her drives or transcending them, she's raising issues that are charged with philosophical import. But, in her view, they're not academic matters. They're matters of life and death. Appreciating their philosophical significance can enable one to realize their universal relevance, without in any way diminishing their existential resonance. In the ancient world, those willing to explore, both existentially and intellectually, such upsetting, gut-wrenching questions were called lovers of wisdom.

In our epoch of professionalized scholarship, developing wisdom is not often associated with "doing philosophy." But only a philosophical exercise of intellect can cultivate it. For, as Aristotle explained, what distinguishes wisdom from other kinds of intellectual excellence is its capacity to integrate—its capacity to see life as a meaningful *whole*.[15] A dialogue with Twelve Step spirituality can help reawaken in philosophy its original passion for meaningful, mindful wholeness. A dialogue with philosophy can enliven Twelve Step spirituality by integrating intelligence more actively into it. The meeting may begin awkwardly, but it has the potential to engender a conversation that is at once intellectually illuminating and existentially gripping.

In our brief description of a Twelve Step meeting at the beginning of this introduction, we left one of its most significant traits unmentioned. Twelve Step fellowships are deeply democratic in spirit. "Anonymity" doesn't just mean that last names aren't to be used. It means that social, economic, and educational distinctions don't matter. There are no Twelve Step officers or avenues for advancement. There is instead a shared sense of fallibility and ignorance before inexhaustible mysteries.

Usually, at the beginning of a Twelve Step meeting, a speaker who has volunteered to do so beforehand sounds the issue or theme that will be its focus, and those present are invited (not required) to improvise on it. In this respect, a Twelve Step fellowship is similar to the jazz ensemble, another unprecedented creation of democratic culture. In both, the individual is encouraged to solo—to speak in his or her singular, inimitable voice. But the solo is evoked by and contributes to an ongoing conversation. Each person has the opportunity to add his or her inimitable voice to the whole that the assembled members of the group are creating.

Much the same holds true for this anthology of essays about Twelve Step spirituality. Each of us contributing to it has his or her own distinctive sense of how best to meet the exigencies that move us to philosophize. Indeed, each of us is inclined to define rationality in a way that is inextricably tied to the philosophical positions we have adopted. Among us philosophers, agreement is rare and differences flourish. While scientists also have their serious disputes, they rarely concern the scientific method itself. But in philosophy, where even basic assumptions are questioned, method is itself subject to challenge, and there is no authority, no meta-viewpoint, no recognized principle of adjudication, that can be used to resolve the contention that ensues. This is especially true of philosophy in our pluralistic, post-structural age, where there are many different, but no privileged, conceptions of rationality, and many philosophical methodologies, all of which are historically conditioned and subject to human fallibilities.

This anthology reflects the postmodern historical context in which it has been created. Our contributors draw upon an array of different methodologies and represent a wide range of European, Asian, and American philosophies. Some of our authors proceed analytically, in accord with the mode of philosophizing now dominant in English-speaking countries; they concentrate on a particular concept or conceptual problem in the hope of reaching a more richly nuanced understanding of it than common sense can provide. Others proceed phenomenologically: they attempt to describe the nature of lived experience from the point of view of the person engaged in it. Some contributors find in a particular philosophical tradition or ancient text a perspective that helps shed light on Twelve Step principles and practices. Others are influenced by the insights and viewpoints of recent philosophers whose provocative originality has opened new paths of thought.

As we've said, this diversity is similar to what one encounters at a Twelve Step meeting, where each contribution to the conversation reflects the unique experience, history, and attitude of the speaker. Here, as there, one might expect such diversity to produce only a cacophony of voices, each with its own sense of rhythm and reason. In our postmodern age especially, dissonance is often the impression produced by gatherings of philosophers. But we believe the reader will find here something subtly but significantly different— something that is also similar to what one finds at Twelve Step meetings: a unifying passion that animates the diversity. The philosophers who have contributed to this anthology employ different perspectives and speak in a variety of philosophical languages. But all of us are drawn to venture beyond the exclusively academic boundaries that often inhibit philosophizing in order to explore, and perhaps shed some light on, what the spiritual life entails.

In fact, one of the most striking and perhaps surprising features of this anthology is that it demonstrates how thinkers with profoundly different worldviews can come to recognize that spirituality is deeply meaningful and even indispensable to human flourishing. Included among our contributors are not only theists but also naturalists inclined toward agnosticism and atheism; admirers of Stoic, Confucian, and Buddhist sages; and thinkers deeply influenced by Nietzsche, existentialism, and postmodernism. Because of their different methods and metaphysical orientations, our authors develop quite different interpretations of what spirituality means. They offer different paradigms of spiritual excellence and employ different concepts to explore what spiritual development entails. But all of them share the conviction that spirituality is deeply human and profoundly important. That there exists such a consensus among philosophers whose views are otherwise so different and even incompatible is quite remarkable. Their essays can help to free us from a narrow conception of spirituality and from the questionable assumptions we often make about it.

Indeed, the diverse approaches to spirituality collected here suggest that spirituality not only is compatible with but also requires a multiplicity of perspectives. When we address spirituality, diversity of viewpoint may be more than an inescapable feature of our emerging global culture; it may be a prerequisite of philosophical perspicacity. For the wisdom to which philosophy and spirituality both aspire requires insight into human life as a whole—and that whole is a complex unity of many aspects and dimensions to which only a multiplicity of perspectives can give us access. What philosophy and the spiritual life alike require is not a uniform approach but nuance and lucidity, heightened self-awareness and humble probity, careful expression and judicious assessment. What the essays in this anthology have in common is a determination to *bring thought to life* in both senses of the phrase—a determination to enliven thought by bringing it into relationship with the lived experience of Twelve Step spirituality, *and* a determination to enrich these experiences by bringing to them a rigorous philosophical thoughtfulness. For the reader, this anthology is meant to be a provocation to wisdom—a catalyst for lively thought and thoughtful living.

As the cumulative effect of the essays in this volume makes clear, the Twelve Steps themselves are distinct but not separate from each other: performed consistently over time, they can reshape one's life into a dynamic whole. With this whole in mind, we have arranged the essays in a sequence that will, we hope, illuminate the logic of the Steps as it gradually unfolds in and through the practitioner's performance of them.

We begin, as the Steps do, with the recognition that addiction renders one powerless. Included in this first section are essays that explore the paradox of addiction mentioned above; but they do so from the viewpoint of the Twelve Step experience and Twelve Step insights. Acknowledging powerlessness is the hinge on which the entire Twelve Step program of recovery depends. Given its pivotal and controversial character, we think it especially crucial to shed philosophical light on it. The first two essays in this section address the issue directly. The third and fourth explore the vulnerability that makes us susceptible to addiction—and also capable of recovering from it.

Once addiction is acknowledged, Twelve Step spirituality would have us turn to a "higher power." If Step One is its hinge, Steps Two and Three constitute the turning point of Twelve Step spirituality as a whole and probably the most controversial of its recommendations. Our second group of essays tackles the question of what this turn entails. Two of our authors emphasize that this issue is a testing ground for the program's avowed openness to diverse viewpoints. The essayists in this section themselves represent such diversity. While they don't all agree about the nature of the "higher power" to which the Steps would have us turn, they agree that the authenticity of the turn itself is crucial.

It's appropriate, then, that the third group of essays attempts to plumb the critical role that authenticity plays in recovery. Philosophers have frequently remarked on the uncanny fact that even though we *are* our selves, *knowing* our selves and being true to our selves can be exceptionally difficult. Addiction adds to what is already a very arduous task an entirely new layer of daunting complexity and harrowing confusion. The essays in this section don't pretend to solve the paradoxes of the addictive self. But they do help to deepen our appreciation of these paradoxes. And while there are some serious disagreements among the authors in this section, all of them share the conviction that being one's self requires entering into a thoughtful relationship with one's self.

The fourth section of the anthology is devoted to one of the deep paradoxes that govern the Twelve Step approach to selfhood, namely, the conviction that being one's self *requires* connecting with others. Twelve Step spirituality insists that recovery isn't a solitary achievement. The essays in this section attempt to lay out the logic underlying this conviction, and try to show how various Twelve Step traditions, including the sponsor-sponsee relationship, put it into action.

Finally, in the fifth section of the book, we consider the overall impact that the Twelve Steps can have on one's life. To describe and explain this impact, the first two essayists draw upon traditions of moral philosophy that describe the good life as the practice of virtue and emphasize the importance of practical wisdom. The final essay puts flesh on the skeleton of recovery by showing the crucial role that gratitude plays in it. All the essays in this section breathe new life into the philosophical discourse on character.

Since all of us share the hope that the essays collected here will be read by individuals interested in the Twelve Steps in particular and spirituality in general, we have worked diligently to make them accessible to those without advanced philosophical training. On occasion, a somewhat specialized philosophical idiom is employed to communicate insights that ordinary language cannot effectively convey. But even when such an idiom is used, we do our best to keep our philosophizing close to lived spiritual experience. As happens in every conversation about mortally serious and difficult matters, this one will prompt those listening to it to occasionally ask, "What do you mean?" and to occasionally exclaim, "I disagree!" This is one of the reasons why our book is only a beginning.

One great poet, composing a eulogy for another in dark times, wrote these still relevant and compelling words: "In the deserts of the heart / Let the healing fountain start."[16] Philosophy and Twelve Step spirituality are fed, we believe, by the same spring. It runs in each of us, though often so far underground that we're oblivious to it. We hope this book will help those who read it come a bit closer to the source.

NOTES

1. We should also mention the interdisciplinary field of addiction studies.

2. *The Spirituality of Imperfection,* the wonderfully insightful work by Kurtz and Ketcham, does begin to explore the philosophical import of the Twelve Steps. But it relies heavily on narratives drawn from various spiritual traditions and does not try to develop a full-fledged philosophical articulation of pivotal Twelve Step concepts.

We should also take note of the efforts that have been made to connect the Twelve Steps to particular religious traditions such as Buddhism and Christianity, since these efforts often involve some philosophical exploration. See, for example, Griffin, *One Breath at a Time,* and Rohr, *Breathing under Water.*

3. Even Jacques Derrida and Emmanuel Levinas rely on intelligence and rationality in their attempt to persuade their readers to recognize the inescapable limits of these powers. See Derrida, *Writing and Difference,* 280–81.

4. While we mean to emphasize that Twelve Step practices do not have a religious dimension, we do not at all mean to imply that these practices cannot be fully integrated into a religious life; one can do so without in any way falsifying either the practices or the religion.

5. In saying this, we do not mean to associate philosophy with the conception of universality espoused by the Western Enlightenment. We mean only to emphasize that philosophizing involves theorizing in a way that exclusively personal self-reflection does not.

6. Here we are drawing on the distinction Bernard Lonergan makes between "the world mediated by common-sense meaning" and "the world mediated by systematic meaning." See Lonergan, *Method in Theology*, 304.

7. See Kurtz, *Not-God;* Travis, *Language of the Heart;* and White, *Slaying the Dragon.*

8. See, for example, "The Task of Becoming Subjective," in Kierkegaard, *Concluding Unscientific Postscript.*

9. See the discussion of *akrasia* in book 7 of the *Nichomachean Ethics.*

10. We will mention some of the noteworthy work that has been done and indicate its relevance, if any, to Twelve Step spirituality.

Herbert Fingarette's attack on the disease concept of alcoholism in *Heavy Drinking* in the late 1980s precipitated much controversy. While Fingarette is a philosopher, his book was largely a review of the scientific literature on addiction at the time of its writing. He presents a very brief (and highly stereotyped) description of AA and appears to be unaware of the fact that AA literature describes alcoholism as a spiritual, not a biological, disease.

Bruce Wilshire's *Wild Hunger* traces modern addiction to the loss of an ecstatic relationship with nature. His book devotes only a few paragraphs to Twelve Step spirituality. In *Addiction and Responsibility,* Francis Seeburger develops an existential theory of addiction that is very consonant with the Twelve Step understanding of it. While he adverts to the Twelve Steps, he develops his own Buddhist-based conception of recovery. The Poland/Graham interdisciplinary anthology, also entitled *Addiction and Responsibility,* contains a few philosophical articles, including Nancy Potter's "Grounding for Understanding Self-Injury as Addiction or (Bad) Habit," which criticizes the "master narrative" (202) of AA, and Richard Garrett's "Addiction, Paradox, and the Good I Would," which testifies to the assistance Twelve Step spirituality can provide to addicts. The latter contains a brief but nuanced description of the Twelve Step view of addiction. Finally, Kent Dunnington's *Addiction and Virtue* uses Aristotle's theory of incontinence and Aquinas's theory of virtue to develop an explanation of addiction that takes into account the role that both choice and compulsion play in it. Dunnington is deeply respectful of Twelve Step spirituality and often draws upon it to support his analysis, although he offers criticism of it once his theorizing takes a theological turn.

11. Kurtz, "Alcoholics Anonymous and the Disease Concept of Alcoholism," *Alcoholism Treatment Quarterly* 20, nos. 3/4 (2002): 5–39. With regard to the question of

whether alcoholism is a disease, Kurtz insists that AA simply has no opinion. On the few occasions when AA literature uses the concept, it does so for the purpose of communicating the fact that addiction is a compulsion over which the addict is powerless.

12. Seeburger's language is existential rather than spiritual, but his entire analysis is focused on the whole person and the primacy of meaning in human life.

13. See Hadot, *Philosophy as a Way of Life* and *The Present Alone Is Our Happiness.*

14. See, for example, Cavell, *Quest of the Ordinary.*

15. Aristotle, *Nichomachean Ethics,* 1140a–1140b.

16. W. H. Auden, "In Memory of W. B. Yeats."

# PART ONE

# Facing Powerlessness, Experiencing Empowerment

J. JEREMY WISNEWSKI

# Being Powerless to Change
## The Wisdom of the First Step

STEP ONE: We recognized that we were powerless over our addiction—that our lives had become unmanageable.

> It is very fitting that this collection begins with Jeremy Wisnewski's philosophical reflections on his own ordeal of addiction and the breakthrough made possible by his acknowledgment of it. Drawing on the work of Martin Heidegger, the great twentieth-century German thinker, Wisnewski describes the "world" of addiction phenomenologically: he helps us see it "from the inside"—from the addict's own perspective. This approach enables him to show how taking the First Step is an excruciating struggle. But it is also an opening to possibility, as Wisnewski, with an assist from the American pragmatist William James, explains. This is the first of our many encounters with Twelve Step paradoxes.

There are times when there is nothing else in the world. Everything points either to it or away from it. It is the color spectrum that allows you to see the bright and the dull. That is the core truth of addiction.

To be addicted is to live in a world colored by one's object of addiction—it appears everywhere, in everything, behind each emotion, before each decision. Addiction comes in myriad forms, but these forms seem to share a common structure: addiction organizes one's entire existence—it is the force around which a life comes to orbit. It defines how one sees one's possibilities, one's potential actions, and even one's relationship with others. Every addiction has its own peaks and valleys—and each object of addiction displays things in its own unique way. Some addictions are not as disruptive or chaotic as others—but they all *organize* things, highlighting what's important and what is merely incidental.

Addiction is an imperialist. It colonizes every aspect of a life. In the most severe cases, nothing remains untouched. Addiction is not content to stay in its own arena, happily consuming its object when possible. It must reach out—it must become the center—and it will take a backseat to nothing. This is why, for the addict, to give up the addiction is not a simple matter. Everything must change. The center must be found again. This is why, for the addict, a world without the object of addiction is an almost unintelligible world—a distant shore, a greener pasture.

The addict is powerless over his addiction. He *is* his addiction. It demarcates the boundaries of his experience, of what is intelligible and what is not. To begin to overcome addiction requires seeing this, and all that it means: to know one is addicted is to know that there is nothing one can do—that one's entire world is owned by a substance, and indeed exhausted by it.

And herein lies the essential irony of addiction, as well as the wisdom of the First Step: it is only by recognizing that one is no longer in control—that one lives under the thumb of a tyrant—that one can begin to find the world again.

## Addicted Phenomenology: The World of the Addict

I have been a recreational drug user for most of my life. I first went to a drug rehabilitation institution when I was thirteen years old. I went again at fifteen. Most of my drug use has involved fairly common substances—alcohol and marijuana. There have been periods, however, when my drugs of choice were on the harder side: LSD, PCP, and hydrocodone have all been central features of my life at various times. Indeed, it might be more accurate to say they *were* my life.

In each of my addictions, I found a similar situation: my life became organized around my addiction. The actions that were most palatable were those that allowed me to indulge my habits, regardless of what other values I once had. I have lied to and stolen from family members, all the while claiming to love them and to recognize the importance of honesty. I have tried to deceive doctors in order to get prescriptions. I have sold things of great value—even if they did not belong to me—just to get the money needed for my immediate gratification. The values the addict once held most dear are soon eclipsed by the immediate needs that constitute the addict's world.

The world of the addict is a world of consumption and subterfuge. Addiction doesn't simply make one do one's drug of choice with more frequency—though it certainly does that; it also changes the way one understands and feels about more run-of-the-mill activities. Life is organized around opportunities for use, or around the creation of such opportunities. The most disturbing thing about the addict's behavior is not simply what he will do. While I am now disturbed by my own past actions, I am far more disturbed by the fact that these actions seemed *necessary,* even *right,* at the time I decided to do them. Addiction doesn't simply lead you to do things you regard as unacceptable; it changes what you count as acceptable in the first place. Addiction doesn't just alter our actions; it alters how we *perceive* actions in general.

Addictive behavior constitutes the world of the addict. A "world," in the phenomenological sense of the term, is the context within which one acts—a context that defines what matters and that makes certain courses of action stand out above others. When the philosopher Martin Heidegger says that human beings are "being-in-the-world," this is exactly what he has in mind.[1] To be human is to exist within a context that organizes our activities and gives sense to our lives. For the most part, the world we occupy is a familiar and intelligible one, and this familiarity and intelligibility make it possible for us to act with the fluidity that accompanies normal activity.

The addict's world has a distinct character, but it too is a structural whole like the world of the non-addict. In everyday language, we speak of "the world of business," "the world of fashion," and "the entertainment world." Such phrases capture, albeit crudely, Heidegger's central idea: to be in a world is to be absorbed in it—to experience certain things as important, and others as not. In the business world, for example, the importance of profit and loss stands out in a way that it does not in the world of concern captured by the word "poetry." Worlds organize experience, make them intelligible, and accentuate certain things over others.

In an important sense, then, we live in different worlds—but this should not be exaggerated. As Heidegger argues, our being is a "being-with" (*Mitsein*); our world is a with-world (*Mitwelt*).[2] In watching the Olympics, to take an easy example, one sees precisely how much is shared. The space of concerns that motivate the Olympian is worlds away from my own concerns, but I am able to understand it—to inhabit it vicariously, as it were. As I watch gymnasts, I am quickly brought to see precisely those things that are of concern to the gymnast: the slight bounce of a landing, the grace of a motion, the need to get every movement exactly right without appearing stiff or inelegant. The "world of the athlete," in other words, is not my own, but it is one I can understand and, indeed, one I can appreciate.

To talk of the "world of the addict," then, is not to talk of a world totally unintelligible to the non-addict. In many ways, the non-addict understands implicitly what the addict's world is like: it has a central element (the object of addiction) that makes certain actions more apparent than others, that organizes one's time, and that constitutes the addict's sense of what's important. In a fundamental respect, then, the world of an addict is like the world most of us inhabit: for some, a career makes our actions intelligible and gives us a sense of what's important; for others, one's family centers things; for still others, it is athletic accomplishment, or music, or food.

But for all the structural similarity, the world of the addict is not *identical* to the world of the non-addict. In addiction, there can be no happy balance between one's addictive behavior and other activities. While one can have a successful career and also a wonderful relationship with one's family, occupying the domestic and the commercial world successively and with equal dedication, addiction will not be made to play second fiddle. In addiction at its worst, every other care and concern is subordinated to a central obsession: consumption of the object of addiction. Indeed, the intelligibility of other things becomes indexed to what one craves: one works *in order to* have money to use; one's relationships become a means to fulfilling one's desires—a source of support for one's habits, whether the support be financial, emotional, or even spatial (after all, one must use somewhere).

Addiction comes in many forms, and I have no desire to be overly reductionist. My addiction to hydrocodone was of a remarkably different character than my addiction to PCP: the urges in PCP were stronger; the situation seemed more desperate. I did more that I regret to satisfy the addiction. Physical addiction may well influence and shape an addict's world in ways we may not find in psychological addiction. Similarly, addiction to legal substances (as opposed to illegal ones) may change certain features of one's phenomenological world simply by virtue of the social milieu in which one acts. These are important differences, but they should not be allowed to mask an underlying similarity: to be addicted to something is to understand oneself, and everything around one, in a particular way—it is to inhabit a world where satisfying one's addiction occupies a central position, eclipsing other ways of acting, other values, and, indeed, other worlds. For the addict, we might even say, the world he finds himself in is not even *his* world—he lives only to serve his master, in a world that makes him powerless to do otherwise. The addict finds himself thrown into a world he never directly chose, constituted by desires and values that he does not necessarily want to have, and powerless to change that world without losing the very things that allow him to understand himself as he does.

## Addicted Logic: The Decision to Quit

And then things become too much to bear. One recognizes, at a distance, that one's addiction is out of control. Small events become opportunities to engage in one's addiction: a trip to the grocery store is a chance to get high in the car without having to explain one's need to get high; a social evening becomes a reason to partake in one's substance of choice—after all, this *just is what I do* to relax. A bit of stress becomes an excuse—I work so hard, I deserve a break. It happens with such ease that soon there are *only* excuses: one is using constantly, and one sees faintly, from the backseat, as it were, that addiction is driving one to its destination.

And when you've decided to give it up—well, you don't really know if the decision is a real one until after you spend some time away from all the resolutions. When (and if) you give it up, *that's* when you know whether or not you *actually* made that decision—there, on that day, when you swore oaths to yourself, weak-kneed but strong-willed, or at least pretending to be.

That's the thing about addiction. The decision to quit is always somehow tentative. "I'm going to do it!" the addict says, already counting up the exceptions, tallying them next to the days it would be *better* to quit. "I've decided to quit," the addict says, "but I will do it only after the weekend." The decision to quit is, ironically, usually a decision not to quit *yet*.

And strangely, the decision to quit produces the desire to do more of the very thing one will quit. The "last hurrah" is planned. When it is over, though, it wasn't quite big enough to really be the last one. The date on which one will quit is pushed back into an indefinite future. The addict who sees his problem is always going to quit, and always at some point in the future. By planning to quit, he acknowledges that his behavior is out of control but only in an impractical way. If he realizes that he is unable to put his plan into action, he acknowledges his powerlessness in a much more primal way. However, if he *does* quit for some amount of time—a week, or a month—he is liable to find reason to celebrate his accomplishment by doing the very thing he is celebrating not doing.

This is addicted logic: at its center is one's addiction, looking always for a reason to use again. Here we see again the extent to which the world of the addict is constituted by her addiction. Even reasoning all too often turns out to be servicing one's addiction. But the reasoning of the addict is not an *exceptional kind* of reasoning. Indeed, it is the normal form of reasoning, but at its most primitive form: we want something, and we invent reasons (or discover them—describe it as you like) to justify getting what we want. As Hume tells us, "Reason is, and ought only to be the slave of the passions."[3] Whatever else one thinks of Hume's claim, this much is clear: addiction thrives on enslaving.

Addicted logic is dialectical. It returns again and again to the object of addiction. As it discovers reasons to quit, it supplements those reasons with their opposites. A reason to continue throws itself into the mix of reasons to quit—and if not a reason to continue, a reason not to quit *just yet*.

The addict is a torn beast. His desire for his substance—and "desire" is still too weak and generic a word—is so strong that he knows he must quit. And he does *want* to quit, but it is a want that must exist alongside his desire to continue. He has not forsaken the drug, he has only sworn off it temporarily, and only tentatively at that. He will not do what he wants; he will do rather what he does *not* want to do—he will *refrain*. He will stare at his desire, only to finally give in to it—to treat himself, just one more time; to have a(nother) farewell hurrah; to celebrate his most recent victory by conceding defeat. He has proven he can quit, and therefore deserves to reward himself with what he cannot have.

And here are the facts the addict confronts: using this will kill you and you do not want to die; but you *want* to do what will kill you.

Addicted logic is a failure of practical reasoning, to be sure. No wonder Plato saw the mind as having separate parts, each vying for control of us.[4]

These are the facts: death is irreversible; you will lose time you would have had with your children, your family, your friends. But desire is not tamed by the recitation of reasons.

The addict's reasoning reveals the extent to which he is powerless over his addiction. Those who do not know addiction sometimes say, not intending to be smug, things like "Just quit" or "Just choose to stop." They imply that using reason is an easy thing—indeed, that reasoning is somehow a magical power that stands outside of one's world, ready to sweep in like a guardian angel, to save one from oneself. They imply that reasoning is neutral, that it is not influenced by one's phenomenological world—by those things that make the world intelligible, meaningful.

But such a view misunderstands both the extent of powerlessness in addiction and the way that addiction becomes *who one is*. To give up one's object of addiction is to willingly step into an abyss—into a context where nothing makes sense any longer, and in which one must again learn how to live.

## Acknowledging Powerlessness: The Wisdom of the First Step

To fight addiction, one must admit that one is not in control. Indeed, one must admit that the drug is in control. In recognizing that the drug is in control—that we are not in control of ourselves—we become empowered and yet remain as helpless as we have ever been. Ironically, it is often the inability to recognize one's powerlessness that increases it: if I can quit anytime, there's no need to quit now. But this is not, nor has it ever been, a simple matter of choosing. One's powerlessness is revealed to one, and in the light of such powerlessness, we become able again to act as ourselves.

"We recognized that we were powerless over our addiction—that our lives had become unmanageable."[5] So runs the First Step of a Twelve Step program, its point of departure. I have tried to sketch this powerlessness briefly, from a phenomenological point of view. To be addicted is to be unable to understand oneself apart from addiction—it is to have one's desire for the object of addiction surface everywhere, and manipulate everything. In thinking about the way in which addiction insinuates itself into the lives of the addicted, I find myself surprised that anyone ever manages to escape it.

But perhaps that is the point. You *don't* escape it—not completely, not ever. To recognize one's powerlessness, I think, involves recognizing precisely this: I am not in control, not capable of partaking in my objects of addiction moderately or occasionally. I have battled addiction most of my life. Indeed, that way of formulating my relationship with addiction already shows my weakness. To say I have battled it might suggest that the battle is over. It isn't— not by a long shot. My addictions are still with me, sometimes dormant but always waiting to seize upon any weakness.

This is part of the hard-won wisdom of the First Step. To recognize that one is powerless is to recognize that one cannot simply decide to quit. It is to recognize that one's life orbits around a central star, the object of addiction; everything else is subservient and secondary. It is to recognize, fundamentally, that who one is—one's self—is not what one thought. To recognize that one's life has become unmanageable is to recognize that what one does is out of one's control and, indeed, that it cannot be brought back into control simply by applying those management strategies so familiar to all of us—the use of reason, of punishment and reward, of detached reflection.

And yet, when you realize you're powerless—really realize it—something changes. One encounters the world differently—one sees oneself and the possibilities available to one in a different light. Implicit in the First Step is a way of understanding the self—who one is and what one is capable of—that is essential to facing one's addiction. This same view of the self, I would like to suggest, is to be found in a great many religious and moral traditions. The wisdom of the First Step lies, at least partially, in a recognition that the self can imprison, that it can blind us to the world as it exists apart from our individual desires and commitments.

The philosopher and psychologist William James describes the liberating effects of acknowledging one's smallness—one's powerlessness—in his masterful *The Varieties of Religious Experience*. Although the context is quite different, James's account of the experience of religious conversion captures what I regard as a central feature of the recovering addict's changing world.

On James's account, part of the collective experiences of those we call "saints" involves a changed understanding of the self and its significance. The saint has "a feeling of being in a wider life than that of this world's selfish interests; and a conviction, not merely intellectual, but as it were sensible, of the existence of an Ideal Power."[6] To be a saint, in other words, involves seeing the world *differently*. Rather than understanding everything in terms of what I want, or what would benefit me, I see the world as much larger than those things that will affect me either directly or indirectly.

It might be tempting to read James as advocating a belief in a divine being—a temptation many also have in reading the Second Step of Twelve Step Programs: "We came to believe that a power greater than ourselves could restore us to sanity."[7] In both cases, however, the temptation should be resisted. As James goes on to say, "In Christian saintliness this power is always personified as God; but abstract moral ideals, civic or patriotic utopias, or inner visions of holiness or right may also be felt as the true lords and enlargers of our life."[8] The core of saintly experience is *not* belief in a divine being, but a recognition that what matters in the world is not exhausted by an inventory of what one desires. In the world of the addict, as we've seen, everything is reduced to the object of addiction—no values can be found that aren't ultimately subordinated to the desire to *use*. The world of the saintly character, by contrast, is a world where one's personal desires matter very little—they are but a small part of a much larger world, comprising much more important goals, values, and ends.

The experience of the saint, James goes on to say, involves "a sense of the friendly continuity of the ideal power with our own life, and willing self-surrender to its control."[9] This "self-surrender," James contends, involves "an immense elation and freedom, as the outlines of the confining selfhood melt down."[10] The difference between the saintly character and the non-saint becomes clearer when we consider how it affects the place of the self in the world, understood phenomenologically. Selfhood is *confining*—it marks the boundaries of one's concerns, the limits of one's world. In James's view, the "liberation" one experiences is not the liberation of an individual self from some oppressive exterior force: one is liberated *from one's self-centeredness*—from the habitual patterns of action that had characterized one's previous (non-saintly) existence.

Acknowledging that one is no longer in control—and, indeed, never really has been—creates the possibility of resisting one's addiction. The liberation in question, much as in the case of James's saint, is *not* a liberation from addiction itself. It is, rather, a liberation from a pattern of seeing and understanding things that has made one's addictive behavior appear to be the only real possibility. It is a liberation, in other words, from the addicted self-centeredness that one has become, and from the world that is organized around it.

This experience of liberation, I think, often accompanies the acceptance of the First Step. I am not liberated from my addiction, because the addiction constitutes me essentially. When I accept the First Step, I accept that *I am addicted, and will always be addicted.* I am liberated, rather, from *myself*—from the hubris of believing that I am in complete control of myself and my actions, and that I am capable of directing myself without any external help. A recognition of powerlessness is emancipatory in the sense that it frees me from illusions that, in fact, have perpetuated my addiction—that I can stop when I want to, that my will is stronger than my urges, and so on.

The acceptance of the First Step thus marks a kind of phenomenological shift in which one experiences one's agency—and one's world—in a qualitatively different way. One recognizes the limitations of one's will, and through this recognition, one's previous and future actions are understood in a new way. This new self-understanding helps us recognize the ironic fact that the belief that we have ultimate control over our actions might actually help to further restrict our actions (thinking we are capable of stopping our addictive behavior whenever we want to, simply by force of will, effectively hinders us from stopping). The addict does not give up her personal desires—the addict still wants to use, after all—but those desires are understood in a new way, and seen as occupying a much more regional place in the enlarged world the addict now occupies. Importantly, empowerment in relation to one's addiction (the feeling that one can *live with* one's addiction—that it is not all hopeless) is not the same as simply exerting a counterforce upon some thing that has colonized one's life. The recovering addict is one who recognizes that addiction *cannot* be beaten—that it is a burden one must bear continuously ("one day at a time," as Twelve Step participants say). Like cancer, addiction is always waiting to come back.

Acknowledging powerlessness, then, amounts to a shift in the way one perceives and understands the world. It can liberate precisely because it frees one from those ways of understanding the world in which everything is reduced to my desires and the means by which I can satisfy them. In seeing my own powerlessness, I see that the world—and, indeed, even my actions—are not entirely in my control. There are forces at work in the world over which I exert no influence and, indeed, cannot exert influence. I come to see my ability to influence my own behavior as limited in ways I could not see before.

The recognition of powerlessness is liberatory, but it is not escape. Indeed, to understand the nature of addiction is to understand that one *cannot* escape it. This is the wisdom captured in the practice of referring to addicts as *recovering* rather than *recovered*. To see one's powerlessness is to see that one's struggle will never be complete. Liberation from addiction is not something achieved and then forgotten. It is, rather, something that must be achieved *continuously*. If one could beat addiction firmly and finally, one would indeed have power over addiction. To see one's powerlessness is to see that every victory is a partial and tentative one; it is to see that any ground we have gained over the years can be lost in a single moment of weakness.

The First Step of Twelve Step programs is one that demands we see the world we inhabit in a different way—one in which we acknowledge our own smallness, and our corresponding inability to control all aspects of the life we are living.

There are many kinds of addicts, and many kinds of addiction. There are also many ways to cope with addiction. I have tried here to capture something about the experience of addiction, but I don't pretend to speak for everyone.[11] I have likewise tried to capture something about the change in one's experience of oneself that accompanies accepting the First Step. But, again, I don't pretend that this is the only way to grapple with an addiction, or that I have discovered an experience that absolutely everyone will have. I do nevertheless hope that I've captured something of importance about the world the addict inhabits, as well as how this world changes as we seek to change ourselves.

I began by claiming that the core truth of addiction could be found in the way it colonizes every aspect of one's life. This truth, I think, is counterbalanced by another, more hopeful one: addiction doesn't have to dominate us; we are not condemned to live only in its world. Change is possible through the recognition that we are powerless to change on our own. Indeed, being powerless is itself a key to change, provided that we can recognize our powerlessness.

This, I think, is the paradoxical wisdom of the First Step.

NOTES

1. See Heidegger, *Being and Time,* 78–148.

2. Ibid., 149–68.

3. Hume, *Treatise on Human Nature,* 2.3.3, 415.

4. See Plato, *Republic,* books 2 through 4.

5. *Alcoholics Anonymous,* chapter 5.

6. James, *Varieties of Religious Experience,* 272.

7. *Alcoholics Anonymous,* chapter 5.

8. James, *Varieties,* 272.

9. Ibid., 273.

10. Ibid.

11. Herbert Fingarette's *Heavy Drinking* goes to great pains to make the point that there is no single condition called "alcoholism" and hence no single solution to "alcoholism." In Fingarette's view, we should not think of heavy drinking as a disease at all—it is a way of life. In this essay, I adopt an agnostic stance on this issue. It's nevertheless worth remarking that my own account fits with Fingarette's in many respects: to be a user is to organize one's life around a substance (using becomes a central activity). Quitting is never simply a matter of choosing to quit; one must reorganize one's life. I have spoken of this in terms of addiction. The question of whether or not addiction is a physiological condition in the case of alcohol is beyond the scope of my current concerns. Even if it is not, I see no harm in using the term "addiction" to describe the patterns of habitual action that come to dominate the life of the user.

MARY JEAN WALKER

# Powerlessness and Responsibility in Twelve Step Narratives

Most of us recognize that addiction saps freedom. But we also tend to think that someone saddled with an addiction should and can do something about it. Ever since Aristotle and the ancient Greeks first examined "weakness of will," philosophers have grappled with this dilemma. The very first of the Twelve Steps raises the issue, and our next two essays address it from two quite different perspectives. The Australian philosopher Mary Jean Walker begins by describing the conundrum and then assesses some of the ways commonly used to try to get past it. Eschewing these, she argues that the narrative theory of identity developed by the contemporary philosopher Paul Ricoeur enables us to resolve the dilemma. The fact that Twelve Step practitioners tend to love telling stories gives great credibility to this provocative proposal.

The literature of Twelve Step groups such as Alcoholics Anonymous contains apparently contradictory implications regarding powerlessness and personal responsibility. In this essay I examine the treatment of these concepts in Twelve Step literature and their implications for the self-conception of people in these programs. In the first section, I examine the literature to demonstrate that addicts are presented as powerless over, yet responsible for, their addictive behaviors. In the second section, I outline two potential ways people in Twelve Step programs might reconcile this contradiction within their self-conception, but I argue that neither is satisfactory. In the third section, I draw on Paul Ricoeur's theory of narrative identity to develop an account of how someone in a Twelve Step group could coherently understand herself as both powerless and responsible.

## Powerlessness and Responsibility

Admitting one's powerlessness is the First Step in Twelve Step programs. In explaining this Step, Twelve Step literature presents the addict as having been taken over by a substance or a compulsion: "Alcohol . . . bleeds us of all self-sufficiency and all will to resist its demands."[1] Powerlessness is described as the result of a condition of both the mind and the body: "We were the victims of a mental obsession[;] . . . first we were smitten by an insane urge that condemned us to go on drinking, and then by an allergy of the body that insured we would destroy ourselves in the process."[2]

Steps Two and Three further confirm addicts' powerlessness by having them accept that outside help is necessary for them to change their behavior, and decide to "turn over" their will. These Steps are presented as a means of attaining humility and overcoming egotism, an antidote to the arrogance that is associated with addiction. Addicts are typically "defiant" and need to replace such defiance with "reliance," or replace doomed attempts at independence with an acceptance of dependence.[3] Attempts at independence are criticized as attempts to play God (a project typical of addicts), while "dependence, as A.A. practices it, is really a means of gaining true independence of the spirit."[4] The positive sense of dependence is explained by comparisons to our dependence on electricity and modern medicine: these too enable other kinds of independence.

The recognition of powerlessness is emphatically presented as necessary for recovery: "Admissions of personal powerlessness turn out to be the firm bedrock upon which happy and purposeful lives may be built."[5] Sobriety or recovery will be precarious if the addict does not recognize his or her powerlessness—but admitting powerlessness enables a new sense of empowerment to emerge.

However, there is a different and apparently contradictory line of thought in Twelve Step literature, which places strong emphasis on responsibility. This line of thought is evident in the diagnostic statements linking alcoholism to various negative character traits and tendencies, and is continued in later Steps. In Step Four, addicts are to take an inventory of their past wrongdoings and character flaws.[6] The literature explains the purpose of this Step by presenting these moral, emotional, and spiritual deficiencies as driving their addictive behavior. Thus, only by remedying these can they recover.[7] Step Five directs addicts to share the results of this inventory with another person, in order to correct their tendencies to be overly harsh or lenient in self-examination.[8]

Steps Six and Seven focus on identifying and removing defects of character. Steps Eight and Nine involve identifying, then making amends to, people the addict has harmed. Steps Ten through Twelve ask the addict to engage in ongoing processes of moral self-assessment and spiritual development, and to help other addicts.[9]

This moral content implies that addicts are responsible for their past actions. In identifying, confessing to, and then making amends for their actions, addicts come to recognize their responsibility for those actions. And such recognition is presented as necessary for addicts to recover.

Thus, addicts in Twelve Step programs are told that they are powerless over some actions and that they are responsible for those actions.[10] Both ideas are presented as not only true but *useful,* or therapeutic. Since people in Twelve Step groups may feel guilty or remorseful about their behavior, believing one is powerless can help by providing relief. Fingarette has argued that the guilt experienced by addicts is likely to obscure good self-understanding because, in order to escape it, addicts may engage in self-deception, convincing themselves that their behavior is not problematic and hence making it more likely that they will continue it.[11] So temporarily suspending feelings of guilt by admitting powerlessness may help addicts acknowledge a need to change. Fingarette's point also indicates the purpose of the belief in responsibility. Many people in Twelve Step programs are likely to have evaluated their addictive behavior negatively—even if they have also deceived themselves about it by blaming others or dismissing problems related to that behavior as bad luck.[12] Accepting responsibility for the behavior, when added to this negative evaluation of it, provides a reason to alter it. While belief in one's powerlessness on its own could become an excuse for continuing the addictive behavior, accepting responsibility prevents this.[13]

Thus, either belief on its own could end up contributing to continuation of the addictive behavior: powerlessness without responsibility could be used as an excuse, while responsibility without powerlessness could encourage self-deception. Both are needed in order for either belief to have its therapeutic value.

## Reconciling Powerlessness and Responsibility

The problem, of course, is that, according to most philosophical as well as commonsense notions of responsibility, actions for which we are responsible must be freely performed, while actions over which we are powerless are not freely performed, and so we are not responsible for them.[14] I will now discuss two ways addicts could make sense of these beliefs that are suggested by empirical sources. Neither method, I argue, satisfactorily accounts for the presentation of these ideas in the AA literature. But they are instructive for identifying what sort of account is required to make sense of this literature.

First, people might make distinctions about degrees or kinds of responsibility, or factors that mitigate responsibility, in such a way that the beliefs are not in conflict. This approach might draw on the idea, for instance, that while it was possible for addicts to have acted differently, it is understandable that they did not, given that they had an illness that predisposed them toward certain actions. Such a view may be consistent with our usual thinking about how coercion or incapacity can mitigate responsibility. Or it may be consistent with philosophical approaches that distinguish between different senses of responsibility. Drawing on a view developed by Gary Watson, for example, we might distinguish responsibility as "attributability" from responsibility as "accountability." We "attribute" an action to someone when we recognize that she performed it. We hold her accountable for it when we regard punishing her, or at least disapproving of her, to be justified.[15] Perhaps addicts are responsible in one sense but not in the other: their actions are attributable to them, but their powerlessness blocks responsibility in the accountability sense. Some such approach might make sense of some of the ways recovering addicts speak. For instance, some Twelve Step program attendees reportedly make a distinction between responsibility and blameworthiness.[16] Alice King, describing her acceptance of being an alcoholic, states that it "was not my fault, but it was my responsibility."[17]

Any solution that involves distinctions about degrees of responsibility, however, would be at odds with the way that powerlessness and responsibility are discussed in AA literature. Alcoholics in AA are taught they are powerless and that they need to take responsibility; no limitations are placed on either idea. Any way of understanding how powerlessness and responsibility can be simultaneously self-attributed needs to account for this absoluteness.

Distinctions about *kinds* of responsibility are also problematic. For instance, if addicts thought themselves responsible in an attributability sense, but not an accountability sense, this would mean they are not responsible in a sense that is robust enough to license others to respond in the ways they usually do in holding someone responsible. Nor is attributability sufficiently robust to justify the actions that are recommended in the Twelve Step literature, such as confessing and making amends. And it is difficult to see how a sense of responsibility robust enough to justify confession and amendment would not be at odds with the belief in powerlessness.

A second possibility arises from reports that people in Twelve Step groups engage in talk of different selves. Some speak of an "addictive" self and another, more authentic self.[18] This enables descriptions of inner conflict involving an "inner addict" who wants to continue the behavior in opposition to the desires or values of the more authentic self. Engaging in such talk could provide addicts a way to experience desires to drink as "not really their own," but as a symptom of their illness, and a way to acknowledge past addictive behaviors while believing that these behaviors were not expressive of their "real" self.

Such talk may initially seem to offer a solution: perhaps powerlessness could attach to one of these selves and responsibility to the other. This talk is also suggestive in light of philosophical approaches that consider responsibility to attach to those actions that are "one's own"—that is, actions that express the agent's self, character, rational judgments, or evaluative commitments. "Self-disclosure" theories of responsibility propose that we are responsible for actions that are expressive of our identities in these senses, although not for actions that are "not our own" (such as reflex or accidental actions).[19]

Again, however, this does not do justice to the Twelve Step literature, which attributes both powerlessness and responsibility directly to the addict. Consider: If the addictive self is the one to whom the addictive traits belong, then only the addictive self, not the authentic self, is responsible for them. But the addictive self is powerless, and so cannot be responsible either. That is, this way of thinking confirms addicts' powerlessness to the extent of saying that certain actions are not even part of their identity. But for responsibility to be applicable, ownership of action is required. Further, it is hard to see how it can be therapeutically valuable for the addict to speak of her powerlessness and responsibility if she attributes them only to her less authentic self. Thus, any reconciliation of powerlessness and responsibility needs to account for how addicts could "own" their addictive behaviors, while also regarding themselves as powerless over them.

## Appropriating Responsibility

So far we have assumed that considering oneself powerless over, yet responsible for, the same actions involves a contradiction. This assumption relies on the premise that one is only responsible for actions that are freely performed. While this is not contentious on many philosophical and commonsense notions of responsibility, it can be disputed.[20] In this section I draw on Ricoeur's theory of narrative identity to explain how it is possible to "take" responsibility by appropriating certain actions as one's own, irrespective of whether or not they were freely undertaken.

The motivation to examine narrative identity in relation to Twelve Step groups comes from noting that their practices involve constant use of personal narratives. They are used in bringing people into the program, describing progress, and making sense of experiences of addiction and recovery. The constant exchange of personal stories within Twelve Step group practices provides templates for self-understanding to members, so that throughout their recovery they may reinterpret themselves and their lives using Twelve Step concepts.[21]

Ricoeur argues that because narrative is the imitation of action, we can articulate our lives using narrative form.[22] A life, like a narrative, takes place over time and contains a sequence of events. Constructing a narrative out of a sequence of events involves connecting them together in ways that enable us to make sense of them in light of each other, so that the narrative as a whole provides a context in which particular events are intelligible. In a similar sense, persons interpret their own lives within self-narratives that make their lives intelligible to them.

A criticism of this approach to identity is that lives are much messier than narratives. Any life will contain disruptions and inconsistencies. Events that are out of one's control or that have nothing to do with one's own "story" will inevitably play a large role in one's life. Ricoeur responds to this point by developing an account of the unifying capacity of narrative. Narrative, he argues, has the capacity to unify discordant events into a whole, combining diversity, variability, discontinuity, and instability into unities. It achieves this through what Ricoeur calls "emplotment."[23]

Emplotment is the arrangement of actions and events into a plot. Arranging events into a narrative form involves interpreting them, since a bare recounting of events would not make them intelligible.[24] For intelligibility, we need to connect events to each other in some way. This involves picking out which events are relevant to the narrative, what their relevance is, and how they connect to other events. In the process of emplotment, then, we interpret our lives in certain ways, giving individual events meaning.

Emplotment is a means of unifying diverse elements, because narrative is able to present these elements as parts of a whole—the narrative itself. Emplotment thus "configures" different events into a narrative unity.[25] For this reason Ricoeur calls narration a "synthesis of the heterogeneous."[26] In the same way, in interpreting ourselves and our lives narratively, we connect diverse events together as a unity, making sense of ourselves as wholes.

Notice that the personal unity that narrative self-interpretation confers does not depend on our having any actual consistency or continuity in our lives, character, or values. Rather, it depends on our self-interpretative practices: in seeking to understand ourselves, we actively synthesize heterogeneous elements by seeking to make them intelligible in light of each other. Chance events, or discordances, are configured into parts of our narratives in virtue of our activity in interpreting them in light of other events in our lives.[27]

This implies that events over which we have no control can nonetheless become part of our identity. As an example, consider Genevieve Lloyd's discussion of Spinoza's expulsion from the Jewish community. Lloyd explains that although the expulsion "shattered the external forms that had hitherto given his life meaning," Spinoza embraced the change as one that gave "greater clarity to the directions of the life he was already leading," and thereby "reshaped his life and identity in a direction that was by no means alien to him."[28] That is, he incorporated the expulsion into his self-interpretation, taking it to express elements of his identity, even though it was no action of his own. By appropriating this necessity, Spinoza transforms an external event into something that makes sense in light of other events in his narrative, and in turn contributes to the intelligibility of other events in his life. By emploting the event, two very different aspects of his life—orthodox Judaism and beliefs that directly conflicted with it—become part of a whole, different parts of one narrative.

If we can actively appropriate chance events into our identity by interpreting them in terms of their role in our narrative, we could also actively appropriate actions over which we think of ourselves as powerless. Rather than being responsible only for free actions, we may assume responsibility for some action because we recognize that it plays a role in our identity: it is something that makes sense in light of other events in our narrative, and it contributes to the context that makes other events intelligible. This involves not just a recognition of responsibility for some actions, but active self-interpretation that configures those actions into part of one's story. Appropriating responsibility through the actions recommended by the Twelve Steps—careful moral inventories, apologizing, and making amends—is part of making the past behaviors part of one's story, part of oneself.

Although this may not be consistent with our intuitions about freedom and responsibility, it is consistent with our intuitions about *identity* and responsibility: we are responsible for those actions that are our own.

As an example, consider an alcoholic who has neglected her family while drinking. As a participant in a Twelve Step program who is trying to cease this behavior, she comes to believe she was powerless over it. She admits her powerlessness and then reconfirms it by seeking the help of a power outside herself and attempting to turn her will over to it. She finds this view a relief, and it helps to prevent her from falling into her usual pattern of self-recrimination, followed by further drinking. But she also expresses her belief in her responsibility for the neglect by listing it when she undertakes Step Four, and by apologizing and endeavoring to make amends to her family when doing Steps Eight and Nine. This appropriation of responsibility helps motivate different future behavior.

In the view developed here, this would involve regarding her addictive behavior as expressive of her identity, even though she had no power over it.[29] This self-interpretation reconfigures the addiction so that it is no longer only an outside force that takes over her but also something that forms part of, and plays a role within, her life story. Note that this does not mean the addiction is no longer an outside force over which she had no control. If this were so, it would diminish the point of the admission of powerlessness, and in any case it would not be consistent with the literature. Rather, she has brought the addiction into her narrative through the behaviors suggested in the Twelve Steps and is interpreting its role—and the role of enacting a Twelve Step program—in her life. Although powerless over the addictive behaviors, she is nonetheless responsible for the behavior (and for that powerlessness) because it is hers.[30]

This explanation thus makes sense of the features of the literature that were not accounted for in the ideas explored in the second section. It does not rely on distinctions about kinds or degrees of responsibility, because it involves free appropriation, not just recognition, of responsibility. And it enables both powerlessness and responsibility to be attributed to one agent with a unified identity that incorporates disparate elements.

## A Final Note on Freedom

Thus, the narrative conception of identity offered by Ricoeur can explain how an addict could accept both powerlessness and responsibility in a way that does justice to the Twelve Step literature. People may freely choose to appropriate responsibility for actions even if they also take themselves to have been powerless over those actions.

While I cannot explore the implications of this discussion for questions about freedom and responsibility more generally here, the discussion does connect Twelve Step thought to certain nonstandard ways of thinking about freedom and autonomy. Lloyd argues that the notion of freedom implicated in her discussion of Spinoza, and in Spinoza's own philosophical thought, is opposed to the Cartesian notion of freedom that identifies it with the will and opposes it to necessity.[31] Spinoza denied the possibility of free will in the Cartesian sense because he regarded the human will as subject to the same necessities as the rest of the natural world. But he presents an alternative, Stoic conception of freedom: we are free when our actions result from our own nature, even though our nature is a necessity for us.[32] And there is a sense in which this is precisely what people in Twelve Step programs learn to do: to understand how both their addictive behavior and their need to remain abstinent are reactions to their own "nature," their identity as addicts. They may thus regard being an alcoholic as a necessity but nonetheless freely appropriate this aspect of their identity, and as such appropriate responsibility for it.[33]

NOTES

1. Alcoholics Anonymous Australia, *Twelve Steps and Twelve Traditions*, 21.
2. Ibid., 22.
3. Ibid., 27–31, 35–36.
4. Ibid., 36–37.
5. Ibid., 21.
6. Ibid., 48.

7. Ibid., 43–44.

8. Ibid., 59–60.

9. Ibid., 6–8.

10. For more general discussion of addiction and responsibility, see, e.g., Stephen Morse, "Hooked on Hype: Addiction and Responsibility," *Law and Philosophy* 19, no. 1 (2000): 3–49; Michael Corrado, "Addiction and Responsibility: An Introduction," *Law and Philosophy* 18, no. 6 (1999): 579–88; and the papers in *Addiction and Responsibility,* edited by Poland and Graham.

11. Fingarette, "Alcoholism and Self-Deception." See also Mary Jean Walker, "Addiction and Self-Deception: A Method for Self-Control?," *Journal of Applied Philosophy* 27, no. 3 (2010): 305–19.

12. Autobiographical accounts in *Alcoholics Anonymous* often note such strategies (e.g., 275, 333, 479, 515), and they sometimes present failure to take responsibility as part of what was wrong with their authors' drinking.

13. See Neil Levy, "Self-Deception and Responsibility for Addiction," *Journal of Applied Philosophy* 20, no. 2 (2003): 133–42, and Peele, *Diseasing of America.*

14. There are other senses in which the AA literature implies that alcoholics have free will. Step Three describes turning over the will as a decision, implying that alcoholics do this freely. My thanks to the editors for this point.

15. Gary Watson, "Two Faces of Responsibility," *Philosophical Topics* 24, no. 2 (1996): 227–48. See also Angela Smith, "Control, Responsibility, and Moral Assessment," *Philosophical Studies* 138, no. 3 (2008): 367–92; and Coleen Macnamara, "Holding Others Responsible," *Philosophical Studies* 152 (2011): 81–102. Watson's view is somewhat more complex in its details than discussed here, though the "self-disclosure" view he develops it to defend is discussed further below. Self-disclosure approaches typically distinguish between *judgments* of responsibility and our *practices* of holding responsible, which involve having certain reactive attitudes and treating the person accordingly. The distinction is drawn from Peter Strawson, "Freedom and Resentment," *Proceedings of the British Academy* 48 (1962): 1–25. A perhaps similar distinction is used by Francis Seeburger (*Addiction and Responsibility,* 175–89), who links recovery to taking responsibility by drawing on a distinction between "reacting" and "responding." I take Seeburger's position to be consistent with my discussion below, though his descriptions of "responding" and its link to responsibility are phenomenological and do not provide a conceptual explanation of this link.

16. Diamond, *Narrative Means to Sober Ends,* 106.

17. King, *High Sobriety,* 269.

18. Michael Larkin and Mark Griffiths, "Experience of Addiction and Recovery: The Case for Subjective Accounts," *Addiction Research and Theory* 10, no. 3 (2002): 303; Diamond, *Narrative Means to Sober Ends,* 120–23. On narratives about finding a true self

in recovery from addiction, see Mariana Valverde, "Experience and Truthtelling: Intoxicated Autobiography and Ethical Subjectivity," *Outlines* 4, no. 1 (2002): 3–18.

19. Watson, "Two Faces"; Smith, "Control."

20. Self-disclosure approaches allow that we may be responsible for actions that are nonvoluntary (i.e., not deliberately chosen or consciously controlled, such as acts of omission, or having certain attitudes as a result of failing to reflect), though not for actions that are *in*voluntary (which would not be connected in the right way to our identities for responsibility to be applicable). The view developed below is close to self-disclosure views, though I argue that what occurs in Twelve Step programs is better understood as an appropriation rather than a recognition of responsibility.

21. See Carole Cain, "Personal Stories: Self-Understanding and Identity Acquisition in Alcoholics Anonymous," *Ethos* 19, no. 2 (1991): 210–52; Maria Gabrielle Swora, "The Rhetoric of Transformation in the Healing of Alcoholism: The Twelve Steps of Alcoholics Anonymous," *Mental Health, Religion and Culture* 7, no. 3 (2004): 187–209; and Nancy Potter, "Grounding for Understanding Self-Injury as Addiction or (Bad) Habit," in Poland and Graham, *Addiction and Responsibility*, 201–24.

22. Ricoeur, *Oneself as Another*, 157.

23. Ricoeur, "Life in Quest of Narrative."

24. Ricoeur, "Narrated Time," *Philosophy Today* 29, no. 4 (1985): 259–72.

25. Ricoeur, *Oneself as Another*, 142–43.

26. Ibid., 141.

27. Ricoeur, "Life in Quest," 21–22.

28. Lloyd, "Shaping a Life," in Mackenzie and Atkins, *Practical Identity and Narrative Agency*, 257.

29. That AA members do come to view alcoholism as central to their identity is well established in anthropological and sociological studies (e.g., Denzin, *Recovering Alcoholic*, and Jensen, *Storytelling*).

30. Some may worry that this picture would still involve a sense of responsibility that is not robust enough to make sense of actions like apologizing and making amends. I regard these actions themselves as a way of freely appropriating a more robust sense of responsibility via active self-interpretation, and hence consider this worry unfounded. In *taking* responsibility by apologizing and making amends, Twelve Step participants alter how they regard their past actions and characteristics and the sense in which they consider them "their own." Thus the practice differs from either making judgments about responsibility, or responding to such judgments, which have been the focus of discussions within the moral responsibility literature. Indeed, this literature has focused on holding *others* responsible, rather than the role of responsibility evaluations in our self-conceptions. I do not have space to further discuss how this idea would sit within the literature on moral responsibility, but my view would align with self-disclosure views of responsibility, so

that this worry is a version of the view that self-disclosure theories of responsibility are not robust enough to license our practices of holding others responsible. For an argument in favor of this view, see Wolf, *Freedom within Reason;* for responses, see Watson, "Two Faces," and Smith, "Control."

31. Lloyd, "Shaping a Life," 257–58.

32. For instance, the modern individualist notion of autonomy (which has Cartesian underpinnings, and in which freedom is closely connected to control) has been critiqued for its inability to account for the many ways in which our autonomy depends on others. There are alternate ways of conceptualizing autonomy that resonate with the AA literature by making it compatible with dependence (see, for example, essays in Mackenzie and Stoljar, *Relational Autonomy*). Ernest Kurtz's discussion of AA's place in intellectual history (*Not-God,* 175–79) is also suggestive of the need to reconceptualize autonomy in approaching AA thought, though he appears to retain the assumption that autonomy is necessarily opposed to necessity. Further exploration of what notion of autonomy would best fit with AA thought might interestingly draw further on Spinoza's neo-Stoic approach.

33. I would like to thank the volume's editors, Jerome Miller and Nick Plants, for their helpful comments on several versions of the essay.

# Vulnerability, Addiction, and Recovery

Like Mary Jean Walker, Corbin Casarez finds the Twelve Step insistence on powerlessness and responsibility philosophically perplexing. But unlike her, he traces
both to a source innate in human existence, namely, the vulnerability that is constitutive of us. This, he argues, enables us to explain both how we succumb to
addiction and how we're able to transcend it. After developing an existential account of addiction, Casarez draws upon the later work of Heidegger and the
postmodern thought of Jacques Derrida to show how the same vulnerability that
makes us liable to addiction enables us to access possibilities that have the potential to be healing.

The First Step in Twelve Step programs is to admit one's powerlessness in the
face of addiction, and many of the other Steps require dependence on assistance from others and a Higher Power for healing and recovery. This admission and dependency are considered essential for confronting addiction. Yet
one who is unable to resist temptations would seem incapable of free choice
and action, which are often considered prerequisites for responsibility. This
poses an interesting philosophical problem: can one who professes powerlessness against temptations and dependency on a higher power be responsible for
her behavior, attitudes, and character?

One answer will not suffice: claiming that "powerlessness" affects only
one part of a person's life (the addiction) dismisses too quickly the serious
challenges that an addict faces. Addiction affects personality, relationships,
opportunities—in short, one's entire life. Yet in order to hold a recovering addict accountable for his decisions, Twelve Step programs must maintain that
addicts have some form of responsibility, even for the First Step of admitting
powerlessness. The tension between acknowledging the power of addiction
to interfere with all aspects of a person's life and believing that an addict can
recover through continued commitment to the Twelve Step process is only
successfully resolved if both aspects are duly considered.

I believe that vulnerability, understood as an essential human capacity, can account for both the reality of addiction and the possibility of recovery, without ignoring the pull of addiction or the addict's responsibility to commit to recovery. Vulnerability, construed as the capacity to expose oneself to the risks of being harmed, also opens one to the possibilities of response and healing. It can account for the powerful lure toward certain destructive behaviors as well as the responsibility to trust others and engage in the recovery process.

## Powerlessness and Responsibility

The free will–determinism debate is a provocative and much-discussed philosophical topic. My interest here, however, is not to defend a particular stance on the nature of freedom, but rather to examine a paradox that arises within the framework of typical intuitions regarding responsibility. According to these intuitions, responsibility entails the power to do otherwise than one did. When we consider addiction, however, intuitions diverge as to whether or not the addict has the freedom or responsibility to resist the temptation of the addictive substance or process ("object" for short). If one wants to maintain that the addict is responsible for recovering from addiction, one seems to encounter a paradox.

First, let me emphasize that we are talking about someone who is *already* addicted. The issue is not whether someone is responsible for becoming addicted—for the initial decision to use a potentially addictive substance, and so on. The question here is whether or not someone who is already addicted can be responsible for resisting temptations and seeking recovery. If responsibility requires the ability to do otherwise, the question can be reframed: does addiction eliminate the addict's responsibility? According to the above-mentioned intuitions, we are already assuming that the addict's decision-making ability is constrained in relation to the addictive object and that this constraint is what differentiates the addict from a non-addict in the same situation. If the addict is not free in the face of the addictive object, then it seems that the addict is not responsible for resisting temptation and seeking recovery. Some will affirm this conclusion and may consequently advocate social engineering or physiological intervention to break the irresistible temptation of the addictive object. Others, by contrast, argue that the addict's freedom is only partially restricted, so the addict is still capable of resisting temptation by mere willpower. This perspective tends to moralize the addict's choices, blaming her for moral failure whenever she succumbs to the temptation of the addictive object.

Both of these approaches seem facile in light of addicts' testimonies and contemporary discussions regarding addiction. The more convincing accounts of addiction affirm that nothing forces an addict to succumb to temptation *and* that an addict is not capable of resisting temptation on his own. Moreover there seems to be little doubt that it is possible for an addict to engage in a process of recovery from addiction, whatever form this recovery might take. This suggests that the addict's responsibility is inhibited but not annihilated with regard to the addictive object.

Since the focus of this anthology is Twelve Step spirituality, let us consider the characterization of addiction, specifically alcoholism, in *Alcoholics Anonymous* (also known as "the Big Book") to try to get a clearer understanding of the issue of responsibility from it. According to it, alcoholics *"have lost the power of choice in drink. Our so-called will power becomes practically nonexistent."*[1] Story after story describes how an alcoholic resolves to stop drinking but later finds himself drunk and wondering how it happened. Self-imposed rules (for example, only drinking on trips) don't work. Despair over one's deteriorating or devastated situation doesn't provide enough motivation and strength to prevent relapse. Knowledge (about one's health, addiction, or susceptibility to certain contexts and triggers) imparted by doctors, family, or Alcoholics Anonymous is insufficient.[2] Testimonies repeatedly affirm that the alcoholic is unable to drink casually or maintain abstinence on her own, regardless of how long she remains sober. Nevertheless, these testimonials are provided by recovering alcoholics, so the very people who describe themselves as powerless against alcohol offer hope to other alcoholics by living a life of recovery. According to this hope-inspiring process, recovery begins with an admission of powerlessness.

These two affirmations, that the addict is powerless against the addiction and that the addict can opt to overcome the addiction, produces our paradox. Alcoholics Anonymous and other self-help organizations and programs rely on the addict's decision to seek and commit to recovery. According to Twelve Step programs, the addict must choose to adhere to the program, which is another way of saying that the addict is responsible for choosing recovery over continued addiction. Yet the First Step of these programs is an admission by the addict, in good faith, that the addict is powerless over the addictive object. *How* can someone who is powerless to resist an addictive object then choose recovery over addiction? Vulnerability, I suggest, accounts for both the overpowering allure of addictive objects for addicts and the possibility of recovery initiated by an acknowledgment of powerlessness. Vulnerability, however, must be understood in a more complete sense than it usually is.

### The Meaning of "Vulnerability"

Vulnerability is commonly understood as weakness, passivity, and the absence of power. When power, equated with strength, influence, or control, is held in high esteem, vulnerability understood as weakness not only will not be admired; it will be despised. From this perspective, the notion that vulnerability might be a positive capacity seems far-fetched. Nevertheless, I believe that vulnerability not only is a positive capacity but is even essential to human beings.

Attending to the etymology of the word "vulnerability" can help us reconceptualize its relation to power and responsibility. The Latin source of the term is *vulnerabilis,* from *vulnerare,* which means "to wound." Furthermore, the Latin root *vulnus* ("wound") is shared both by "vulnerability" and "vulnerary," the latter term signifying remedial properties or potency. Something whole may be wounded, and a wound may be restored. Both the ability to be wounded and the ability to heal depend upon the openness of the self. Something that is invulnerable cannot receive a wound; it is not exposed to this risk. Only something vulnerable is exposed to the risk of being wounded, and only a wound can be exposed to the vulnerary cure.

Vulnerability is closely linked to exposure and openness. Its receptivity is not, however, necessarily a passivity. Though one can be exposed passively, one can also expose oneself reflexively, that is, actively. "Exposure" has not carried the same stigma as "vulnerability," or at least it has not been restricted to only a negative meaning.[3] A weak spot can be exposed, but so can film, and it is only through this exposure that film can record an image. Exposure is bidirectional. On the one hand, I can bring something hidden out into the open; what is exposed impacts its environment, or its concealed impact is now revealed. On the other hand, what is exposed can now be affected by the environment in a way it could not before. Exposure allows something both to affect and to be affected by its context. Sometimes the active role of exposure is emphasized, and sometimes the passive, but exposure makes both activity and passivity possible simultaneously. It is this bidirectional nature of exposure that makes vulnerability more than just weakness.

Though power is often understood as strength, a more inclusive conception of "power" acknowledges the potency of potentiality. The notion of "power" is often applied to the *force* that effects some actualization, but just as important are the *conditions* and *capacities* that enable the actualization. This is not an abnormal sense of "power." An engine's capacity for combustive output is quantified in horsepower even when the engine is not running; what is quantified in this case is not actual output, but potential. The capacity to act is legitimately understood as power.

Vulnerability is such a capacity. Indeed, vulnerability is an essential human capacity to act upon and to be acted upon by one's environment.[4] Because vulnerability is an essential human capacity, no human being can be invulnerable in the fullest sense. "Invulnerability" when applied to human beings is not the lack of this capacity for exposure but rather a relatively diminished level of vulnerability (usually involving resistance to a particular factor or threat). Since invulnerability is just lessened vulnerability, it is only properly attributed when one is less exposed to one's environment and so has a reduced capacity for interaction. The more vulnerable one is, the more one can be affected by, and can affect, one's environment. Human beings are essentially open to their contexts, but the degree to which one is open can vary.

## Vulnerability to Addiction

Now we shall apply this understanding of vulnerability to the addict's situation. Even though I have emphasized at length that vulnerability is a capacity, a type of potentiality, and therefore a positive notion, we should not forget that vulnerability as exposure risks being wounded. Addiction is an example of vulnerability's negative potential, though perhaps not in as straightforward a way as one might expect. One way to understand addiction is as a doomed attempt to overcome vulnerability.

Being vulnerable means being exposed to the elements of one's context: the surrounding objects, conditions, and forces to which one is related. This exposure to one's context makes one susceptible to addictive influences. There are many ways in which we are exposed to our contexts: physiologically, culturally, conceptually, and so on. For example, we can interact with our context by ingesting alcohol, assimilating our behavior to others' expectations, or explicitly entertaining the thought, "Alcohol would relax my nerves right now." As these examples suggest, the variables in the context to which we are exposed are numerous and complicated, and our interaction with them depends also on our exposure to past contexts and the anticipation of being exposed in the future. Exposure to a particular context allows a multitude of conditions to overlap and interact with one another; these conditions, filtered by our level and mode of exposure, enable diverse actualizations even in similar situations.

The complexity of our relations within various contexts can help account for the variety of responses to the stimuli and conditions to which we are exposed. Genetics, education, religious beliefs, social networks, and many other factors have a great effect on how each individual responds to her environment. One person may find an addictive object unappealing while another person finds it immediately irresistible, or an individual can respond differently to the same object on two different occasions. Some temptations are widespread, and some appeal only to certain individuals primed in certain ways. When one is exposed to a context, one is not just exposed to the potentially addictive object. One is also exposed to other objects, activities, and people; in addition, one is influenced by one's own beliefs, values, practices, habits, and proclivities. The fact that different people have different temptations, and that the same person may find the same object sometimes tempting and sometimes not, demonstrates that the conditions for forming an addiction vary case by case and cannot be entirely explained by the addictive object itself.

So what do addictive situations have in common? In such complex and variable contexts, it is unlikely to find one single factor or set of factors common to all of them. In his existential account of addiction, Francis Seeburger locates the commonality not in the environment but in the addict's orientation toward her environment. On this account, addiction results when one abandons the responsibility to choose. This "disownment," as Seeburger calls it, is produced by a "*lack* of any clear sense of meaning in life" and the need to fill that gap with something that organizes one's world so as to provide a sense of order and control, even though that sense is illusory.[5] Addiction replaces the uncertainty and insecurity resulting from a lack of meaning by which to organize one's life. What rushes in to provide this illusory sense of order and control may vary from person to person, and individuals may develop more than one addiction. The addictive object enables one to organize one's life around it, evade difficult choices, and quiet existential questions. For an addict, the object of addiction provides a focal point around which life can be centered: fetishizing the object, fantasizing about past and future encounters with it, and shaping present behavior and attitudes toward the next opportunity to experience it seem to provide one with structure and direction.

What is particularly striking about Seeburger's account is the suggestion that addicts are attempting to control their lives, but do so by means of surrender, giving themselves over to the objects of addiction. As I have already noted, the human capacity to interact with our context makes us susceptible to environmental influences. Vulnerability exposes humans to the risks inherent in their environments, and it does not guarantee that our choices will always be the most satisfying or productive ones. Vulnerability as a capacity enables us to make both wise and poor decisions, so it does not in itself provide a meaning by which to organize one's life. For the addict, the risks involved in responding to one's environment without a guaranteed meaning seem unbearable. The object of addiction simplifies the situation by calling one to surrender to its temptation. In this way, the risk of addiction to which we are all vulnerable is disguised as a means to avoid the risks inherent in vulnerability itself, though of course this requires that one completely submit to the addictive object.

Thus, we could characterize addiction as the surrender of one's responsibility to an addictive object in order to avoid risk. The addict is motivated to restrict his own responsibility by the desire to make sense of the many choices and risks present in the environment. Once this choice to submit to the addictive object is made, it is difficult to overturn. That is, once the addict is addicted, addictive behavior is no longer an expression of one's response to the environment. The addictive object has been granted an overpowering influence that organizes the addict's orientation in each context. The misguided pursuit for control (invulnerability) leads to powerlessness; the addict cannot resist the addictive object as long as it determines how the addict reacts to the environment.

Notice the distinction here between response and reaction. If vulnerability enables one to respond to one's environment, addiction causes one to react instead. The ability to respond includes sensitivity to multiple factors and multiple ways of engaging in a context. One can orient oneself in different ways in each context, and how one does so determines which responses will be available. Addiction narrows the environmental factors to those that reinforce the addiction; thus, an addict's response is limited to reacting to these factors in particular ways. Reaction is a type of response, but it is the type of response that occurs when one relinquishes responsibility. The addict has not overcome the vulnerability essential to being human, but has surrendered to factors in the environment in order to avoid the risks inherent to this vulnerability.

This appears to validate the widespread understanding of vulnerability as weakness. One's vulnerability to addictive influences leads one to being "wounded" psychologically, biologically, and existentially. It must be noted, however, that the risk of addiction is possible because of a capacity for interaction with one's environment, and that this capacity is not only negative. Vulnerability may admit of the possibility of addiction, but only as one possibility among others. To focus on the negative possibilities of vulnerability blurs the positive possibilities also available; it is to these possibilities that we now turn.

## Vulnerability as Capacity for Response

The risk of being wounded is inherent to our essential vulnerability. Nevertheless, the capacity of vulnerability makes it possible for one to become engaged in one's context. This engagement exposes us to the risks of being wounded, but it also enables us to impact and interact with our environment. The vulnerability that makes addiction possible is more primordially the ability to respond. This responsibility precedes (logically and structurally, if not temporally or consciously) the reduction of one's choices to that of addictive reaction. An examination of the broader capacity of vulnerability reveals the responsibility, however diminished it may be in the addict, essential to each of us. Though this is an uncommon way to understand vulnerability, the work of Martin Heidegger and Jacques Derrida supports it.

Heidegger provides resources for adopting this conception of vulnerability, though he tends to speak in terms of resoluteness, projection, and releasement. Still, his language occasionally approaches the characterization of vulnerability offered here. For instance: "Letting-be, i.e., freedom, is intrinsically exposing, ek-sistent. Considered in regard to the essence of truth, the essence of freedom manifests itself as exposure to the disclosedness of beings."[6] Freedom, in this passage, is portrayed the same way that I have characterized vulnerability, as exposure. For Heidegger, one who is free is exposed to the meaningfulness of entities and can make sense of the world by virtue of these meanings. This exposure is not, however, a passive receptivity to singular meanings that dictate our reactions. Entities are polysemic, offering different possible meanings for those who expose themselves to the entities' disclosure. In other words, we can understand our contexts in various ways, since it is possible for things to show up for us with different meanings, suggesting multiple possibilities for orientation and response from among which we can choose.

Though this receptivity to the possible meanings of entities is not purely passive for Heidegger, there is a danger in trying to control the activity of world disclosure. In his critique of Nietzsche's "will to power," Heidegger asserts that the nature of will to power is to exceed itself in willing mastery.[7] The attempt to control the meaningfulness of entities and to master one's environment can never be fully satisfied; this will to power seeks more and more mastery until it is itself enslaved by the will to mastery. Instead of finally obtaining control over one's world, one succumbs to the drive to control inherent to the will to power. The proximity of this critique to Seeburger's analysis of addiction is enlightening. Futilely seeking control over the risks inherent to one's essential vulnerability, the addict submits to an object under the delusion that it will organize the world in a meaningful way. In so doing, the addict finds that responsibility is transformed into reaction.

This danger, however, reveals a more essential potential. The risk that one will be controlled by the impulse to control is made possible by one's exposure to the disclosure of entities in their polysemic meaningfulness. The latent possibilities in one's context are revealed by virtue of one's exposure to it, and the response of seeking mastery is not the only response possible. Acknowledging one's vulnerability and attending to the context, one reveals the inherent risks and possibilities of that context. While one's essential capacity for vulnerable exposure is never eliminated, it can be embraced or suppressed. In this sense, one "becomes vulnerable" (even though one is always vulnerable) the more one accepts the risks and possibilities inherent in being exposed.

Attending to the possibilities opened up by vulnerability does not in itself disclose any particular response as clearly the morally prescribed course of action. As Jacques Derrida has often argued, responsibility and decision cannot be prescribed, calculated, or driven by categorical principles and still survive as a decision. Such responses are again reduced to reactions, even if the actions entailed are viewed positively. That is, the prescription, calculus, or principle organizes the world in advance so that only one path is possible. True responsibility cannot be determined in advance in such a way. "If an event worthy of this name is to arrive or happen, it must, beyond all mastery, affect a passivity. It must touch an exposed vulnerability, one without absolute immunity, without indemnity; it must touch this vulnerability in its finitude."[8] In order for an event to truly rupture any chain of reactions, one must be vulnerable to the various possibilities in one's context, including the "unforeseeable" ones.[9] In the language we have already been using, one must recognize that essential vulnerability and the will to control one's context are incompatible, even when control takes the form of morality, law, politics, medicine, or education. Derrida states this concisely in his essay "Force of Law": "There is no *justesse*, no justice, no responsibility except in exposing oneself to all risks, beyond certitude and good conscience."[10] Being exposed to risks is not a flaw of humanity; it is the essential openness to the world that makes action and response possible. Again, vulnerability must be understood as primordially a positive capacity that entails the risk of negative consequences.

Vulnerability is rooted in exposure—exposure to risk but also to opportunity. According to David Dobbs, recent behavioral studies have indicated that the genes responsible for neurosis, depression, and violence in an impoverished environment are also responsible for adaptation, innovation, and leadership in a nurturing environment.[11] In contrast to the idea that one's genes provide a steadfast and predetermined reaction to changes in the environment, the "orchid hypothesis" suggests that genetic combinations enable one to respond adaptively to environmental interventions in either positive or negative ways. Genetic responsiveness, rather than genetic determinism, provides a picture of hereditary traits that sidesteps the nature-versus-nurture debate by proclaiming "both." Dobbs argues that this new understanding of genetics reveals a new role for vulnerability in our self-understanding: "Risk becomes possibility; vulnerability becomes plasticity and responsiveness."[12] The risk of exposing oneself to the world, of being vulnerable, opens one up to the influential conditions in that environment, both positive and negative. In contrast to a complete passivity, this risk is partially an active pursuit: it makes one "not just more vulnerable but more plastic" so that one can "feel a heightened sense of agency."[13]

Heidegger, Derrida, and Dobbs have each in their own way indicated the vulnerability essential to human beings. This vulnerability does risk being wounded by harmful features of our environment, but at a more basic level it makes possible responsive interaction within various contexts. In the addict's case, attempting to minimize the risks inherent in vulnerability eventually leads to a relinquishing of responsibility, surrendering the power to make decisions to some limiting object. The resulting powerlessness experienced by the addict is the futility of the effort to control one's situation and to eliminate potential risks. Still, the capacity to respond remains for the addict. This responsibility can be embraced by practicing a humility that acknowledges the influence exerted on the addict by the addictive object. In acknowledging our essential vulnerability, we expose ourselves once again to the positive possibilities available in our environments. Thus, the First Step in Twelve

Step spirituality restores an awareness of one's essential vulnerability and reacquaints the addict with her potential for real response—including the possibility of recovery.

NOTES

1. *Alcoholics Anonymous,* 24. Emphasis in the original.

2. Regarding the insufficiency of self-knowledge to prevent addictive behavior, see ibid., 39–42.

3. This connotative difference is demonstrated (and perhaps reinscribed) by Bruce Wilshire in his discussion of vulnerability in *Wild Hunger,* 56–58. In these few pages, Wilshire points out that exposure can be frightening, leading to withdrawal or servitude; while doing so, he identifies vulnerability with the body's dependence on its environmental context, and implies that our primal response to such dependence is negative. Wilshire's description of our response to being exposed dovetails with Seeburger's existential analysis regarding the roots of addiction (which I discuss below). I will argue against reducing vulnerability to its negative connotation, as Wilshire seems to do. Our essential vulnerability entails both the danger *and* the potential inherent in exposure.

4. In saying that vulnerability is essential to human beings, I am not saying that it is only or even primarily a human capacity. I am simply restricting the discussion to humans in order to focus on the addict's potential for responsibility.

5. Seeburger, *Addiction and Responsibility,* 106 (emphasis in the original). Regarding "disownment," see 89–92; the argument that addiction provides a sense of control is made at 128–30.

6. Heidegger, *Pathmarks,* 144–45.

7. Heidegger, *Off the Beaten Track,* 174–76. This critique, located in the essay "Nietzsche's Word: 'God is Dead,'" is expounded in even more detail in Heidegger's essay "The Question concerning Technology" (found in *Question of Technology*) and in his lectures on Nietzsche.

8. Derrida, *Rogues,* 152.

9. Ibid. Derrida specifically claims that this "unforeseeability" comes from the other, but the hermeneutic of the Derridean "other" (especially in light of his interactions with Emmanuel Levinas) is a complicated one. It is fair to say that "the other" can refer to that which is not reducible to oneself, and vulnerability expands this class by exposing oneself bidirectionally to one's context.

10. Derrida, "Force of Law."

11. David Dobbs, "Orchid Children," *Atlantic Monthly,* December 2009, 52.

12. Ibid.

13. Ibid., 60.

JEROME A. MILLER

# Addiction and Tears

Jerome Miller's essay may be read as an attempt to draw out the radical implications of Corbin Casarez's proposal that we rethink addiction and recovery in terms of vulnerability. Miller argues that Twelve Step spirituality is philosophically revolutionary because it challenges the privileged role that self-control has played in the traditional understanding of moral character. Proceeding phenomenologically, Miller argues that the heart, understood as the vulnerable core of the self, is more primordial than the controlling ego or appetitive desire. It is the source of the self-donative passion awakened in us by the mysteries that have the power to move us to tears and so to melt our addictions.

A friend of mine, for many years a drug addict, once confided to me that being the lead speaker at a Twelve Step meeting was the most terrifying experience of his life. This admission resonated with me. The prospect of expressing oneself at a meeting can be dreadful, in part because one knows one is liable to break down and weep. But the revolutionary character of Twelve Step spirituality is due, I believe, to its discovery that the flow of tears has an uncanny power: it can melt addiction. The trauma of sobbing can be redemptive. The philosophical question is, How is this possible? Is there a way to explain the surprising connection between sobriety and tears?

This is not a connection that our philosophical tradition prepares us to make. From its inception, Western culture has considered self-control—including control over one's tears—the indispensable lynchpin of virtuous character. It teaches that addiction can be overcome through willpower, sobriety achieved through self-mastery. Twelve Step spirituality challenges these convictions. It encourages us to accept our vulnerabilities instead of resisting them. Understanding it requires nothing less than a paradigm shift in our understanding of our selves. In what follows, I try to explain the logic of this shift and the reasons that make it, in my view, rationally compelling.

## The Project of Control

The concept of self-control is a puzzling notion because it requires us to think of the self as both the controll*er* and the controll*ee*. Plato, the first philosopher to explain the concept, recognized this apparent contradiction and developed the strategy that has long been used to resolve it: *divide the self into parts.*[1] Those of us who get angry at ourselves for yielding to impulses can easily recognize the parts Plato distinguished.

(1) The rational part of the psyche provides us some understanding of the moral ideals that ought to govern our conduct. As the only part of the psyche capable of knowing these ideals, it's entitled to be the controll*er* who rules over the other parts of our subjectivity and makes them conform to moral exigencies. Self-control is logically and psychologically possible because rationality can operate independently of the parts it is supposed to govern. In Western culture, reason will retain the morally and culturally privileged role Plato gives it long after Plato's own metaphysical understanding of the soul is abandoned.

(2) The appetitive part of the psyche is the locus of those desires that, when left unsupervised and uninhibited, lead us to do morally horrific acts. Desire is hydra-like. There's no boundary or measure immanent in it, and hence no possibility that is off-limits to it. It is capable of doing *anything.*[2] Desire pursues whatever it seeks with the intention of seizing hold of it and never letting go of it. It follows that a desire is an incipient addiction. It can't wait to get what it wants and possessively holds onto it once it has acquired it.

(3) Located, as it were, between reason and appetite is *thymos*—what we call emotion. Although Plato describes it as the natural ally of reason,[3] he also insists that, like appetite, it needs to be rationally controlled. Emotion is wedded to reason insofar as our way of judging a situation determines what emotion it calls forth in us. (For example, I get angry at myself for drinking to excess only if I believe such behavior reprehensible.) But since emotions can themselves become excessive and cloud reason, they too have to be moderated and restrained.

I have described Plato's moral psychology in some detail because we still tend to divide ourselves into reason, emotion, and desire, although the tectonic shifts of culture have significantly altered what they mean to us.[4] In the modern world, the psyche is no longer considered subordinate to an eternal Logos. The individual claims autonomy for both reason and freedom, and works to make the historical future conform to human planning. But different as this modern project of control is from Plato's conception of virtuous self-rule, it is still reason that aspires to govern and still the compulsions of desire that are perceived as a threat to it. One would think that the autonomous ego, once installed as the ruling principle of culture, would have no difficulty getting rid of addictions that are so antithetical to it. But, in fact, the opposite seems to have happened. Instead of disappearing, addictions have proliferated. Obsessed as our culture is with control, it has proven to be strangely incapable of mastering them. One can't help but wonder if some terrible irony of which we are oblivious is at work here—some irony that makes our very project of control the seedbed of our compulsions.[5]

## Impassioned Vulnerability

The suggestion that the project of control may itself lead *to* addiction, rather than away from it, may initially seem highly implausible. But it becomes more credible once we examine the kind of pleasure on which our addictions fixate.

Pleasure is most satiating when it covers and saturates the whole floodplain of consciousness. Such pleasure has many modalities: it can be intense but short-lived (orgasm), or mellow but prolonged (the experience of being stoned). Whatever the modality, pleasure of this sort pleases by engulfing awareness. The contents of consciousness dissolve into the immediacy of the experience. The world that is ordinarily the object of our senses disappears. All that is other and beyond us evaporates. Pleasure, when totalizing, suspends the other-directed focus of conscious living. Flooded by it, we have no psychic distance from it. This is precisely why such pleasure is the perfect refuge—the ideal haven.[6] It provides the absolute relief, the total escape. We can relax in it, unwind in it, sink down in it, as in a womb. We never feel safer, more invulnerable, more impenetrable, than when we're enveloped by it.

If this description of the most addictive pleasures is accurate, it requires us to challenge theories that portray the id of appetite as a primal, primordial part of the psyche. To the addict desperately trying to master addiction, desire does feel like an inner beast, insatiable and untamable. But if desire craves pleasure because it provides perfect refuge, then pleasure-seeking is an exercise in *repression:* it's a recoil from the world—a flight from the alterities we encounter in it. And repression is not primal or primordial but secondary and derivative. For repression is consequent to, and a response to, what it is trying to repress. It's our attempt to flee what has the potential to upset us, overwhelm us, traumatize us. If pleasure represses, our desire for it is motivated by our terror of being devastated, our dread of alterity, our anxiety in the face of the unprecedented, unpredictable future.

That we are, in fact, always susceptible to trauma, always liable to be devastated, is a given. It's not a psychic eccentricity or symptomatic of some pathology. It's due to our primal and primordial vulnerability—to the fact that the very core of our being can be not only moved by but overcome by all that is sublime and beautiful, wonderful and dreadful, enlivening and horrifying. We are always already thrown open to—caught, as it were, in the throe of—realities that transcend us and have the power to overwhelm us. Intentionality—our very capacity to be conscious of the wondrous and terrifying, the inspiring and the devastating—is inherently traumatizing because it involves us in mysteries that exceed our comprehension, and so makes us participants in an inherently dangerous, unpredictable drama. Consciousness renders us vulnerable to the forbidding alterity of the world. We are always already caught in the throe of realities that are beyond us and too much for us.[7] We're always already in over our heads.

Where in us should we locate this primal opening, this radical vulnerability? In what part of the Platonic psyche is it housed? We may be inclined to identify it with the rational part, since it is intelligence that enables us to recognize overwhelming mystery *as* overwhelming mystery. But we can't overlook the fact that the wondrous and the dreadful, the aweful and horrific, have an emotive as well as a cognitive import. In fact, they reverberate throughout our entire being. Our experience of them goes all the way down in us. Any theory that divides the psyche into parts cannot account for the fact that vulnerability affects our being *as a whole*.

Many religious and spiritual traditions rely on a kind of communicating that speaks from the vulnerability at the core of our selves, instead of covering it up. It's called "speaking from the heart." *Cor,* the Latin word for "heart," is the source from which our word "core" derives. As used in spiritual traditions throughout the world,[8] "heart" does not signify one bodily organ or psychic capacity. It does not mean the emotions in contrast to the "head" or reason. It means the very center of our being—the center to which all our capacities, including intelligence and reason, belong. We are *all* heart because our being as a whole is bound to and affected by the vulnerability at the core of us. This vulnerability is the source of all our affections. It's the spring from which passion flows.

As its derivation from the Latin *passio* suggests, passion begins passively: it starts when our being is affected by some reality other than ourselves. It follows from this that the primordial characteristic of passion is suffering. We are its patients, not its masters. Passion is evoked in us—called forth in us—by what overwhelms us. This is why we imagine falling in love as an arrow that pierces the heart, causing it a mortal wound. Whether we're talking about falling in love with another person or with literature, with mathematics or baseball, with pottery or the stars, it's something that happens *to* us rather than something we cause. Passion is born in us when astonishment overcomes us.

But vulner*ability* suggests something different from sheer passivity, and so did the word "suffering" as it was originally used. To "suffer" did not mean only to undergo; it also meant to *allow*. Since passion is engendered in us by something beyond us that astonishes and overwhelms us, we can't manufacture it. But insofar as we *let* ourselves be affected, we are active in our very passivity: we *open* ourselves to, begin to give ourselves to, that which is moving us. The motion that we're moved to make is self-donative. To do an act wholeheartedly is to devote oneself entirely to what one loves, to give oneself to it without reservation, inhibition, restraint. The impassioned violinist gives herself wholly to the music and holds nothing back; the impassioned hiker brings a child's spendthrift enthusiasm to her walks. Although it is the poignancy of the music, the morning glory of the mountain trail, that inspire us to expend ourselves on them, this self-expenditure crucially depends on our willingness to make it.[9] Here is the uncanny paradox: impassioned living involves our giving ourselves to that which moves us in our deepest vulnerability.

This vulnerability is the rub. It's precisely our weakness, our susceptibility to wounds, that we're tempted to—and able to—flee. We're tempted to flee because wounds can be traumatizing. We're able to flee because we can refuse to suffer our vulnerability, even though it is constitutive of us. While we cannot produce passion or manufacture our enthusiasms, we *can* close ourselves off to whatever might awaken them. We cannot cause ourselves to fall in love, but we *can* protect ourselves from ever being pierced. We can suffer our vulnerability—or recoil from it and repress it.

Such repression involves disassociating ourselves from vulnerability so that we can operate independently of it and dominate it. We achieve such independence by making the rational ego the control center of our psyches. In our society, we take the existence of such an ego for granted and assume that its formation is a natural, inevitable part of maturation. But, in fact, the formation of the ego as a control center is not a psychic necessity. It's a consequence of organizing the psyche around the goal of control that dominates our culture. This organization is achieved by a strategy of "divide and conquer." The "I" has to separate itself from the heart, the core of the self. It has to use reason to plan its project of control and the will to operationalize this project. It has to turn the different capacities of intentionality (rationality, imagination, emotion, and sensation) into distinct "parts" of the psyche that function separately from each other. The psyche as a whole is thereby reconfigured so that it no longer *is* a whole, and so is no longer liable to be wholly affected by anything. In the self as so reconfigured, there is no place for our primordial vulnerability. The very purpose of the reconfiguration is to repress it.

It is not difficult to discern the principal consequence of this repression. Passion depends on and arises from our primordial affect-ability. We cannot repress this affect-ability, cannot put a tourniquet on our hearts, without profoundly diminishing our capacity to be moved. It's true that the tourniquet rarely works quite as efficiently as we would like. The circulation of the affections is not entirely stopped. But when the psyche is organized around the project of control—when the clenched fist of the rational ego replaces the vulnerability of the open heart as its governing principle—the passion that escapes the tourniquet has itself been shaped by the desire to repress. It was no accident that Plato thought of anger when he wanted to show that emotion is one component of the partified psyche. Anger is our emotional response to losing what we're determined to possess. Through it we aspire to regain control by attacking and repressing whatever has taken control from us. Anger is the tightening of an already clenched fist. And if the ego has difficulty controlling its anger, this is because the anger is fueled by the ego's very determination to be in control.

However, keeping one's fist clenched, as the project of control requires, is an endless, exhausting business because we cannot ever eliminate the possibility of failure from our lives. The world in its alterity is always resisting our control; the unprecedented future is always upsetting our plans, instead of conforming to them. Interruptions are always happening, and crisis can begin to brew at any time. Our therapeutic culture provides us techniques we can use to cope with, handle, manage, the psychic dis-ease such contingencies provoke. But coping mechanisms, however sophisticated, are never foolproof. Our vulnerabilities are not as easily overcome as our technological successes lead us to expect.

So it is that we look to pleasurable sensations for relief from the tension we experience as rational egos.[10] To provide such relief, pleasure has to be saturating. It has to fill every nook and cranny of the psyche where fear or anxiety, worry or insecurity, may lurk. But the desire for such pleasure is not primal in us. It does not spring from an id that is more primordial than any other dimension of the psyche. For such desire is itself repressive and presupposes what it is desperate to repress—the vulnerability that *is* primal and constitutive of us. It is true, of course, that the pleasures which saturate consciousness make us *feel* good. But this feeling is a sensation, not an emotion. Far from being an affect—a passion evoked in us by a reality beyond us—saturating pleasure provides us refuge from alterity and temporarily protects us from all our affections. In fact, the experience of such pleasure is entirely compatible with, and an extremely effective way to disguise, the profound anomie, the utter absence of affect, that, in our culture, is called "depression."

It is, then, a grave mistake to suppose that the pivotal psychic drama involves a struggle between the rational ego and the id for control of the psyche. For each of these is itself a modality of control, and both collaborate in repressing the impassioned vulnerability that is more primordial than either. The fundamental human choice is not between reason and desire, self-mastery and appetite, repression and permissiveness. For desire, appetite, license are themselves repressive exercises in control, and the project of control, even when it employs intelligence and rationality, is itself governed by desire—more specifically, the desire for invulnerability. There is an alternative to living as a rational ego or as an uninhibited id, but to access it one has to abandon the addiction they share: the addiction to control itself. Trying to overcome this addiction through willpower, trying to master it by further tightening one's fist, cannot possibly have any effect except to exacerbate it. In fact, *any* action that we who are addicted to control may be inclined to undertake is going to be governed by the very addiction we are attempting to break.

Once we realize this, we're compelled to acknowledge the terrible fact that we can do precisely *nothing* to get past our addiction. And here at last, after a rather circuitous journey, we reach the First Step of Twelve Step spirituality: admitting that addiction renders us impotent. In a culture that prizes control above everything, admitting even to oneself that one is impotent can be excruciating. In the age of Cialis and Viagra, this condition seems to be easily reversed. But if the culture of control keeps on inventing new technologies, devising new coping mechanisms, inventing new pleasures and security devices, it does so precisely because no remedy for our impotence and fallibility is ever going to be infallible. We are powerless over our addiction to control. And no matter how obsessively we pursue it, control is itself powerless over our vulnerability. We can flee it but not escape it; we can repress it but never master it. All the strategies we employ to disassociate ourselves from it are applied too late. Our hearts are always already exposed, always already susceptible to being pierced.

Impotence, then, is no physiological quirk; it's not a consequence of pathology, either physical or psychical. It's the result of the vulnerability we can neither escape nor master because it's the very core of ourselves. It's the awful truth we have to face if we're to face who we are.

## The Gift of Tears

My drug-addicted friend who was panic-stricken at the thought of leading a Twelve Step meeting was terrified of speaking from the heart. This terror is understandable. For when one's heart is in one's mouth, the words one intends to say are liable to disappear into sobs. Weeping differs from crying. When one cries, there's a rent in one's composure—a quivering lip, a slippage of breath, a trickle of tears; but one's self-possession remains essentially intact. But when one weeps, one's being as a whole temporarily breaks down. The ego, the control center of the psyche that's usually so proficient at keeping emotion in check, collapses. The body shudders under a weight it can't bear. Weeping is, as it were, the signature of human vulnerability. It's the paradigmatic idiom of human suffering. It testifies more eloquently than speech to the depth of our affections.

This description of weeping seems to confirm the suspicion that it is *sheerly* emotional and irrational. Such an assessment of it is long-standing. In one of Plato's earliest dialogues, Socrates rebukes his friends for weeping in response to his imminent death.[11] In the eyes of the Platonic Socrates, such uninhibited emotion demonstrates an egregious lack of philosophical equanimity, a failure to exercise the kind of rational self-control that the philosopher, above all, is expected to possess. According to Plato's diagnosis of it, weeping causes the emotional part of the soul to subvert the right rule of reason. We would expect him to say the same of the addict who breaks down when trying to speak at a meeting. Rational speech is submerged, it seems, by a flow of irrational feeling.

Twelve Step spirituality rests, however, on a very different conception of human interiority. According to it, the project of self-control that has for so long been considered the only possible antidote to addiction is itself a modality of addiction. "White-knuckling," the determination to master one's weaknesses through willpower, cramps the spirit instead of liberating it.[12] Like every addiction, it shuts down our receptivity and closes us off to what is beyond us. It is devastating to acknowledge that this is the case—devastating to realize, after years of trying to master addiction, that one has only been vacillating from one modality of control to another without ever *opening* oneself to anything beyond oneself. Such a realization may very well lead one to weep. But far from being irrational, such weeping is set in motion *by a profound insight that affects our entire being.* This cannot happen if the psyche is divided because then the impact that insight can have on us is restricted, compromised, aborted. If truth is to live in us, our entire being has to be open, receptive, vulnerable to it. Weeping under the impress of an insight means that truth has finally broken through our defenses and reached our hearts. To weep for this reason, in this way, is deeply, profoundly, preeminently sane.

When we're weeping because we're finally realizing what a mess we've made of our lives, all we can see is our impotence, our weakness, our terminal failure. We do not yet realize the great irony from which all of Twelve Step spirituality derives: the fact this very breakdown of our previously self-assured ego, this very inability to control our tears, is *opening* us to the Influence of sublimities that transcend us. But if we do break down at a Twelve Step meeting, the members of the fellowship are likely to respond in a way that surprises us—and helps to revolutionize our point of view. When we see the eagerness with which they welcome our tears, the empathizing embraces they offer us, the gratitude they express for our willingness to expose our fallibilities, we may start to suspect that our breakdown has the potential to be a breakthrough. According to the logic that governs the human heart and Twelve Step spirituality, it is only in and through our vulnerability that we can begin to access an Influence greater than ourselves.

My argument may seem to have jumped too quickly to this encouraging, hopeful possibility. But we can, I believe, confirm that it is a *real* possibility by considering what can lead us to weep. We weep only when overwhelmed. And we can be overwhelmed only by something that affects our whole being—our whole world. While failure at one thing isn't devastating, a failure that affects *everything* is. Sickness leaves the structure of our lives intact; a terminal illness doesn't. Contrary to what the Platonic Socrates argues, our own death or the death of someone who means the world to us is a preeminent reason to weep: weeping shows we realize, in the core of ourselves, the *import* of what is happening. Weeping, then, is a response to the *important,* the *ultimate,* that which is of *transcendent,* transformative *significance.*

This is why, in addition to the weeping that pours out our griefs, there is weeping that expresses the deepest of human joys. I referred above to our symbol for falling in love—a heart with an arrow through it. This suggests that love is itself a kind of death—a devastating wound from which we don't recover. But what flows from this wound are tears of gladness evoked in us by the goodness of the beloved. C. S. Lewis says that the experience of such radiance leave us "surprised by joy."[13] When falling in love, we're stunned into silence by a reality of transcendent importance whose existence was previously unknown to us. Such experiences suggest that the ultimately important—the ultimately meaningful and ultimately worthwhile—is no abstraction. It is an active, living reality capable of suddenly rupturing our lives open to a joy even more piercing, more overwhelming, more life-altering, than death. Whenever and wherever the transcendently important appears in our lives, it brings us down to the bottom of our impotencies. The great irony is that wholehearted acceptance of these impotencies clears a place in us for empowering grace. Our own life is lifted out of the shallows and becomes charged with the ultimate significance it now serves. As recipients of the grace dispensed by the transcendently important, we can play the role of impassioned collaborators in the gift economy that it creates.[14]

I have been speaking of the transcendently important, the ultimately worthwhile, that which is preeminently significant. The Twelve Steps refer to this as "God." I'm reluctant to use this term here because it has become something like the supreme cliché and hence no longer has the power to take us by surprise, to shatter our expectations, and throe us open to the unforeseen. One distinguishing characteristic of the Holy—the Transcendently Important—is that it never loses its capacity to shock us and shake us utterly. We cannot possibly know ahead of time how or when it will arrive, because it comes to us from and as an unprecedented future that undoes all our plans and defies all the strategies we use to try to control it. The Transcendently Important breaks in upon us without our being able to predict it, and so always amazes us as something miraculous. The Twelve Steps describe it as a "higher power." But what is most astonishing about it is that its power derives from its poignancy—its capacity to touch, with excruciating tenderness, the heart of our deepest vulnerability.

Nothing testifies to the poignancy of its power—and the power of its poignancy—so eloquently as the impact this power has on our addictions. For most of us, nothing we've ever experienced in our lives can compare to the inexorable, irresistible power they have over us. Nothing in the world even approximates the strength of their grip on us. But there is something active in the world that they cannot withstand. Addiction refuses to yield to a clenched fist but the excruciating tenderness of love can melt it. It is this tenderness and the tears it wrings from us that open the arteries and allow our affections to circulate again. The quarantine that kept the parts of psyche separate from each other is thereby lifted. We become the heart we have spent our lives fleeing. Addiction was never part of it. It was only the tourniquet. The free flow of the affections makes it unnecessary. This flow starts with a cataract of tears. When no dam is built to restrain it, it turns into a river of gladness.

I began by speaking of what is most revolutionary about the Twelve Steps—the fact that they do not try to overcome addiction through the will to control. In our culture of clenched fists, this is incomprehensible. But to go all the way down in us, sanity has to be heartfelt. And sanity becomes heartfelt only when we allow what is Transcendently Important to reverberate all the way down to the very bottom of our vulnerability. There, and only there, can the Transcendently Important come to *matter* to us. We might say that the Twelve Steps carve a kind of pathway to the heart—a kind of riverbed that allows love to pour into us. They don't tell us when or how such love will happen, nor do they pretend to comprehend it. Sanity, they suggest, requires that we entrust ourselves to Mystery. There is more wisdom in this poignant trust than in any other human potency.

NOTES

1. See Plato's *Republic,* 430e–431d and books 2–4, in *Great Dialogues,* for the tripartite theory of the soul.

2. See ibid., 571c–d.

3. Ibid., 441a.

4. For a recent argument in favor of Plato's tripartite division of the psyche and reason's right to govern it, see Dent, *Moral Psychology of the Virtues*.

5. In what follows I will be arguing in support of Francis Seeburger's contention that "all addicts are addicted to 'control'" (*Addiction and Responsibility*, 129). Insofar as this is the case, it is not so surprising that a culture obsessed with control is pervaded by addiction.

6. This account of pleasure has been influenced by Spalding Gray's *Impossible Vacation*.

7. I have developed this insight at some length in *Throe of Wonder*, where I argue that wonder, dread, and awe give us access to mysteries that transcend us. These experiences, as I understand them, are similar to the kind of ecstatic experience that Bruce Wilshire describes in *Wild Hunger*. However, I emphasize, in a way that Wilshire does not, the irreducible alterity of the other as other.

8. See Michael Meslin, "Heart," translated by Kristine Anderson, in Eliade, *Encyclopedia of Religion*, 234–37.

9. In *Spirituality of Imperfection,* Kurtz and Ketcham distinguish willingness from willfulness.

10. I should emphasize, however, that, in my view, escape from the world (especially its traumatizing alterity) is the principle objective of the addicted psyche; saturating pleasure is only a means to it. For this reason, the pursuit of escape can remain addictive even when it does *not* result in pleasure. As Seeburger says (*Addiction and Responsibility,* 6–9), one can become addicted to addiction itself.

11. See *Phaedo,* 117c–e, in Plato, *Great Dialogues*.

12. See, for example, "On the Move," in *Alcoholics Anonymous,* 491: "After white-knuckling it for almost two years in A.A., I finally broke down and saw that I could not stay sober all by myself, but I was terrified of going back to drinking."

13. Lewis, *Surprised by Joy*.

14. See Hyde, *Gift*.

# PART TWO

# A Power Greater Than Oneself?

# An Inclusive Spirituality?
## Naturalism in the Twelve Step Tradition

As the essays in the first section of this anthology have implied, and as the first three of the Twelve Steps themselves suggest, acknowledging one's own power-lessness can lead one to ask whether there exists "a power greater than oneself." If the Twelve Step affirmation that there is such a power has long been a source of controversy and confusion, it is in part because the Twelve Steps do not clarify what this "power" is. Gerald Cantu, the first of our contributors who tries to shed some philosophical light on this issue, draws attention to the conflicts that it provoked even when the Twelve Steps were being formulated. Cantu examines the early history of Alcoholics Anonymous for the purpose of determining just how philosophically inclusive the Twelve Step tradition is. He ends by arguing that a psychological interpretation of religious experience makes it possible for those with a naturalistic worldview to take spirituality seriously.

The Twelve Step program is more than just a form of therapy designed to help addicts achieve and sustain physical sobriety. It is a spiritual program designed to reach the goal of sobriety by realizing its *summum bonum,* a sober and spiritually whole life achieved through a sequence of spiritual experiences. As Twelve Step literature states, "A.A.'s twelve steps are a group of principles, spiritual in their nature, which if practiced as a way of life, can expel the obsession to drink and enable the sufferer to become usefully and happily whole."[1] The title of the present anthology calls attention to the spiritual nature of Twelve Step fellowships. The question I would like to address in this essay is, How inclusive is the spiritual culture of the program they follow?

We begin with a distinction between various forms of inclusion. (1) *Institutional inclusion* concerns the codified requirements for membership in a community. An institution is inclusive of an individual if that person meets the requirements for membership. (2) Inclusion on a personal level is manifested in *spiritual receptivity*, an attitude of respect for a differing worldview based on the recognition that it provides an adequate path to spiritual realization. (3) Another dimension of inclusivity is the *philosophical compatibility* of different cultures. This concerns the logical relations between their fundamental tenets. One system of belief is inclusive of another if its *summum bonum* can be realized by a person who remains committed to another system.

Each of these forms of inclusion, and their relationships to one another, are interesting topics in themselves. The question under consideration in this essay, however, concerns the extent to which the *culture* of Twelve Step spirituality is inclusive. Therefore, the primary focus will be on the third form of inclusion, with only incidental discussion of spiritual receptivity and institutional inclusion.

In the rest of this essay, I will argue that Twelve Step culture is inclusive enough to encompass both non-natural and naturalistic worldviews. By a "non-natural worldview" is meant a worldview that is committed to the existence of a reality over and above the natural world accessed directly by the senses, or inferred to exist by the sciences on the basis of what is directly sensed (such as the quantum universe). Faith is defined non-naturalistically as belief that this higher supra-natural reality exists.[2] A naturalistic worldview is committed to the belief that the world accessed directly by the senses, or inferred by the sciences on the basis of observation, is the only one that exists or is known to exist. Non-natural faiths include Christianity, Catholicism, Islam, Judaism, Sikhism, Mahayana and Tantric Buddhism, Vedanta, New Thought, and New Age, all of which have the common feature that they are committed to the existence of a non-natural realm. Naturalistic worldviews are those associated with agnosticism and atheism. I aim to show that Twelve Step culture is inclusive enough to encompass all faiths and worldviews enumerated above.

The structure of the essay is as follows. In the first part, I shall explicate how the inclusivity of Twelve Step culture encompasses all non-natural faiths. In the second, I will show how Twelve Step culture is inclusive of naturalistic worldviews as well.

## Twelve Step Spirituality's Inclusivity of *Faith*

Twelve Step spirituality is a religiously inclusive culture. It is inclusive of all non-natural faiths and accommodates a wide variety of temperaments. In a passage that shows a remarkable degree of religious pluralism, Bill Wilson states, "While A.A. has restored thousands of poor Christians to their churches, and has made believers out of atheists and agnostics, it has also made good A.A.'s out of those belonging to the Buddhist, Islamic, and Jewish faiths."[3] Twelve Step spirituality does not require a practitioner to renounce a currently held faith. On the contrary, practitioners are encouraged to return to whatever faith is a real option for them. It is striking that not one passage with a contrary message can be found in Twelve Step literature, whereas a plethora of passages can be cited that endorse inclusivity, acceptance, and respect. To quote one: "We think it no concern of ours what religious bodies our members identify themselves with as individuals. This should be an entirely personal affair which each of us decides for himself in the light of past associations, or his present choice. Not all of us join religious bodies, but most of us favor such memberships."[4]

The basis of this inclusivity is the metaphor of a broad "Realm of Spirit." In *Alcoholics Anonymous,* Bill Wilson says, "To us, the Realm of Spirit is broad, roomy, all inclusive; never exclusive or forbidding to those who earnestly seek. It is open, we believe, to all men."[5] This is in stark contrast to the sort of teaching found in traditional, sectarian religiosity, which tends to insist on one path to God, truth, and salvation—an attitude embodied in Matthew 7:14, which says that "the gate is narrow and the way is hard that leads to life, and there are few who find it."[6] There is a long and interesting story to be told about the basis of this inclusivity,[7] but the scope of this essay requires focus on more proximate causes.

The proximate cause was Bill Wilson's[8] decision to side with the religiously liberal members of the early Twelve Step fellowship, and against the religious conservatives, when it came time to give a final formulation of the spiritual concepts of the Twelve Step program. The religious conservatives wanted a Twelve Step spirituality that was unambiguously founded on orthodox Christianity. The religious liberals wanted a theology-free program. The latter got their way. Bill Wilson authored the text of *Alcoholics Anonymous* in consultation with the members of AA. (He also made unilateral decisions where necessary.) When it came time to decide on the final language for the published version, Wilson relates, "[There] were conservative, liberal, and radical viewpoints. . . . The liberals were the largest contingent and they had no objection to the use of the word 'God' throughout the book, but they were dead set against any other theological proposition. They would have nothing to do with the doctrinal issues. Spirituality, yes. But religion, no—*positively* no. Most of our members, they pointed out, believed in some sort of deity. But when it came to theology we could not possibly agree among ourselves."[9] What Wilson fails to mention in this passage is that he himself was a religious liberal. From his cultural milieu, Wilson imbibed the spiritual musings of Ralph Waldo Emerson and the Transcendentalists—seminal influences on his own spiritual development.[10]

There are two components of this milieu that will be underscored here as particularly influential on Twelve Step spirituality. The first was Emerson's idea that God could be found anywhere in nature, including ourselves. This influence had the effect of making Twelve Step spirituality receptive to all forms of religion, which are essentially reflections of the human search for the divine.

Another important idea in New England spirituality is that faith cannot be legislated. Although faith is essential, the particular shape of anyone's faith and the kinds of spiritual beliefs one has are matters that can only be determined by the individual. One can see this idea percolating in Bill's recollections of "his [grandfather's] insistence that the spheres really had their music; but his denial of the preacher's right to tell him how he must listen."[11]

These ideas are the basis of the complete freedom that is given to members of the Twelve Step fellowship to work out their own spiritual concepts as they practice Twelve Step spirituality's program of action. As Wilson says, "Whether we agree with a particular approach or conception [of another's form of spirituality] seems to make little difference. Experience has taught us that these are matters [for] . . . each individual to settle for himself."[12] What we get in the attitude of Wilson, then, is a capacious spirituality that is constantly seeking and that gives the individual the final authority on what he or she comes to believe about *the* spiritual realm. This has made Twelve Step spirituality a highly flexible practice that can accommodate a wide variety of temperaments.

Interestingly, this puts Twelve Step spirituality in the same class as the mature spiritual traditions, which tend to be attuned to the fact that individuals are different. People have different desires, different cognitive abilities, and different sensibilities. Hinduism, for example, draws a distinction between individuals who are led more by their heads than by their hearts. The former tend to deal with wisdom on a very abstract level and see the content of insight non-dualistically. The latter tend to be dualists and devotionalists and are encouraged to choose a preferred manifestation of God and to remain devoted to it throughout their lives.[13] A spiritual practice that is broad enough to include different kinds of personality in this way is all the better for it, and Twelve Step spirituality is certainly inclusive in this respect.

## Twelve Step Spirituality and Naturalism

We have seen, then, that Twelve Step spirituality is inclusive of all non-natural faiths. Does Twelve Step's inclusivity extend to naturalism, including the naturalism of the atheist and agnostic?

Institutional inclusion is generally understood to be accomplished by following the principle that each individual can conceive of God as she wishes. This principle has the effect of including naturalists in Twelve Step spirituality. However, although Wilson was sympathetic to naturalists in the early years of the fellowship, he did not have an attitude of spiritual receptivity to their worldview, as I shall now go on to argue.

The phrasing of Step Three—"God *as we understood Him*"—is designed to make it possible for naturalists to commit to a spiritual program of action, and it was an outcome of the larger controversy over the final language of Twelve Step spirituality involving liberals, conservatives, and "radicals"— the naturalists who were representative of the left wing of the fellowship and who wanted any mention of God stricken out of the Steps. As Wilson puts it, "This was the great contribution of our atheists and agnostics. They had widened our gateway so that all who suffer might pass through, regardless of their belief or *lack of belief.* God . . . was now expressed in terms that anybody—*anybody at all*—could accept and try."[14] These naturalists in the early Twelve Step fellowship were, of course, Wilson's friends, and his abundant sympathy for all people led him to decide on Step Three's final phrasing, so they would not be left out. However, despite language allowing the naturalist to proceed with the spiritual program of action while maintaining naturalistic beliefs, Wilson's attitude does not entail spiritual receptivity toward naturalists, for it is connected with an attitude that fails to recognize that naturalism is an adequate path to spiritual realization. The preponderance of textual evidence suggests that Wilson wanted to make it possible for naturalists to begin practicing the program by adopting a naturalistic higher power, but this was a way of proceeding that Wilson thought would be provisional.

He hoped and expected that practitioners would come to believe in *some* form of non-natural faith as they progressed through the program of action.

Notwithstanding Wilson's lack of spiritual receptivity to naturalists, the phrasing of Step Three is part of a broad and inclusive philosophy of Twelve Step spirituality. Wilson did have an essential part in synthesizing the various elements that make up this culture, which *is* inclusive of naturalists, as I now endeavor to show.

As I indicated earlier, one worldview is inclusive of another worldview if a person subscribing to the latter can realize the *summum bonum* of the former without being logically compelled to renounce the fundamental beliefs of the latter. *The* summum bonum *of Twelve Step spirituality is a sober and spiritually whole life achieved through a spiritual experience. Any naturalist can partake in this* summum bonum *without being required to retract her naturalistic beliefs because of the psychologized conception of spiritual experience on which Twelve Step spirituality is based.*

Every founder leaves his or her stamp on the movement he or she creates and sets a pattern that followers attempt to realize for themselves. Wilson had a spiritual experience, which he self-effacingly characterized as a "hot flash." In a moment of depression, Bill appealed to God. "The result was instant, electric, beyond description. The place seemed to light up, blinding white. I knew only ecstasy and seemed on a mountain. A great wind blew, enveloping and penetrating me. To me, it was not of air, but of Spirit. Blazing, there came the tremendous thought 'You are a free man.'"[15] After his experience, Wilson promptly and enthusiastically began serving other alcoholics. Wilson's pattern of conversion followed by service was thus set.

Wilson fortunately recognized that a spiritual experience of his variety would not be replicated by all who are in need of the benefits of recovery. He set out to correct the idea that recovery from alcoholism was to be achieved via his brand of spiritual experience in *Alcoholics Anonymous's* important appendix titled "Spiritual Experience." There Wilson writes:

> The terms "spiritual experience" and "spiritual awakening" are used many times in this book which . . . shows that the personality change sufficient to bring about recovery from alcoholism has manifested itself among us in many different forms. . . . In the first few chapters a number of sudden revolutionary changes are described. . . . Many alcoholics have . . . concluded that in order to recover they must acquire an immediate and overwhelming

'God-consciousness' followed at once by a vast change in feeling and outlook.... [These] transformations, though frequent, are by no means the rule. Most of our experiences are what the psychologist William James calls the 'educational variety' because they develop slowly over a period of time.[16]

With respect to spiritual experiences, then, Wilson distinguishes between "dramatic" spiritual experiences like his own, which are characterized by intense emotional valences and immediate shifts of perspective, and "educational" spiritual experiences, which lead to more gradual shifts in perspective and changes of habits through the methodical application of a spiritual practice. What is common to both kinds of experience is a shift within the psyche from the experience of negative emotions and ideas—pessimism, dejection, anger, and disturbance—to the experience of more positive emotions and ideas—happiness, joy, sympathy, love, compassion, and peace of mind. What Wilson accomplished with this distinction was a flexibility that allows the details of the general pattern of recovery to be filled in with different kinds of experiences, both in terms of the kind of spiritual experience one has and how one goes on to be of service to other addicts.

Spiritual experiences are open to naturalists on account of the fact that Twelve Step spirituality employs a psychologized conception of them. This conception derives from modern psychology—and more specifically from its naturalism. Theoretical discussions of the naturalized conception of the spiritual experience can be found in John Dewey's *A Common Faith,* Erich Fromm's *Psychoanalysis and Religion,* Abraham Maslow's *Religions, Values, and Peak Experiences,* and William James's *Varieties of Religious Experience,* the last of which was a direct influence on Wilson's understanding of spiritual psychology. These psychologists recognized the value of spiritual experiences and formulated methods for studying them while maintaining an agnostic attitude regarding their causes, or the cognitive meaning attributed to them, even though those who undergo the experiences may attribute them to a non-natural source. We see this attitude in William James's chapter on conversion: "To be converted, to be regenerated ... are so many phrases which denote the process, gradual or sudden, by which a self hitherto divided ... becomes unified.... This is at least what conversion signifies in general terms, *whether or not we believe that a direct divine operation is needed to bring such a moral change about.*"[17] James and the other psychologists I've mentioned were able to study the spiritual experience by dissociating the experience itself, which occurs as a matter of fact, from the intellectual accretions—the cultural interpretations—attached to it. To be sure, there is always some intellectual component connected with such an experience, but that component, which is a product of whatever family of concepts happen to be in use in the given culture, can be separated from the experience itself.

We got a glimpse of the psychologized conception of the spiritual experience in the appendix "Spiritual Experience," quoted above, but there is a remarkable passage that makes explicit reference to such a conception in the text of *Alcoholics Anonymous*. When a patient who was being treated by the distinguished psychologist Carl Jung for alcoholism asked whether there were exceptions to his fatal prognosis, Jung replied, "Yes, there [are]. . . Here and there . . . alcoholics have had what are called vital spiritual experiences. To me these occurrences are phenomena. They appear to be in the nature of huge emotional displacements and rearrangements. Ideas, emotions, and attitudes which were once the guiding forces of the lives of these men are suddenly cast to one side, and a completely new set of conceptions and motives begin to dominate them."[18] The Twelve Step program is, in fact, a set of exercises that aim to bring about a spiritual experience in this psychological sense. It is a discipline that is known through experience to lead to certain kinds of effects. The effects are those that occur within the psyche, and the causes of these effects are the practices that constitute the spiritual program of action, including the Twelve Steps themselves.

It might be objected that Twelve Step spirituality is a practice designed to bring about faith. This raises the suspicion among naturalists that the program is designed to lead them to non-natural beliefs, which would create resistance in their minds to Twelve Step spirituality. This suspicion would be justified if Twelve Step spirituality were a devotional practice that *is* meant to guide the practitioner toward faith—in the Trinity, for example—by means of a set of rituals and exercises. In a devotional tradition, those who are of little faith are encouraged, at the outset, not to worry about the absence of faith and to proceed with the practices, which are alleged to produce the desired beliefs as they are carried out. If Twelve Step spirituality were a devotional practice of this sort, the practitioner would be led through a set of exercises—self-examination, the making of amends, the deepening of one's spiritual consciousness—that are designed to deepen one's faith in a higher power, or God, in the non-natural sense. But while Twelve Step spirituality may appear to be such a devotional practice, and is certainly compatible with one, the institutions of Twelve Step spirituality are in fact highly flexible spaces in which different forms of practice are allowed to coexist. Devotional approaches are but one type of practice. Characterizing Twelve Step spirituality in the devotional terms above would be like describing a beautiful forest on the basis of one of its trees. The description would carry some truth, but it would represent only a partial account. Left out would be the great diversity of the forest's flora and fauna. Separation of the term "God" in Step Three from any particular content has had the effect of making the program experimental and non-devotional for a great many people. The devotional attitude is guided by practice toward some preconceived insight, but since the Twelve Step program does not aim for any specific insight, there is no particular content to which the practitioner is being led.

One can, then, pursue Twelve Step spirituality with a purely experimental attitude, testing its spiritual practices to determine whether they lead to spiritual experience in the psychological sense, while maintaining a naturalistic attitude. Some insights of Aldous Huxley are apposite in this context:

> We see that there is no conflict between the mystical approach to religion and the scientific approach, because one is not committed by mysticism to any cut-and-dried statement about the structure of the universe. You can practice mysticism entirely in psychological terms, and on the basis of a complete agnosticism in regard to the conceptual ideas of orthodox religion, and yet come to knowledge—gnosis—and the fruits of knowledge will be the fruits of the spirit: love, joy, peace, and the capacity to help other people.[19]

Huxley was speaking of mystical spirituality here, but such an attitude can be applied to Twelve Step spirituality as well. It is possible to carry out the practical program without being committed to any particular worldview. If one carries out the practice of Twelve Step spirituality even with a naturalistic attitude, one will obtain the fruits of the program: a spiritual experience, characterized as a shift from the psyche's experience of negative emotions to the experience of more positive emotions.

Rather than leading to some preconceived insight, then, Twelve Step spirituality is a practice that fosters honesty and the inclination to self-examination whereby each individual can come to the consciousness of his or her own belief—whether that belief be natural or non-natural. William James distinguished between "tender" and "strong" temperamental attitudes, and claimed that natural and non-natural worldviews are determined not purely theoretically but also by one's temperament. Naturalism, then, is not only a theoretical worldview but also a temperamental attitude. Twelve Step spirituality's ability to accommodate this temperament shows the remarkable extent of its inclusivity.

NOTES

1. *Twelve Steps and Twelve Traditions*, 15.

2. The uses of "non-natural" and "faith" in this paper are purely technical, not evaluative. Belief in a supra-natural reality is not unnatural in the sense that it is abnormal, and faith may obviously be defined in a way that does not necessarily imply belief in a supra-natural reality. For instance, Paul Tillich defines faith as "ultimate concern" (see *Dynamics of Faith*), while Erich Fromm defines it as the embrace of an "ultimate object of devotion" (see *Psychoanalysis and Religion*). The main division I intend to keep in focus, however, is that between belief in a non-natural reality and the lack of this belief. For this, I use non-natural as opposed to natural worldviews and refrain from using a more expansive conception of faith.

3. Bill W., *As Bill Sees It*, 20.

4. *Alcoholics Anonymous*, 28.

5. Ibid., 46.

6. English Standard Version.

7. A longitudinal account would connect the spiritual milieu of New England with Vedanta's entry into the American spiritual consciousness. For background, see Goldberg, *American Veda*.

8. Wilson was the cofounder of AA and the person primarily responsible for synthesizing the various psychological, religious, and philosophical ideas, thereby forming Twelve Step spirituality as we now know it.

9. *Alcoholics Anonymous Comes of Age*, 162.

10. For a discussion of the different elements found in Vermont's spiritual milieu, see the interview of Susan Cheever by Krista Tippet, "The Spirituality of Addiction and Recovery," May 15, 2008, http://www.onbeing.org/program/spirituality-addiction-and-recovery/229.

11. *Alcoholics Anonymous*, 10.

12. Ibid., 50.

13. See Smith, *World's Religions*, 26–50, for a discussion of Hinduism.

14. *Alcoholics Anonymous Comes of Age,* 165.

15. Bill W., *Three Talks to Medical Societies,* 14.

16. *Alcoholics Anonymous,* 183.

17. James, *Varieties of Religious Experience,* 189 (italics added).

18. *Alcoholics Anonymous,* 27.

19. Huxley, *Human Situation,* 215.

# Atheism and Twelve Step Spirituality

In this essay, a natural follow-up to Gerald Cantu's, Sean McAleer explores the boundaries of the Twelve Step tradition by arguing that atheism is philosophically compatible with it. He draws support for his position from a surprising source—the philosophy of science. His analysis suggests that Twelve Step practitioners can do something comparable to what scientists do when they speak of what is unobservable without affirming that it actually exists. McAleer ends by explaining why open-mindedness on the question of God is especially in keeping with Twelve Step spirituality, a view entirely consonant with Cantu's claim that pluralism is a hallmark of the Twelve Step tradition.

In offering a plan for recovery from addiction, the Twelve Steps offer "a design for living" that even non-addicts might find attractive. Indeed, the spirituality of the Twelve Steps seems to recapture a vision of philosophy as a way of life rather than a merely academic discipline: the "Twelve Steps are a group of principles, spiritual in their nature, which, if practiced as a way of life, can expel the obsession to drink and enable the sufferer to become happily and usefully whole."[1]

But the atheist or agnostic seeking relief from addiction and attracted to the design for living embodied in the Twelve Steps might despair at discovering that most of the Steps refer in some way to God. How can an atheist sincerely and coherently turn her will and life over to the care of God or ask God to remove her shortcomings if she doesn't believe in God? It seems that atheism is incompatible with Twelve Step spirituality.

Despite its surface plausibility, I think this view is mistaken. In what follows, I draw from philosophical reflection on the nature of science and the mind to show that atheism is fully compatible with Twelve Step spirituality.

Before we begin, we should get clear about terms. "Theism" and "atheism" typically refer to the God of the Western theological tradition, who is seen as all-knowing, all-powerful, and all-good. But we should think of them more broadly, as referring to any sacred and supernatural entities or forces or dimensions—Western or Eastern or whatever—to which one can pray, devote oneself, and so on. Theists believe that this kind of being exists, atheists believe no such beings exist, and agnostics are neutral, withholding belief altogether.

## Orthopraxis versus Orthodoxy

One reason in favor of the compatibility view—the view that atheism is fully compatible with Twelve Step spirituality—is that Twelve Step spirituality is primarily a matter of right action rather than right belief, of *orthopraxis* rather than *orthodoxy*. If what one believes matters far less than what one does, an atheist's lack of belief in God need not prevent her from meaningfully and sincerely practicing the Steps and living a contented sobriety, for she can take action in the absence of belief.

Both the foundational texts of Twelve Step spirituality as well as the practices of many Twelve Step meetings bear out this primacy of action over belief. For example, the Third Tradition specifies a desire to stop drinking, rather than theistic belief or indeed belief of any kind, as the only requirement for membership in AA.[2] To the extent that belief is important to recovery and Twelve Step spirituality, it need only be the belief expressed in the preface to the Big Book: "Yes, I believe this program can work for me too."[3] Many AA meetings begin with someone reading "How It Works," which details a program of action rather than a litany of beliefs of the sort one finds in the Nicene or Apostle's creeds. And it is noteworthy that the "spiritual awakening" of Step Twelve is the result of taking action rather than the result of having certain beliefs.

But even if we grant the primacy of action over belief, how can an atheist coherently practice the Steps, since so many of them refer to God? The Second Step refers to "a power greater than ourselves"; the Third and Eleventh Steps refer to "God as we understood him"; the Fifth, Sixth, and Seventh Steps mention "God" or "Him." Even the inclusive qualifier "as we understood him" does not seem broad enough to include atheists.

## Theological Anti-Realism

As the God of the Twelve Steps is "God *as we understood him*," perhaps the atheist can find a way to understand God that simultaneously respects her nonbelief and allows her to meaningfully practice the Steps. This seems like a tall order, but the chapter "Working with Others" emphasizes that the newcomer "does not have to agree with your conception of God. He can choose any conception he likes, provided it makes sense to him."[4] Strange as it may initially seem, considering how philosophers make sense of science can help us see how atheism is compatible with this Twelve Step policy of toleration.

The aims of science and the ontological status of the entities described in scientific theories are among the central issues in the philosophy of science. Scientific theories often explain observable phenomena by appealing to phenomena—entities, processes, and structures—that aren't directly observable, a practice that raises the question of how we should think about those unobservable phenomena. *Realists* think that the unobservable entities the theories postulate (for example, electrons, quarks) really exist, that they are part of a true story about what the world is really like. *Anti-realists,* by contrast, typically don't believe in the unobservable entities a theory postulates, since they take scientific theories to be merely useful tools for organizing, classifying, and predicting our experience of the world and do not think they aim at the literal truth about things.[5]

One of the leading anti-realists in contemporary philosophy of science is Bas van Fraassen, whose "constructive empiricism" holds that scientific theories aim not at truth but at *empirical adequacy.* A theory is empirically adequate when it accurately predicts observable events such as the motions of the planets or vapor trails in cloud chambers or the data gathered from a particle accelerator. But whether a theory is *true* and not just empirically adequate turns on whether *unobservable* entities like quarks are real or merely useful fictions. While realists think that such unobservable entities are real, an anti-realist like van Fraassen sees no need to think this, since a theory can achieve its aim—which for van Fraassen is not "a literally true story of what the world is like"[6] but merely empirical adequacy—without them. It's as though there's a tax you must pay, as a scientist or philosopher, if you insist that an unobservable entity is real. Why pay the tax if you don't need to? Thus, van Fraassen is more cautious than his realist counterparts, declining to make the inferential leap into the existence of unobservables. Readers familiar with Occam's Razor will notice it at work here: to commit oneself to the real existence of unobservables would multiply entities beyond necessity, since their reality isn't needed for a theory's empirical adequacy.

Needless to say, many philosophers disagree with van Fraassen's view: Some are skeptical that a sharp distinction between what is observable and what is unobservable can be meaningfully drawn; others are convinced by arguments favoring realism, for example by the argument that a theory is empirically adequate only because it is true. Anti-realists, by contrast, think that a theory can be good and useful without being true. Fortunately, we need not settle the dispute between realists and anti-realists here. For our purposes it is enough that anti-realism is a reasonable view, as even many of its detractors admit.

Perhaps our atheist, hoping to practice the Steps despite a lack of belief in God, can adopt van Fraassen's anti-realist stance and take the Twelve Steps to aim not at truth but at the spiritual analog of empirical adequacy: does working the Steps lead to sobriety and serenity? Just as the constructive empiricist accepts that a scientific theory is empirically adequate without believing in the existence of the unobservable entities of which it speaks, our atheist can accept the Steps as spiritually adequate without believing in the unobservable entity—God—to which they make reference. Without something like van Fraassen–style anti-realism, the atheist seeking to practice the Steps seems to be caught in the sort of self-contradiction that Lieutenant Scheisskopf's wife, a character in Joseph Heller's *Catch-22,* finds herself trapped in: "'I thought you didn't believe in God.' 'I don't,' she sobbed, bursting violently into tears.' But the God I don't believe in is a good God, a just God, a merciful God. He's not the mean and stupid God you make Him out to be.'"[7]

In adopting a van Fraassen–like strategy, the atheist can be seen as embracing *theological fictionalism.*[8] Just as a scientific anti-realist can regard a theory's unobservable entities as helpful fictions, the theological anti-realist can interpret God in a similar way. We don't think novels and movies are not good because they're fictions, and the scientific fictionalist does not think a scientific theory is not good and useful because the unobservable entities it speaks of are not real. And the same can be said for the atheist hoping to practice the Steps.

A distinction between *acceptance* and *belief* can be of great value to the atheist who wishes to practice the steps despite her disbelief. As one eminent philosopher sees it, "To accept that $p$ is to have or adopt a policy of . . . postulating that $p$—that is, of going along with the proposition (either for the long term or for immediate purposes only) as a premise in some or all contexts for one's own and others' proofs, argumentations, inferences, deliberations, etc. . . . Acceptance implies commitment to a policy of premising that *p*."[9]

The atheist does not *believe* the proposition that God exists, but she can *accept* it in the above sense and thus do the things her theistic fellows do, such as making a decision to turn her will and life over to the care of God, seeking through prayer and meditation to improve her conscious contact with God, and so on. Thus the distinction between belief and acceptance can allow the atheist "to hold two opposed ideas in the mind at the same time, and still retain the ability to function," an ability that, according to F. Scott Fitzgerald, is "the test of a first-rate intelligence."[10]

An important difference between belief and acceptance is that believing something, unlike accepting it, is not under our direct voluntary control: you cannot believe something merely by willing yourself to do so. This isn't to say that you can't through your voluntary actions make it more likely that you believe *x* rather than *y*. Your choosing to watch only one cable news channel or to read only certain books will no doubt influence what you believe. The point is that what we believe isn't directly up to us; it's not a matter of choice. Acceptance, by contrast, *is* voluntary; accepting something is an act we perform rather than a passive state we find ourselves in.

The connection between acceptance and commitment to action is important, for accepting something typically structures one's deliberations and actions. I might be unsure of whether you'll keep your promise to join me for a canoe trip; indeed, I might believe that you won't show up, given past experience. But despite my lack of belief, I can accept the premise that you will join me and then act accordingly, by driving to your house, for example, or bringing an extra life vest. I am not merely pretending that you will join me; nor am I formulating a hypothesis that you will join me, to be tested by ringing your doorbell. Similarly, a scientist who accepts a theory is committed to a program of research that will include some kinds of experiments and not others. This isn't to say that accepting a theory or proposition involves dogmatically holding it, come what may. Rather, one takes the matter as settled for the purposes at hand, be they scientific or practical.

So the atheist, who may have felt that her lack of belief in God was incompatible with practicing the Twelve Steps, has a philosophically respectable way to render her disbelief compatible with her practice. She cannot by force of will believe in God, given the involuntary nature of belief. But she can make a decision to accept the existence of God despite her disbelief. Thus she can do things like seek through prayer and meditation to improve her conscious contact with God because she finds the Twelve Steps spiritually adequate: "It works—it really does."[11]

So the atheist's lack of belief in God need not preclude her from meaningfully and coherently and sincerely practicing the Steps. For just as a scientific anti-realist who accepts a theory as empirically adequate can regard the unobservable entities the theory speaks of as helpful fictions, the theological anti-realist who regards the Twelve Steps as spiritually adequate can regard the God posited by the Twelve Steps as a helpful fiction, which she accepts but does not believe in. The atheist who embraces a van Fraassen–inspired theological fictionalism will find that her atheism need not preclude her from meaningfully practicing the Twelve Steps.

## Theological Reductionism

Attending to the philosophy of mind also lends support to the compatibility of atheism and the Steps. The mind-body problem—the question of the mind's relation to the body—has long been a central philosophical concern: Are the mind and the body distinct substances? If so, how do they interact? Are minds capable of existing apart from bodies? These questions take on increased urgency as the success of the physical sciences pushes many philosophers toward materialism, now more commonly (and accurately) referred to as *physicalism*, the view that only physical forces and entities are real.

Some philosophers think that ordinary psychological states like belief and desire will find no place in a fully worked out scientific picture of the mind, and thus hold that we should eliminate these "folk" psychological notions. These *eliminative materialists* take the same attitude toward the mental as most people take toward unicorns, thinking that if some kind of thing doesn't exist, we should remove it from our ontology—our list, so to speak, of what exists. Beliefs and desires are fictions, eliminativists hold, but not helpful ones, and elimination is the proper response to unhelpful fictions, whether the fictions are unicorns, phlogiston, astrology, or minds.

Other philosophers agree that these commonsense notions and their objects are problematic for a physicalistic worldview, but rather than eliminating them or treating them as fictions, they think they can be fully explained in terms of—and thus reduced to—physical entities, states, and concepts, which are not by their natures so problematic. On this view, mental processes and events are really physical processes and events, processes of the nervous system. Thus, a pain I experience is real, but it is identical to and thus reducible to a state of my brain or nervous system.

Still other philosophers think that the mental can be neither reduced to the physical nor eliminated. Such philosophers are *dualists,* often because they find it impossible to account for consciousness in purely physical terms. They are *substance dualists* if they think that the mind and the brain are two distinct kinds of substance or thing, or *property dualists* if they think that mental properties are distinct from physical properties, even though the mind and brain are not distinct substances.

Needless to say, we have barely scratched the surface here; the point of this discussion has been simply to distinguish reductionism from eliminativism. On the assumption that most theists hold that God is a nonphysical substance and that many theists believe they have nonphysical souls, it seems safe to say that most theists are substance dualists. Most atheists, by contrast, are monists, believing that only physical, natural substances are real. Moreover, they are theological eliminativists, holding that the word "God," like the word "phlogiston," doesn't ultimately succeed in referring to anything real. Many atheists—think here of the most public ones like Richard Dawkins and Christopher Hitchens—think that, far from being a useful fiction, the idea of God is not merely unhelpful but is downright harmful. Here, I wish to consider the often neglected option of *theological reductionism,* in which the atheist who hopes to practice the Twelve Steps regards God as reducible (say) to the principles and fellowship of AA, just as one might regard the mental as reducible to the physical.

The great American philosopher John Dewey can be seen as offering a reductive understanding of God: "It is this active relation between ideal and actual to which I would give the name 'God.'"[12] Dewey was concerned to distinguish *religion,* with its commitment to the supernatural realm, from the *religious,* which, in the words of a commentator, consists of "unifying experiences focused on ideals, experiences in which there occur enduring changes in ourselves that enable us to live better, deeper, fuller lives in harmony with the unchangeable forces in the universe . . . [experiences] in which a person is profoundly moved by some ideal end or ends in such a manner that the self is unified in some more or less enduring way and the person's life becomes better and more properly adjusted to the conditions and forces in the universe that affect him."[13] Similarly, the theologically reductive atheist can understand God as the principles and fellowship of AA, and, believing that the principles and fellowship of AA can restore one to sanity and make one "usefully whole," such an atheist can decide it is appropriate to turn his or her will and life over to the care of the principles and fellowship.

However, the reductive atheist still faces a roadblock, namely, the possibility that reducing the divine to the human may preclude one from sharing the core belief that "no human power could have relieved our alcoholism."[14] And while atheists clearly can improve their conscious contact with the principles and fellowship of AA through meditation, as the Eleventh Step suggests, it's not clear what role prayer can play in their spiritual life, given their reductive understanding of God. This is at least one place where the non-eliminative, non-reductive fictionalism toward God, modeled on van Fraassen's antirealism, has an advantage.

The difference between the reductionist and the fictionalist is subtle, but not so subtle as to be nonexistent. Unlike the reductionist, who reinterprets talk of God in physicalistic terms, the fictionalist does not engage in a project of reinterpretation but takes God-talk at face value, thinking it false, strictly speaking, but very useful nonetheless. Theists and reductionists agree that a sentence like "God removed my defects of character" is true, but they mean very different things by it because of their different understandings of what the word "God" means. Theists mean that a not-directly observable, supernatural being intervened in their lives and removed their defects of character; reductionists mean that their defects were removed by the principles and fellowship of AA, without making any commitment to the idea that a divine agent has removed them. On the other hand, theists and fictionalists mean the same thing, that a not-directly observable, supernatural being intervened in their lives and removed their defects of character, but the fictionalists do not think this statement says something that is true, since they do not hold that this supernatural entity actually exists.

## Open-Minded Atheism

We've explored two philosophically respectable strategies that the atheist who is attracted to Twelve Step spirituality can adopt. No doubt there are others. But the two we have explored show that atheism is compatible with Twelve Step spirituality.

Having made a case for the compatibility view, I think it's important to distinguish *open-minded atheism,* which remains open to the possibility that theism may be true, from *dogmatic atheism,* which does not. Given the role philosophical thinking about science has played thus far, it is no surprise that the intellectual virtue of open-mindedness, so central to the practice of science, should come to the fore here. At a minimum, open-mindedness involves openness to evidence and argument, requiring both the willingness and the ability to consider the merits and demerits of other points of view and ways of seeing the world, along with one's own.[15] Open-mindedness should not be confused with the absence of commitment or with not taking a stand, intellectual or practical, on an issue: open-mindedness is not neutrality. An open-minded person who believes a theory is true or accepts it as empirically adequate is open to evidence and argument that undermines and disconfirms the favored theory. She is not like "the scientist who refused to perform a certain experiment lest it prove his pet theory wrong."[16]

The virtue of open-mindedness is closely related to the virtue of intellectual humility, which at a minimum requires us to be robustly aware of our fallibility as knowers. We're often wrong about things—sometimes relatively trivial facts like Ty Cobb's lifetime batting average or who directed *Casablanca,* sometimes about more important things such as our interpretations of events and other people's motives. It's not as though I can name five beliefs I now have that I know are false; if I know them to be false, I won't believe them, if my mind is functioning properly. But given my imperfection, I can be confident that some of the things I now believe are false. That is, I have a higher-order or meta-belief about my beliefs: I believe that some of my beliefs are likely to be untrue. An intellectually humble person does not avoid this hard truth and insist that all the beliefs he or she holds are true—that's dogmatism. Nor is the humble person so overwhelmed by the sense of fallibility as to reject all beliefs and become a complete skeptic. The humble person realizes that it is possible to steer a middle course: one can match the confidence with which one holds one's beliefs with the evidence one has for them, acknowledge that one may be mistaken, and always be open to other ways of making sense of human experience.

To a great extent, the theological fictionalism described above embodies the virtue of open-mindedness. In spite of believing the contrary, the fictionalist is willing to accept what she or he does not believe and to act as if it is true.

This is not to suggest that the fictionalist who practices the Twelve Steps in this way is some kind of saint, for the addict is probably driven to this point by addiction: "Under the lash of alcoholism, we are driven to A.A., and there we discover the fatal nature of our situation. Then, and only then, do we become as open-minded to conviction and as willing to listen as the dying can be. We stand ready to do anything which will lift the merciless obsession from us."[17]

The virtues of humility and open-mindedness should be familiar to most people engaged in the Twelve Steps. As the second appendix to the Big Book, "Spiritual Experience," reminds us, "Any alcoholic capable of honestly facing his problems in the light of our experience can recover, provided he does not close his mind to all spiritual concepts. He can only be defeated by an attitude of intolerance or belligerent denial. . . . Willingness, honesty and open mindedness are the essentials of recovery. But these are indispensable."[18]

It would be intemperate to insist that the closed-minded atheist who adopts theological fictionalism or reductionism will be unable to recover. But to the extent that open-mindedness and humility are core values of Twelve Step spirituality, open-minded atheism is surely preferable to its closed-minded cousin.

At the risk of ruffling some feathers, I'd like to suggest that what is sauce for the goose is sauce for the gander: just as open-minded atheism is preferable to closed-minded atheism, so too open-minded theism—theism open to the possibility that it is mistaken—is preferable to closed-minded theism. For it, too, is more consistent with the core values of open-mindedness and humility.

Whatever one's view on that question, I hope to have shown that, initial appearances to the contrary notwithstanding, atheism *is* compatible with Twelve Step spirituality, and that the resources of philosophy can be quite helpful in explaining how this is the case. It's unlikely that the views explored here will ever be in the mainstream of Twelve Step spirituality, but they should certainly be welcomed. For a pragmatic approach to spirituality and acceptance of theological diversity is at the heart of Twelve Step spirituality: "If he thinks he can do the job some other way, or prefers some other spiritual approach, encourage him to follow his own conscience. We have no monopoly on God; we merely have an approach that worked with us."[19] Theological fictionalism and theological reductionism are approaches that might work—and have worked—for others.[20]

NOTES

1. *Twelve Steps and Twelve Traditions*, 15.

2. *Alcoholics Anonymous*, 563.

3. Ibid., xii.

4. Ibid., 93.

5. For an excellent, accessible introduction to these issues, see Gorham, *Philosophy of Science*.

6. van Fraassen, *Scientific Image*, 8.

7. Heller, *Catch-22*, 180.

8. I should point out that van Fraassen himself is a theist and indeed a devout Catholic.

9. Jonathan L. Cohen, "Belief and Acceptance," *Mind* 98 (1989): 368.

10. Fitzgerald, *Crack-Up*, 69.

11. *Alcoholics Anonymous*, 88.

12. Dewey, *Common Faith*, 51.

13. William Rowe, "Religion within the Bounds of Naturalism: Dewey and Wieman," *International Journal for Philosophy of Religion* 38 (1995): 20.

14. *Alcoholics Anonymous*, 60.

15. For an excellent discussion of open-mindedness, see Jason Baehr, "The Structure of Open-Mindedness," *Canadian Journal of Philosophy* 41 (2011): 191–214.

16. *Twelve Steps and Twelve Traditions*, 97.

17. Ibid., 24.

18. *Alcoholics Anonymous*, 568.

19. Ibid., 95.

20. Thanks to Erica Benson, Geoff Gorham, and the editors of this collection for helpful comments on earlier drafts of this essay.

JOSEPH AREL

# Transcending the Power Struggle
## Relating to the Infinite

In his provocative essay on "a power greater than ourselves," Joseph Arel advances a point of view that differs rather dramatically from that presented by Gerald Cantu and Sean McAleer. Opposing naturalism, he argues that if we're to take this phrase seriously, we must identify this "power" with the infinite. However, he makes this claim only after patiently examining how our efforts to rely on our finite abilities to overcome addiction tragically cause us to become enmeshed in a self-defeating struggle with finite forces. While Arel's essay is deeply influenced by Hegel, the great nineteenth-century German thinker, it stays focused throughout on its guiding purpose—unlocking the logic that leads from Step One to Steps Two and Three.

In the following essay, I will attempt to show how the experience of one's own powerlessness can lead one to acknowledge that a higher power plays a fundamental role in one's recovery from addiction. Recognizing this higher power, I will argue, is a step toward correcting an erroneous conception of what is involved in one's own struggle. By properly orienting oneself to the higher power, one can more truthfully orient oneself toward the real character of one's addiction. My exposition will make no attempt, nor could it, to capture everyone's experience of the powerlessness of addiction. While I will be drawing my arguments primarily from Hegel's *Phenomenology of Spirit* and Gregory Bateson's article "The Cybernetics of 'Self': A Theory of Alcoholism,"[1] I will present my argument directly, without navigating through the technicalities and specialized language of their respective philosophies.

## Experiencing a Loss of Control

We experience many things as being within our own control. For example, in the morning, I choose what I want to eat. In the grocery store, my will is what determines what will fill the shopping cart. Yet, at the same time, much of my lived reality lies outside of my grasp. The seasons change regardless of whether or not I want them to, trees grow apart from my knowing about them, and the sun is on a course that I cannot control. I identify these as external and outside of me. I know they are beyond my sphere of control. On the other hand, I cannot remain indifferent to them. Often, we need something from the external world because it is essential to how we are able to live our lives.

Whether or not it rains has been and is a natural phenomenon that is crucial to the survival and flourishing of many peoples. Since the source of rain lies beyond our own agency, but is at the same time quite important, people have had to try to understand how they should relate to it. More precisely, we attempt to relate to the ultimate *source* of the rain. Relating to the ultimate source of the rain has been an important way to establish a spiritual connection to something beyond our own finite agency.

Relating to the "higher power" through nature means that we acknowledge that the enactment of our own wills—our desires and the projects that we have for our lives—is tied up with a causal force that lies beyond our grasp. In this experience of the uncontrollability of nature, we are led to orient ourselves to a higher power by acknowledging that we are powerless over even the immediate world that concerns us.

Another way that we may be led to relate to a higher power is through our own minds. Often, we take the external world of nature to be the site for that which lies outside of our control. We take ourselves, our bodies and our minds, to be within the sphere of our own agency. This gives us a picture of a sphere of control (our minds and bodies) which stands opposed to a sphere we cannot control (the "external" world). However, if we reflect on the experience we have of ourselves, on what lies within this "inner" sphere, we can see that our sense of ourselves as self-ruling agents is more problematic than it may initially seem.

For example, while we would locate our emotions within our inner selves, the experience of emotion tells us that it is not within our control in any straightforward way. We generally do not set out to be afraid, embarrassed, or angry. And, much as we might like, we cannot simply *make* ourselves happy, cheerful, or joyous. Instead of deliberately setting out to have a certain mood or feeling, we simply *find ourselves* angry or happy.[2] What this shows us is that our experience of emotion is that of discovery. An emotion is not a state of being I set out to achieve and am able to accomplish in the way that I can cook a meal or change my oil; instead, emotions *happen* to me.

The experience of mental disability or neurosis is also an experience where I *find myself* feeling a certain way. Those of us who are familiar with these kinds of experiences, and those of us who have experience of addiction, have a very real and pressing experience of not having control over our inner selves. For us, it is easy to recognize the ungraspable and uncontrollable elements within ourselves, just as many people can easily acknowledge the uncontrollable nature of the external, natural world.

The experience of powerlessness with respect to one's own mental health is perhaps the most intimate experience of impotence and powerlessness that one can have. With a thunderstorm, we can recognize that the external world is beyond our power. In response to it, we can retreat into our homes, finding some solace in what we have stored up, some comfort in our families, or some space to ourselves within our own minds. However, to experience one's own mind, and with it one's emotions and desires, as beyond one's control is to find that one does not have a home to retreat into for safety. The most intimate space for retreat is a "place" shown to be foreign to me in the sense that it is ultimately not a product of my own will.[3] This "place" can be experienced as hostile to the interests and goals I have set out for myself. This "house" for my innermost feelings and desires does not have the safety of a home.

In our "inner selves," we experience an ungraspable ground that supplies the foundation for our own agency. Not only are we led to recognize a "beyond" outside of ourselves in nature, we're also led to recognize that there is a "beyond" within our innermost selves. With the experience of needing the rain to come, we can experience the presence of a higher power, the ultimate source for reality. With the experience of our inability to control ourselves, we also find something beyond our control. Thus, we experience the fact that, like the outer world, our inner world is not ultimately of our own making. It makes sense, accordingly, that both of these experiences prompt us to try to figure out how to form a relationship to this higher power.

## The Self as Its Powers

In order to choose how to live our lives, we have to come to an understanding of who we are and what we want out of life. Self-identity is a particular problem for those of us with harmful impulses. Something about who we are makes it difficult for us to carry out what we want to do with our lives. This makes coming to an understanding of who we are a particularly pressing task, because we know that in order to correct whatever it is that is going wrong, we first need to get to know this person who is having these problems.

I may initially try to base my self-understanding solely on my past accomplishments. I could try to identify myself as a person who has received a certain academic degree, who in my youth was responsible for certain athletic accomplishments, or who had, sometime in the past, achieved a certain social standing. However, the memory I have of my past identity cannot change the fact that the actual experience I have of myself concerns *how* I am able to live my life *now*. This involves coming to an understanding of what I can do today and in the future. How I live my life depends on the unique ways in which I choose to cultivate myself and pursue my possibilities.[4] What I *can* do or what is possible for me to do is what defines the experience of my life as it is actually lived. When I try to structure my self-identity around past achievement, all I have is a self-understanding of someone I *was,* when I am trying to get a sense for who I *am* and who I *can be.*

For example, to take pride in "being a father" is not to be proud of having produced human offspring at some time in the past. This achievement is not something I am ever finished with. Instead, if I identify as a father, it is because I identify myself as someone who has the capacity to participate in parenting. If I am simply biologically connected to some human offspring at some point in the past, this may not be relevant to how I identify myself now. Really identifying with this capacity involves identifying with the possibilities that are associated with it. I must think of how to care for my child, not only today but also in the future. Parenting is not a state of having-once-been-a-parent; rather, if I identify as a parent, it is because it is one of the possible ways that I can articulate my life.

Structuring one's identity around past achievement misses the fact that, as humans, we are fundamentally oriented toward the future.[5] As we have seen, to be oriented toward the future is to be concerned with my capacities, with what I can do. Consequently, if I pay attention to how my self-identity is lived out, I come to define my life around particular capacities for acting in the world. The result of this is that I am who I am only insofar as I have these capacities. These capacities are my powers. They are the ways in which I can be effective in and engage with the world.

## The "Power-Not-To" Is a Peculiar Kind of a Power

Usually, the actions we do not do are irrelevant to our experience of ourselves. For example, I do not smoke a pipe, or chew gum, or sleep with a fan on. There are millions of things I do not do that are not a part of my identity. There are also things that used to form a part of my identity but that were, for a time, important for me not to do. I may have had to refrain from eating too many sweets or from cracking my knuckles. For a time, *not doing* these behaviors was a part of who I was, as I was someone who was in the process of choosing to refrain from these behaviors. However, these choices have since receded into the background and eventually became unimportant to me. The result of this is that I am no longer someone who defines himself as having the power not to crack my knuckles; instead, I just do not do it anymore.

However, for the addict, addiction never recedes into the background and never becomes insignificant in the way that an activity that one no longer practices may. As AA will assert, once an alcoholic, always an alcoholic. This means that this "power-not-to" must remain a part of one's identity, because if one forgets about this and no longer makes it a part of one's identity, there are dire consequences.

Most of the powers that make up my identity require that I do something. If I identify as a father, a painter, a reader, and a runner, then I have to engage in parenting, painting, reading, and running in order to confirm to myself that this is who I am. If I take myself to be a runner and I see myself running, I get confirmation that what I took myself to be is actually the case. If I take myself to be a runner but I do not run, I will understandably be insecure about this self-assertion.

The situation is similar with a capacity for resistance, a "power-not-to," one might say. In this case, in order to maintain my identity as the kind of person who has the power to refrain from a certain behavior, I must see myself using this power. If this capacity only exists insofar as I am making this capacity a part of who I am, then in order to reaffirm to myself that I have this power, I have to see it in action.

The "power-not-to" runs into a particular problem that a positive ability or capacity does not. The problem is that my success in exercising this power can deprive me of the opportunity to show myself that I have it. For example, a person may define herself as having the capacity to cure a certain disease. She might spend her life identifying herself as someone who will be able to get rid of this problem. However, the successful achievement of her project will mean that she is no longer needed. Without this disease to cure, her power to cure has no way to actualize itself and she will no longer experience herself as the person she thinks she is; at best, she could identify with the kind of person she once was. This power to cure is meaningless without the disease it opposes. So, the problem is that this power to cure only gains its power from confronting the disease.

Similarly, in a world of pure sobriety, as in a world no longer afflicted by the disease I've cured, there would be no chance to show that I have the power to resist drinking. In this world, the opportunity will never arise for me to prove that I have the "power-not-to." If part of who I take myself to be involves a "power-not-to," then I will want to experience this power of mine in order to confirm its existence. This will prompt me to put myself into situations where I have the opportunity to show to myself that I am still able to resist.[6] If my identity is structured around this "power-not-to," then one success is not enough. In order to show to myself that this is who I *am,* not just who I *was,* then I must *continue* to win this battle, to triumph over the parts of me or my world that are in conflict with my ideal of sobriety.

## Opposing Forces

The challenge to prove to myself that I have the power to resist a temptation leads me into what I call a "struggle of opposing forces."

Most immediately, in my experience of addiction I feel myself drawn to some external object. By "external," I do not mean that there must be some physical object sitting outside of me. It can also be an object of fantasy. In both cases, however, the object of my desire is always something that stands against me and toward which I move. Since the desire for this object only occurs in the presence of the object, real or imagined, I know that I am deeply *affected* by it. The desire is not something that comes about simply on its own; rather, the desire is produced in me by the object.

Since I know that it affects me, I know that it has some kind of power. When I find myself with alcohol as the object toward which I am oriented, I simply find myself drawn to it. I do not first see or imagine it, then stop to decide whether or not I will desire it. I experience alcohol as immediately desirable. The thought of the object and my desire for it are simultaneous. I do not decide to be affected by it; it affects me. I conclude, accordingly, that this power is exerted on me in a way that is beyond my control. My ability to be affected by this substance shows me not just that it has its own power but that it is more powerful than I am.

My experience tells me that I am being controlled by alcohol. However, it would be a mistake to separate the hostile world on the one hand and my vulnerable self on the other. One might oppose the threatening fire to the vulnerable dry wood. However, the fire only gains its ability to be threatening because the wood is constituted in such a way that the fire is able to act upon it so successfully. The wood has a certain power or capacity that, when paired with the fire, makes fire possible. Importantly, the fire does not have its "active" power without the "passive" power of the wood.[7] Only when these powers are paired together do we have fire. Likewise, alcohol is only able to be so powerful, to gain control over me, because my vulnerability, this passive power of mine, gives it this power. Seeing this, I realize that I am not simply overpowered by the object of my addiction; rather, when I am put in relation to it, we become entangled.

While I feel like I am passively being acted upon by different forces in my life, I realize that I myself, with my own powers and vulner-abilities, am fundamentally involved whenever I experience myself as falling prey to the external embodiments of my addiction. In fact, I provide the essential fuel for this cycle of addiction. Thus, while it may at times seem as though I am simply being acted upon by forces too powerful to combat, I realize that this is only part of the truth. The larger reality is that, as a participant in my struggle, the forces that seem to oppose me also draw their strength from my susceptibility to them.

We saw above that in order to prove to myself that I have the "power-not-to," I have to see myself using this power. This challenge draws me into the cycle of opposing myself to what threatens me, and, since my vulnerability and the object of my addiction are intertwined, opposing myself to what threatens me involves opposing myself to my own vulnerability. This is because there is an opposing force within me as well as outside of me. My struggle against both of these forces must be constantly renewed if I am to continue to affirm my "power-not-to." Hence, I am locking myself into a familiar power struggle that my own vulnerability keeps reinforcing. This struggle is doomed to fail because proving my power to resist it necessarily requires that my vulnerable self continues to be affected by it. In other words, success cannot be found within the terms of an opposition of powers because my "active" power of resistance will always be dependent upon my "passive" power of being affected. I cannot turn to my "power-not-to" in order to resolve my situation because this will only lock me into an opposition between the active and passive powers that reinforce each other. I now know that my power to resist will always be accompanied and trumped by my power to be affected. What I am left with is a repeated cycle where the fighting off of my desire will also be the reinforcing of it. Thus, *the power struggle itself inevitably takes on the character of an addiction.*

Entering into this power struggle will mean a constant back-and-forth movement between my vulner-ability to drink and my ability not to drink. Both of these forces are found together, within me, and so the work of proving that I can resist will continue to attach me to the object of my resistance. The challenge to resist that I present to myself encourages me to again reproduce the situation where this challenge is needed. This means that in my challenge, I lead myself right back to my own vulnerability. This would be like chemically treated wood walking through fire in an effort to prove it could resist bursting into flames. The combination of these two powers will only result in fire because they are constituted in such a way that their unique powers feed off of each other. Further, it is only in continually proving to myself that I have the "power-not-to" that I can feel confident that I have the kind of self-control that is necessary for my identity. Thus, if this challenge is essential to my identity, this challenge itself will become addictive.

Additionally, I have to acknowledge that while I can use these powers or capacities in better or worse ways, I cannot decide not to have them. The power to have and not have the powers of desire and resistance is not something within my control. For example, while I have the power to see, this power is not something I had a hand in creating. I can attempt to see more clearly. I can shut my eyes or avert my gaze, but I cannot control the very fact that I have been given this power. Similarly, while there is a range of ways in which I can take up my weakness as well as my ability to control this weakness, the fact that I am so constituted is not something within my grasp. Taking account of this fact encourages me to look beyond myself and my own powers, since I see that there is something beyond my agency and something beyond the struggle of opposing forces that holds sway within me.[8] In other words, confronting my own powerlessness leads me to the source of it, which is beyond my own power.

## Beyond Opposing Forces: Acknowledging the Infinite

We see that the need to identify myself as someone with the "power-not-to" leads me to become dependent on the very passive vulnerability that I oppose. While the need I have to identify with a "power-not-to" encourages me to engage in this struggle, this struggle itself becomes an addictive reinforcement. Consequently, I learn that I cannot continue to engage in this opposition; instead, in order to escape this addictive relationship with myself, I have to relate to a power *outside* of this opposition.

Acknowledging powerlessness involves acknowledging my powerlessness over my own powers. I am not the source for my own powers. They are beyond my control. Orienting myself to this fact involves orienting myself to a power or force more fundamental than the powers I employ. Initially, we may call this a "higher power."

Of course, the "power" of the "higher power" is a different sort of power altogether than the kinds of powers that I have and that draw me towards things in the world. It is not a power that affects things in the world like my will, desires, or even something like the force of gravity or inertia. To give it such determinate content would be to limit it and reduce it to being one among the many powers with which I'm in contention. Instead, we are talking about what is beyond my finite powers, an infinite or beyond that is their source. By acknowledging my own powerlessness, I can recognize the infinite that is implied by the powerless I find within myself.

When I recognize the role of the infinite in my struggle, I can come to realize why help cannot be sought from *within* the cycle of finite, opposing forces. Instead, I am led to something beyond them, to the greater context within which my struggle takes place. Paying attention to the very nature of my power struggle leads me to recognize an infinite that lies beyond and is the ultimate source for this struggle of opposing forces. Since I know that my drawing on my own powers will also draw on my own weakness, I recognize that I cannot look to any of the finite forces involved in my struggle for help. I am led to acknowledge that only "a power greater than myself could restore me to sanity" (Step Two). In the space between Steps One and Two, I experience the movement from the struggle of opposing forces to forming a different kind of relationship to my dependency and power struggle, one mediated by my conception of an infinite. This "relationship" with the infinite is different because, whereas in finite relationships I confront something I can grasp and to which can I can oppose myself with my force, a relationship to an infinite does not carry within it this possibility. Relating to the infinite makes impossible the symmetrical relationship involved in any struggle among opposing forces. This new way of relating to my situation opens up my ability to relate to this ongoing struggle without merely having to assume my familiar position in this addictive and unhealthy opposition of forces. Relating to the infinite can liberate me from the finite relationships that only serve to reinforce my struggle.

## Prayer

At the beginning of this essay, I spoke about the way that we relate to the beyond through the natural world. I am now suggesting that, just as we relate to a higher power by acknowledging an ungraspable source for nature, we can also be led to acknowledge an infinite by facing the elusive and uncontrollable nature of our own mental life.

There are different ways that we can relate to this ultimate source. Step Eleven states, "Sought through prayer and meditation to improve our conscious contact with God as we understood Him, praying only for knowledge of His will for us and the power to carry that out." Having acknowledged our own powerlessness and the infinite to which it opens us, we can turn to prayer as an attempt to properly recognize and connect with this infinite.

There are different ways in which we can relate ourselves to the ultimate cause of the natural world. If we want rain, we can pray for rain, be it silently, through dance, or through song. But what we take our prayer to be doing can vary as well. I may think of prayer as asking for something. In this type of relationship, we might treat prayer as involving a kind of symmetrical relationship where I stand before a being, before whom I call myself "powerless," and ask for help. This is symmetrical in the sense that I am hoping that a change in my part, my asking for something, will result in a change in another being, some being "answering" my prayer. However, the turn to an infinite came about through a fundamentally different relationship to power. As we saw, forming a relationship with the infinite involves orienting oneself toward a reality that is fundamentally different from finite powers and that transcends all opposing forces. This infinite or "higher power," consequently, is not just something "much more powerful" than I am. In relating to the infinite, I am relating to the ungraspable power that grounds and sustains all other powers, including my own power. Since the infinite is not just another kind of finite power, for me to expect to be able to affect this power with my own would be to fall back into the symmetrical relationship of opposing forces. If I am truly "powerless," I cannot effect change in the higher power. Thus, approaching prayer as if I could effect such change does not fully achieve the recognition of the stance of powerlessness (or, perhaps more precisely, of surrender).

To be adequately true to the experience that turned me to the infinite, I have to realize that my prayer will have to take a different form. As Kierkegaard writes in *Purity of Heart,* "The prayer does not change God, but it changes the one who offers it."[9] Step Eleven can show us how to remain true to the recognition that help will not come from within my power struggle; rather, change begins when I begin to more accurately orient myself to the power behind or beyond my own powers.[10] Relating to the infinite, consequently, can liberate me from the struggle of opposing, finite forces because this relationship frees me from the struggle I find when I set myself up against my addiction.

If I am relating to the infinite through nature and hoping for rain, I can pray in the hope of getting what I want from the infinite beyond. This involves supposing a symmetrical relationship, one in which I have the power to change the infinite with my finite powers. But I can also pray in order to orient myself to the fact that I do not control the rain. My songs and dances can teach me to accept my powerlessness over the rain and to come to terms with the fact that I cannot control the weather. Working on this relationship can free me from the anguish of holding myself responsible for what is fundamentally beyond my control. Similarly, I can pray or meditate in order to come to terms with the fact that my own inner mental life is beyond my control, and fighting against this will only keep me within a struggle I cannot win. Prayer, consequently, orients me to the ultimate source, the infinite, that holds sway over the finite world I inhabit.[11]

Relating to the infinite in this way seems to be the kind of prayer that Twelve Step spirituality encourages us to say.

## NOTES

1. This essay appears in *Steps to an Ecology*, 309–37.

2. See Heidegger's *Being and Time* on "state-of-mind" (*Befindlichkeit*) and "thrown-ness" (*Geworfenheit*), sections 29 and 38.

3. Although he is not immediately talking about mental illness, this is the basic structure of the "Unhappy Consciousness" in Hegel's *Phenomenology of Spirit*. Here, consciousness recognizes that its own essential nature is not fully its own.

4. Here, I am drawing on Heidegger's discussion of being-in-the-world. Heidegger claims that the self precisely is its possibilities. See *Being and Time*, sections 12–24.

5. Heidegger will describe the temporality of *Dasein* as fundamentally oriented toward the future, which is implied in the assertion that we should understand ourselves most fundamentally in terms of our possibilities (what we can do in the future). See *Being and Time*, sections 67–71.

6. Bateson, *Ecology of Mind*, 321. Bateson describes this as a "challenge" to oneself. My essay owes a great deal to Bateson's and, in many ways, is an exploration of the central ideas found in his essay.

7. I am here drawing on Hegel's discussion of the "play of forces" in "Force and the Understanding" in the *Phenomenology of Spirit*. One of Hegel's main arguments in this section is that forces have to be seen in their interaction with each other, and to speak of one force without the opposing forces that make it possible is abstract. Most fundamentally, a force only exists in its relation to other forces.

8. Again, Hegel's "Unhappy Consciousness" draws out this structure in rigorous detail.

9. Kierkegaard, *Purity of Heart*, 51.

10. Dunnington makes an even stronger claim in *Addiction and Virtue*. He argues, as I do, that the prioritization of immanence can encourage or support addictive behavior. He writes that "the post-Christian pursuit of flourishing and fulfillment . . . has been reduced to a project of immanence" (144). He goes so far as to claim that "addiction is a product of this modern privileging of immanence at the expense of transcendence. Addicts may be our most forceful and eloquent modern prophets, reminding us of the peril that a denial of the transcendent brings" (145).

11. Though he does not explain exactly how this is accomplished, Dunnington points to this when he considers Paul's exhortation that we should "pray without ceasing" (1 Thess. 5:17). Dunnington describes "worship" broadly, as "the possibility that human persons may experience and live their days as an expression of their relationship with God" (*Addiction and Virtue*, 142).

# "Ordinary" Spirituality
## One Buddhist Approach to Imperfection

While Wamae Muriuki is especially interested in Steps Six and Seven, which concern the removal of character defects, his essay focuses on the question of whether such a moral transformation can be brought about by our own efforts or only by a "power greater than ourselves." Muriuki significantly widens the cultural scope of our anthology by arguing that, on this issue, there is a deep affinity between the "ordinary" spirituality of the Twelve Steps and Pure Land Buddhism. The latter is a Buddhist tradition developed by practitioners who were acutely aware of their own deficiencies. This awareness, which is also prominent in Twelve Step fellowships, led them to believe that it was possible to reach the Pure Land—and moral transformation—only by entrusting oneself to Buddha.

With their focus on acknowledging and accepting one's failings as the basis of recovery, the Twelve Steps have been characterized as a spirituality of "giving up" or "resignation" that is at odds with its goals as a positive spiritual program. Similarly, in the Japanese Buddhist tradition of the True Pure Land School (*Jōdo Shinshū*), the paradoxical statement of Shinran that the proper subject of liberation through rebirth in the Pure Land of Amida Buddha is the "evil person" has been criticized as undermining traditional Buddhist morality. However, both the Twelve Steps and Shinran's Pure Land tradition can be seen as delineating a spirituality of imperfection—one predicated on the conviction that a deep existential awareness of one's brokenness offers a path toward a genuine and sincere morality.

The Twelve Steps are grounded, first and foremost, in an acknowledgment of our helplessness in the face of addiction. Once this difficult truth has been internalized, we recognize that only a higher power (however we conceive of it) can intervene meaningfully in our life, and therefore that we should wholeheartedly turn ourselves over to that higher power. Having done so, we must deeply, honestly, and searchingly make an inventory of our failings; admit these failings to ourselves, to others, and to our higher power; be ready and willing to be rid of these failings; and call upon our higher power to help us do so. An honest assessment of our failings leads to an awareness of how our actions have hurt others. Such an assessment encourages us to make amends to those we have hurt, to continue to be honest and forthright about our failings and mistakes, to deepen our relationship with our higher power, and, finally, to reach out to others who are also struggling.

From the standpoint of those who consider the individual an independent and self-sufficient moral actor who bases her decisions on a defined moral calculus and is accountable for her own decisions, the most problematic of the Twelve Steps are those that call upon us to realize our failings and short-comings, and to rely upon our higher power to remove them. According to these critics, the Twelve Steps, with their emphasis on interiority and self-knowledge, must be matched by positive prescriptions for action (reform) to be done by the moral actor herself. In this view, one's moral responsibility is not discharged merely by an honest assessment of one's failings, including the inability to rectify one's own behavior.

Against this, however, Twelve Step spirituality insists that a "searching and fearless moral inventory" leads to a deep and existential awareness of our brokenness. And this, in turn, opens up a transformed understanding of the self, and a new understanding of moral action. This conviction is shared by the Japanese Pure Land Buddhist tradition of Shinran, which holds that the "do-gooder," or the person who believes in her capacity to be an autonomous moral agent, fails to recognize her deep entanglement in patterns of karmically conditioned behavior. That is to say, both the Pure Land tradition and Twelve Step spirituality recognize that the human condition is not one of autonomy in the sphere of action, but one that is deeply influenced by numerous (and unacknowledged) causes and conditions that themselves shape our actions. It is only in the light of the wisdom and compassion shown us by our higher power that these heretofore unrecognized patterns become clear, and our conviction of ourselves as autonomous moral agents ("do-gooders") can be overturned. Once this has been achieved, the path of an "ordinary spirituality" opens up.

As I am using the phrase, "ordinary spirituality" is characterized by an awareness that striving toward idealized standards of moral and ethical perfection through one's own effort is doomed to fail. For the practitioner of "ordinary spirituality," adhering to these idealized standards involves the mistaken belief that human beings can achieve these ideals through acts of heroic self-will. It is only when the struggle to achieve these ideals founders upon the hard reality of human fallibility that we are confronted with the stark realization that we are, in a word, spiritual incompetents. The path of "ordinary spirituality," as explored by both Shinran's Pure Land Buddhist tradition and Twelve Step spirituality, abandons the notion that living a truly moral life requires the individual to adhere to established moral codes as an autonomous actor, and is instead based upon living in light of an ever-deepening consciousness of one's failings and a thoroughgoing reliance upon a higher power.

## "A Searching and Fearless Moral Inventory"

As Trysh Travis[1] notes, the Twelve Steps' orientation toward interiority has its roots in American religiosity of the early twentieth century. Specifically, one can identify three strains at work in early Twelve Step spirituality. The first of these comes from Oxford Group asceticism. Founded as a kind of first-century Christian fellowship in 1921 by the Lutheran minister Frank Buchman, it came to be known as the Oxford Group in the 1930s.[2] The Oxford Group strove to attain what they called the Four Absolutes: absolute honesty, absolute purity, absolute unselfishness, and absolute love, through the practice of sharing one's sins, surrender to God, restitution, and listening for God's guidance. Further, "Buchman and his followers constituted their identities through a series of rejections—of the rationalized, depersonalized modernity embodied in the organized church . . . and of all those 'who arrogate to themselves the external purity of a lovely flower' but who 'behind the velvet delicacy of its petals [have] heart[s] rotten and worm-eaten.'"[3] Bill Wilson attended Oxford Group meetings, and he incorporated some of the practices of the group into the Twelve Steps.

Secondly, Wilson's formative spiritual experience, Travis argues, resonates most powerfully with Protestant notions of "conviction under the Law." Listening to Wilson recount his experience, we can certainly hear the evangelical overtones in his moment of despair and liberation: "I still gagged badly on the notion of a Power greater than myself, but finally, just for the moment, the last vestige of my proud obstinacy was crushed. All at once I found myself crying out, 'If there is a God, let Him show himself! I am ready to do anything,

anything!' Suddenly the room lit up with a great white light. I found myself caught up in an ecstasy which there are no words to describe. . . . All about me and though me there was a wonderful feeling of Presence."[4]

Travis goes on to argue that "depersonalization and the dissolve of bodily boundaries is liberating—a cause for celebration. . . . A new and miraculous feeling of unboundedness replaces the terrifying isolation that is the marker of modern personhood and social organization . . . [as a result of] having finally surrendered his futile modern selfhood and 'die[d] to the world.'"[5] The moment of existential despair leads to a rejection of the individualistic self, which is liberating rather than negative or nihilistic. The understanding here is that spiritual freedom is to be found in the rejection and abandonment of modern notions of autonomy and self-reliance.

Finally, it is possible to view early Twelve Step spirituality as part of the "New Thought" or "mind-cure" movement that William James described in the *Varieties of Religious Experience*. These movements appeal "to persons for whom the conception of salvation has lost its ancient theological meaning, but who labor nonetheless with the same eternal human difficulty. *Things are wrong with them*. . . . To that enduring human inquiry, New Thought gave a decisive and optimistic answer: 'You *are* well, sound and clear already, if you did but know it.'"[6] As with the Oxford Group, the movement's highest aim was to encourage the believer to give the "little private convulsive self a rest, and find that a greater Self is there."[7]

Since Twelve Step spirituality developed out of a milieu in which the individualistic, autonomous self is problematized, it should be seen as part of a spectrum of practices based on a rejection of this modern conception of the self, and a reliance on a higher power to effect true and lasting change. There are two implications of this Twelve Step approach. First, for Twelve Step spirituality, genuine morality is made possible by a confrontation with the limitations of the self (conceived of as the agent of moral perfection) and a recognition that self-directed effort will fail. Second, it is the very notion of an autonomous self (in the modern sense) that has led to this moment of crisis. In this last respect, Twelve Step spirituality shares much with the approach of the Pure Land Buddhist tradition, which is grounded upon a rejection of the capacity of the individual to effect her own liberation.

## Pure Land Buddhism and Shinran

Pure Land[8] Buddhism is predicated upon the three Pure Land sūtras preached by the Buddha Œākyamuni in India, sūtras that reveal the existence of the Buddha Amitābha (*Amida* in Japanese)[9] and the promise of liberation in his Pure Land, billions of miles to the west. Pure Land belief first arose in India sometime at the beginning of the Common Era, with the seminal sūtras in this tradition composed around 100 CE[10] and translated from Sanskrit to Chinese by the third century CE.[11] These three sūtras are the *Sūtra of Infinite Life,* the *Sūtra of the Buddha Amitābha,* and the *Contemplation Sūtra.* Whereas in traditional Buddhism, nirvana (that is, liberation from the cycle of birth and death) is achieved through the disciplines of ethical precepts, meditation, and the cultivation of wisdom, Pure Land Buddhism offers a simpler path. The goal, here, is not nirvana in the present life, but rebirth in Amitābha's Pure Land through the practices laid out in the Pure Land sūtras.[12] Once reborn there, the believer can quickly attain enlightenment through the direct instruction of Amitābha and the resident bodhisattvas, in a world perfectly suited to uninterrupted spiritual practice.[13]

The *Sūtra of Infinite Life* details the forty-eight vows that Amitābha Buddha took, as a bodhisattva, to establish this Pure Land. For Pure Land practitioners, the eighteenth vow (or the "principal vow") is perhaps the most important. In its first or "causal" form, the Buddha makes his enlightenment contingent upon the liberation of all sentient beings: "Were I to attain Buddhahood, and yet if sentient beings of the ten directions were not to be born [in the Pure Land] even though they were sincere in heart, had faith and joy, and desired to be born in my Pure Land with even ten [moments of mindfulness of the Buddha],[14] then I would not accept true enlightenment. Only those who commit the five damning offenses[15] or slander the true teachings will be excluded."[16]

The second iteration of the vow, the "fulfilled principal vow," recounts the same promise *after* Amitābha's Buddhahood: "If sentient beings hear [Amitābha's] name and have faith and joy, with even a single [moment of mindfulness of the Buddha], and if they extend their own religious merit to others with a sincere heart, and if they desire to be born in that Pure Land, then they will attain birth there and will reside in the stage of nonretrogression. Only those who commit the five damning offenses or slander the true teachings will be excluded."[17] In both versions, all that is required for birth in the Pure Land is "sincerity of heart, hearing Amitābha's name, faith and joy, [a] desire to be born in Pure Land, extending religious merit to others, and [mindfulness of the Buddha]."[18] This simplified path thus opens up the possibility for people of all religious capacities to rely upon rebirth in the Pure Land, and upon Amitābha Buddha's power to ensure their eventual attainment of nirvana.

By the Kamakura period in Japan (1185 CE–1333 CE), there was an increasing sense of uncertainty and doubt as to the efficacy of individual efforts to achieve liberation through traditional Buddhist practice. This doubt was bolstered by the Buddhist teaching that Japan, and the world at large, had entered the period of Final Dharma (*mappō*), that is, a time period after the death of the historical Buddha Œākyamuni, in which two of the three pillars of the Dharma, practice and enlightenment, had been lost.[19] Pure Land scholar Kyōshin Asano argues that the idea of mappō "connoted a break-down in the ability of the Buddhist path itself to overcome impermanence and bring about the attainment of enlightenment," and that this perceived failure forced Japanese Buddhists who were grappling with the very idea of a loss of effective spiritual practice to find new means to achieve liberation.[20]

This need was made all the more salient by the social, political, and environmental catastrophes that wracked Japan during this period. As society collapsed into war and chaos, Japanese Buddhists must have been all the more convinced that they were living in the period of Final Dharma, and so it is not surprising that the Pure Land path, which deemphasized the role of traditional practice and perfection of wisdom, became more and more popular. Deeply affected by his inability to follow the traditional path, the Japanese Buddhist monk Shinran (1173–1263 CE) was one of those who experienced a revolution in his previous understanding of religious practice. His wife, Eshin-ni, recorded one particular episode in one of her letters. She wrote that one day Shinran fell ill, retired to bed with a high fever, and then suddenly recalled an episode that had occurred seventeen or eighteen years earlier. At that time he took it upon himself to recite the three Pure Land sūtras a thousand times "for the benefit of sentient beings," when he suddenly realized that he was making a grave mistake because "the repayment of the Buddha's blessing is to believe the teaching for oneself and then teach others to believe." Reciting the sūtras as if that act would lead to liberation was the product of "self-generated faith."[21] For Shinran, faith, or rather entrusting (in Japanese, *shinjin*), means an utter reliance on what the Chinese Pure Land master Tan-luan identified as "other power" (*tariki*), that is, entrusting in Amitābha's vows to save sentient beings and not on "self power" (*jiriki*), which relies on one's own efforts to effect liberation. As we saw with the Oxford Group and Bill Wilson's experience, the Pure Land Buddhist approach is to recognize and accept the limitations of the self, and self-directed effort, and to rely fully upon a higher power—in this instance, on Amitābha Buddha.[22]

In tandem with this rejection of self-directed effort is Shinran's conviction that he is a thoroughly deluded individual: "I know truly how grievous it is that I . . . am sinking in an immense ocean of desires and attachments and am lost in vast mountains of fame and advantages, so that I rejoice not at all at entering the stage of the truly settled, and feel no happiness at coming nearer the realization of true enlightenment. How ugly it is! How wretched!"[23] This ignorance and delusion extends to the realm of moral reasoning, as he laments, "For if I could know thoroughly, as Amida Tathāgata[24] knows, that an act was good, then I would know good. If I could know thoroughly, as the Tathāgata knows, that an act was evil, then I would know evil. But with a foolish being full of blind passions, in this fleeting world—this burning house—all matters without exception are empty and false, totally without truth and sincerity."[25]

This suggests that there is no way for a person living in the age of *mappō* to know thoroughly and absolutely what acts are good and what acts are evil. In our foolish and deluded existence, everything we do will turn out to be empty and false because we are not living in the clear light of wisdom. Therefore, any individual attempts toward liberation, being founded upon a basic inability to distinguish between right and wrong, are doomed to failure. Further, Shinran's description of the condition of human beings strongly implies that it is the natural condition of human beings in this time period to be irrevocably flawed. Because the causes and conditions of our world make it impossible to distinguish right from wrong, spiritual imperfection is, in Shinran's view, an inescapable fact of our present existence. Ignorance of the true depth and extent of our imperfections leads us to believe that they can be corrected solely through individual effort. But this is a grievous error. "Self power" and self-directed effort must be overthrown in favor of reliance on the "other power" of Amida Buddha, whose vows ensure that the practitioner who relies upon them is unfailingly brought to liberation.

## The Struggle for Righteousness

Shinran was certain that karma impacted one's behavior in the present, which meant that his actions in the present were determined by conditions from the past. He is recorded as saying in the *Tannishō* (A Record in Lament of Divergences), "Good thoughts arise in us through the prompting of good karma from the past, and evil comes to be thought and performed through the working of evil karma. The late Master said, '[Know] that every evil act done—even as slight as a particle on the tip of a strand of rabbit's fur or sheep's wool—has its cause in past karma.'" As he goes on to tell his fellow practitioner Yuien, "If the karmic cause so prompts us, we will commit any kind of act."[26] Thus, for Shinran, it was impossible to conceive of himself or, indeed, of any person living in the age of Final Dharma, as an independent moral agent. Given this state of affairs, our only option is to abandon any idea of ourselves as capable of making independent choices between good and evil. This finds its clearest expression in this well-known passage from chapter 3 of the *Tannishō*:

> People who rely on doing good through their self-power fail to entrust themselves wholeheartedly to Other Power and therefore [are] not in accord with Amida's Primal Vow, but when they overturn the mind of self-power and entrust themselves to Other Power, they will attain birth in the true and fulfilled land. It is impossible for us, who are possessed of [karmic afflictions], to free ourselves from birth-and-death through any practice whatever. Sorrowing at this, Amida made the Vow, the essential intent of which is the evil person's attainment of Buddhahood. Hence, evil persons who entrust themselves to Other Power are precisely the ones who possess the true cause of birth. Accordingly he said, "Even the good person is born in the Pure Land, so without question is the person who is evil."[27]

According to the conventional understanding, birth in the Pure Land, or liberation, must be assured for the "good person," if even an "evil person" will be reborn there. However, in Shinran's understanding, it is precisely the evil person, who has abandoned any notion of herself as a capable moral agent (thereby turning from self power to Other Power), who is the object of Amida's Vow, and is thus assured of birth in the Pure Land. The "do-gooder," who adheres to rigid notions of right and wrong and her own capability to discern the difference between the two, is, in Shinran's view, blind to the reality of the moral universe in which she lives. That is, while the "do-gooder" assumes that one can make free moral choices according to an established moral calculus, Shinran argues that our actions are so conditioned by our karmic entanglements that we could find ourselves doing just about anything, evil or good, despite our best intentions.

Shinran's view here is founded on the fact that human knowledge is necessarily limited—both by the times and context of the Final Dharma period, by the finitude of our knowledge and insight, and by our ignorance of the latent tendencies that condition our behavior. Dan Lusthaus describes these tendencies as "embodied conditionings." That is, "These are the karmic latencies that predispose us to perceive or react in certain ways. They are karmic insofar as they are the product of previous . . . experience, now latent, and insofar as they condition how we re-act or will re-act to present or future . . . experience."[28]

In light of this, the only truly moral action is one that takes as its basis an abandonment of self-directed striving toward the good. For the Pure Land practitioner, this takes the form of a thoroughgoing and deeply existential awareness of the depths of one's entanglement in past karma, and a wholehearted entrusting in the compassionate activity of Amida Buddha as encapsulated in the Vow.[29] This is expressed in the recitation of the phrase *namu Amida Butsu* (I take refuge in Amida Buddha), in what Shinran calls the "one moment" of true entrusting.

## "Ordinary" Spiritualities

So as we have seen, there are deep continuities between Twelve Step spirituality's suspicion of modernist conceptions of the individual as an autonomous self, and Pure Land Buddhism's acknowledgment that self-directed effort in the moral sphere is sure to fail. For both, the notion that one can rely on the self and self-powered effort to find a way out of brokenness is an error. Confronted with the existential reality that one is incapable of finding a way out on one's own, both traditions advocate a "surrender" to a higher power as the only possible solution. Only when the idea of the individualized self has been overturned can the path to a genuine and sincere morality, that is, an "ordinary" spirituality, be cultivated.

This ordinary spirituality opens up in the space previously occupied by false notions of the self and adherence to rigid understandings of right and wrong. For Shinran, this spirituality is grounded in the freedom and naturalness that comes from fully trusting in Amida Buddha. For Twelve Step spirituality, a similar kind of ordinary spirituality comes from surrender to one's higher power. While each path begins with a negation and a rejection of established objectives of moral perfection, each strives toward a life of openness based on a deep understanding of one's flaws, and a responsivity to life's changing circumstances. This path is "ordinary" to the extent that it abandons the notion that the moral life requires adherence to fixed, externalized ideals of conduct, and instead bases itself upon living a life in the light of a deepening consciousness of one's spiritual incompetency, and one's inability to change except through reliance upon a higher (Other) power. Beyond this, the individual is not called to any special kind of activity whatsoever.

Once these external ideals and guides for behavior are discarded, how are we to know how to live the "surrendered" life? For the newly "surrendered," this new freedom can be disorienting and alienating, or could lead to charges of antinomianism.[30] Since the path of ordinary spirituality is internal and psychological, rather than external and based on ideals of perfection, one must rely upon the broader community of others to "model" the ordinary life for them. Within Twelve Step spirituality, we can see this at work in the framework of the meeting: by watching and observing how others live their sobriety, through hearing their stories and testimonials in group gatherings, and, importantly, by recognizing (being convicted) that *you are just like them,* the path to an ordinary spirituality is shaped, guided, and molded.[31]

Overturning the notion of an individualistic, autonomous self opens up our awareness to our fundamental connectedness with, and deep indebtedness to, human and nonhuman others, and is itself the foundation of a truly moral life. Once freed from a false sense of self, and from its demands regarding morality and moral action, one can live out an ordinary spirituality founded on a commitment to the responsivity of action, and to a continual struggle against our habitual tendencies and patterns of behavior. This life involves an ongoing commitment to the difficult affective work of deepening one's awareness and understanding of one's brokenness, and a willingness to model oneself upon the example of a community of others who are struggling in similar circumstances. So it is at once a communitarian model for spiritual life (built upon sharing with others) and also a highly personal model (based upon interiority and affective work). It is necessarily the case that this can only be fully understood while one practices it and faces everyday challenges from a space of responsivity. For both Buddhist and Twelve Step spirituality, the overthrow of the self clears the ground for a spirituality of spontaneity and responsivity, and it is this openness that allows the individual to freely and genuinely respond to changing circumstances.

NOTES

1. Travis, *Language of the Heart.*

2. Ibid., 30–31.

3. Ibid., 72.

4. Ibid., 73.

5. Ibid., 74.

6. Quoted in ibid., 76.

7. Quoted in ibid., 77.

8. "Pure Land" is used to translate the Sanskrit term *Sukhāvatī,* meaning "land" or "realm" of "ultimate bliss." As an epithet, it refers specifically to the Buddha-land of Amitābha (*Amida*), which is characterized by its blissful and paradise-like qualities. Essentially, each Buddha takes a number of vows that detail the locale and conditions within which they will function, and the resultant Buddha-land is established by the fulfillment of those vows. Amitābha's vows specify the establishment of a paradise-like Buddha-land in which sentient beings can quickly practice and attain nirvana.

9. As the bodhisattva Dharmākara, he took forty-eight vows to establish a Pure Land and now, as a Buddha, is identified as the Buddha of Infinite Light (in the Sanskrit, *Amitāyus*) and Life (Sanskrit, *Amitābha*).

10. Galen Amstutz, "The Politics of Pure Land Buddhism in India," *Numen* 45, no. 1 (1998): 70.

11. See Jan Nattier, "The Indian Roots of Pure Land Buddhism: Insights from the Oldest Chinese Versions of the 'Larger Sukhāvatīvyūha,'" *Pacific World: Journal of the Institute of Buddhist Studies,* 3rd ser., 5 (2003): 179–201.

12. Dobbins, *Jōdo Shinshū,* 3.

13. See Inagaki and Stewart, *Three Pure Land Sutras,* 103–8.

14. Dobbins, *Jōdo Shinshū,* 3–4. In the Chinese and Japanese traditions, "moments of mindfulness" encompass a number of possible practices, including visualization and vocal recitation of the name of a Buddha.

15. The five damning offenses are killing one's father, killing one's mother, killing an *arhat,* shedding the blood of a Buddha, and destroying the harmony of the *sangha.* See Dobbins, *Jōdo Shinshū,* 175.

16. Ibid., 3–4.

17. Ibid., 4.

18. Ibid.

19. Kyōshin Asano, "The Idea of the Last Dharma-Age in Shinran's Thought, Part 1," *Pacific World: Journal of the Institute of Buddhist Studies,* 3rd ser., 3 (2001): 53.

20. Ibid.

21. Bloom, *Living in Amida's Universal Vow,* 14–15.

22. Hereafter referred to as "Amida," following the Japanese pronunciation.

23. Shinran, *Collected Works,* 125.

24. "Tathāgatā," or "thus come one," is one of the ten epithets of the Buddha.

25. Shinran, *Collected Works,* 679.

26. Ibid., 670.

27. Ibid., 663.

28. Lusthaus, *Buddhist Phenomenology,* 48.

29. See Ryōshō Yata, Ryōshō, "An Examination of the Historical Development of the Concept of Two Aspects of Deep Belief, Part 1," *Pacific World: Journal of the Institute of Buddhist Studies,* 3rd ser., 3 (2001): 158.

30. Shinran's True Pure Land community did struggle with "licensed evil," the belief that since Amida especially works to save the "evil person," one should deliberately commit evil acts in order to be saved. Shinran's response to these individuals was to say, "Just because there is an antidote, it doesn't mean that you should drink the poison."

31. As Damian Elrath eloquently puts it, "The essence of [Twelve Step spirituality] is conversation, dialogue. . . . Ninety percent of the recovery process is through peers talking with one another. The beginning of all wisdom is self-knowledge. In [Twelve Step spirituality], you connect first with yourself. Then with another human being. Then with your Higher Power. You can't say, 'I love God and hate my brother'" (quoted in Robertson, *Getting Better,* 126).

# PART THREE

# Recovering Selfhood

# The Sober Addict

## A God Brought Low by Grace

Jason Danner's essay provides an ideal transition from our previous section on the "Higher Power," the focus of the first three Steps, to this section on "Recovering Selfhood," which is the primary focus of Steps Four through Seven. Here we explore how Twelve Step spirituality summons us to undo the illusions we have about ourselves and come to an authentic acceptance of who we really are. Danner's essay, similar in some respects to Wamae Muriuki's, provides us a narrative of this journey toward authenticity. He begins by describing how getting "high" enables one's self to feel divine. But the shift to "white-knuckling" sobriety is in its own way self-deifying. The alternative to both, Danner argues, is the experience of grace that involves accepting one's destitution and so recovering one's authentic selfhood.

According to the Twelve Step spiritual program of recovery, the movement from addiction to sobriety is made possible by the help of a power greater than the addict. Since alcoholics seek in the "high" of drunkenness a feeling of being godlike, allowing this Higher Power—as it is known—to work is one of the most critical elements of Twelve Step recovery. But Twelve Step recovery also warns that it is possible to approach sobriety as another kind of high in which the alcoholic views himself as above his alcoholism. Whether seeking a high through alcohol or through sobriety, the addict is attempting to divinize himself—to set himself apart from reality. To recover through the Twelve Steps, one must forswear all highs, all routes of escape from the problematic reality that led to addiction, and accept the inescapability of that situation as the starting point for a new kind of life.

## Playing God: Getting High

"First of all, we had to quit playing God."[1] One frequently hears this line from the book *Alcoholics Anonymous* quoted in AA meetings. It speaks directly to the alcoholic's most basic problem, which is a desire to run the whole show. Implicit in this desire to run the show is a rejection of how things are, a refusal to deal with reality on its terms.

How does alcohol enable the alcoholic to play God? The alcoholic drinks to get high. Height is a spatial quality—a state of being above lower things—and also a way of describing the intensity of an experience. Ordinary "low" life lacks intensity. Ordinary reality feels lifeless. When low, the self feels itself to be just another mundane object among objects, differing from them in the sole regard that it is uncomfortable with this state.

Height is always relative to a low state. It is the seemingly magical gravity-defying ascent from this low state that constitutes the rush of *getting* high. Once high, few things are as thrilling as casting a glance downward at what one is soaring above. Getting and being high are intense experiences characterized by dramatic feelings that provide a strong sense of self-presence.

In this intense state, the self feels himself to be extraordinary, that is, exempt from ordinariness, and in this way, like a god. He is no longer a mere object among objects, but is utterly removed from that status and stationed in the celestial heights. He is the very summit, the focal point of everything. He is playing God.[2]

But the self cannot retain this fullness nor maintain this intensity; it falters, departs, and the fully self-present self disappears. From the heights, it plummets, evacuated of its previous fullness. The higher his rise, the steeper his fall, and nothing leaves him feeling as utterly empty as having felt utterly full.

Above all else, the one who has suffered this terrible descent from the celestial heights desires to return to them. The erstwhile god cannot bear being human. So he gets high again to feel godlike again. And comes down again. And gets high again. And so on. Thus is born the addictive cycle.[3]

## Hitting Bottom

The image of addiction as a *cycle* is misleading; more precisely, addiction is a *spiral*. Addiction *progresses;* it is not simply a matter of getting high, coming back down, and then getting high again. With each repetition of the low-high-low movement, addiction progresses another step. Eventually, the addict repeats this movement until she reaches the point at which she can no longer get high and drinks only to level off the pain of coming down (a pain compounded and exacerbated by the repeated failure of the attempt to soar above it). In this state, the addict doesn't drink to achieve the height of intense self-presence that made her feel divine. Instead, she drinks to annihilate herself, to benumb herself, the locus of the pain that she can no longer rise above. Formerly, she drank to experience herself as a fullness of presence; now, she drinks for oblivion, hoping to rid herself of the self-presence that has become so painful.

Addiction progresses until the addict reaches bottom. Every alcoholic in recovery has a story about hitting bottom. In terms of our discussion thus far, the bottom is the point farthest away from the celestial heights, the consummate refutation of all pretenses to divinity, accompanied by a keen awareness that this state of being on the bottom is inescapable: it is a bottom from which there is no climbing up. Making matters worse, one does not gently touch down on the bottom. One hits it with a ponderous thud after plummeting from the celestial heights. In the experience of the self-deifying alcoholic, she hits bottom at full speed, having traversed the greatest imaginable distance from everything to nothing.

In the stories that alcoholics tell, it is the impact of hitting bottom that shatters their illusion that they can remain above reality. The pain of the impact forces them to recognize that they are not powerful gods but powerless addicts. The obsession with alcohol has not only failed to lead them to the celestial heights; it has delivered them to the deepest of depths.

A powerless wreck on the floor of a profound depth, the alcoholic who has hit bottom is faced with the stark reality that she must change or she will die. Sadly, some are so fragmented and warped by the spiraling of addiction that they are unable to choose anything but the path to insanity or death. They feel so totaled by the impact that they cannot imagine that they possess any resources to mount the effort to change. The reality of their personal powerlessness is so complete that it seems to be the only possible reality. To one accustomed to thinking in terms of high and low, powerlessness is effectively a matter of undergoing the death of what one once considered oneself to be. The impact has shattered one's illusion that one can do anything about reality. The alcoholic's situation is further complicated by the fact that reality has become for her a bottom—a reality much, much worse than the "ordinary" reality of many people's lives or even the desperate reality that one sought to escape through alcohol. The alcoholic even lacks the power to achieve for herself the ordinary reality she drank to escape. Now, for her, there is no more drinking to level off. The spiraling accelerates. The desire to drink maddeningly overtakes all other concerns. Things are grim for the alcoholic who has reached the bottom.

So it is no surprise when she becomes desperate enough to try anything, even the AA program. Perhaps this program will change her. Perhaps it will fix her. Perhaps it will enable her to grab hold of sobriety and hang on to it. Perhaps sobriety will raise her up, off the bottom, out of the depths.

## White-Knuckling: Seeking the High of Moral Perfection

We often associate "sober" with good sense, level-headedness, and clear-mindedness, and "alcoholism" with the senseless repetition of destructive behavior, emotional imbalance, and clouded judgment. Sobriety and intoxication seem to be binary opposites, the former the perfect antidote to the latter. As many alcoholics—recovering and active alike—can attest, nothing kindles a craving for sobriety like the ruinous effects of advanced alcoholism. From the perspective of a craving for salvation from alcoholism, a craving that is born in the depths, the attainment of sobriety naturally seems to be an *ascent* from the depths that enables one to leave behind one's alcoholism, and the bottom to which it led.

But this craving for sobriety is itself a veiled desire for a high—*the high that puts one above one's alcoholism.*[4] This desire lurks behind the phenomenon of what members of AA call "white-knuckle sobriety." When one white-knuckles, one holds on as tightly as possible to one's sobriety out of an unwillingness to let it go and return to the unacceptable state of alcoholism—an unwillingness that is understandable since one is still smarting from the pain of hitting bottom. The white-knuckler thinks her will is the force she must deploy against the slide back into alcoholism. She equates sobriety with simply abstaining from drinking. If she can keep herself from taking that drink, then she won't get drunk. Her alcoholism, she thinks, was the result of a lack of willpower. All one needs to do is to exert more willpower and the problem will be solved. In this scenario, it is one's will, properly focused on the problem of avoiding drinking, that functions as the "higher power" that can keep one from alcoholism. She seizes with all her might the sober self that emerges in the absence of alcohol and thinks that if she holds on tightly enough, she will be able to prevent the re-descent of this self.

This shows how it is possible, and tempting, to understand sobriety as a high. In fact, the alcoholic can view sobriety as the ultimate high insofar as it solves the problem of being stuck in a cycle of highs and lows. In other words, it seems to give the alcoholic precisely what he sought in every drink. From this perspective, sobriety is, in a real sense, the high to end all highs, that is, the state that puts an end to the cycle of getting high and coming down. Intensely gripping his newfound sobriety, terrified of letting go of it lest he lapse back into active addiction, the white-knuckler seeks a kind of power that will enable him to raise himself above his weakness, his powerlessness, once and for all. When he white-knuckles, he is trying to bring his errant will under the lash of his will. He finds his alcoholism, his inability to control his behavior, unacceptable. And when a white-knuckler works the Twelve Steps, he works them *at* himself, *at* his alcoholism.

But the problem is that, for the alcoholic, this *doesn't* work. The white-knuckler cannot stop obsessing about alcohol, whether he drinks it or not. Formerly, he saw alcohol as a solution to his problem of feeling low and ordinary; now, he sees sobriety as the solution to his problem of alcoholism. He is still trying to find a power that will enable him to control his problems. He is still playing God—in this case, a God who has power over alcohol.

### There but for Grace Go I

To sober up, the alcoholic must abandon the idea of sobriety as another high. He must also abandon the hope of moral perfection. According to AA's portrait of recovery from alcoholism, the sober self needs neither highs nor perfection. Indeed, he is advised to eschew these. So, how *does* he get sober? AA's answer is that he gets sober through a grace that comes to him from a power greater than himself.

The Twelve Step spiritual program of recovery from addiction turns on the idea of grace. An elusive concept even for those who accept it as real, grace warrants some explanation. A few years ago, a friend who was struggling with the concept of grace asked me to explain it to him. I told him the story of the grace I received through the experience of getting a tuberculosis (TB) test.

Fate elected that I would suffer from an acute fear of needles. Beginning with a traumatic incident at age five involving a clumsy nurse, a bent needle, a fainting spell, and a hysterical mother, I spent the next twenty-five years morbidly terrified of that slender pointed instrument.

The essence of my terror was this: I was convinced that a needle's puncture would annihilate me. When faced with the prospect of getting a shot, my entire existence would become concentrated on a solitary point: specifically, the point where the needle would meet and poke through my skin, drilling through me. In those moments, it was as if my whole existence was a target for the point of a weapon that always found its bull's-eye. A needle had the power to alter my whole way of being in a moment, instantly paralyzing me with terror. It was the greatest power that I knew.

I prayed *hard* not to be terrified, to be unafraid. My most heartfelt wish was to have power over the needle, to face it with a calm resolve or, better, indifference. I wanted to be able to grasp my existence in such a way that I would be able to fend off the power of the needle to make me afraid. If I could get the proper grip on myself, I would be able to hold in check that quivering, terrified part of myself. I would be able to lift myself above the terror and gain a perspective on it. I could look down on my terrified self and see that it wasn't the whole of me, that the point to which the fear of the needle reduced me wasn't all of me.

During my first year as a graduate student, my terror was brought to a head. My institution required all students to have a TB shot as a way of protecting the campus community from outbreaks of the sickness. In my mailbox in the graduate student lounge, I found a notice informing me that I needed to have the test. It was early fall. I had to have a TB test or lose the stipend and tuition remission that I needed to continue my doctoral studies.

I went to the student health center to see if there was any way of dodging or at least delaying the shot—and admitted my fear to a physician there. She told me that there was a name for my fear but was unable to recall it, so she went to her office to look it up. "Aichmophobia," she said as she came through the door a few minutes later. This effort struck me: like the grumpy nurses I'd previously encountered, she didn't know what it was called, but, unlike them, she went to look it up. It was something no one else had ever done or offered to do and that effort alone meant a lot to me. (It is revealing that a doctor's admission of her ignorance was a pivotal moment in my development!) Learning the name of my phobia was an undramatic but important turn. In learning that name, I also learned that it wasn't just me who suffered from it. Others had this phobia, too. I wasn't the only coward.

The doctor also did something else different. Instead of trying to coax me through the TB test immediately, she told me to come back the following week. I was a little puzzled but glad for the reprieve and, like a student who knows better than to ask the teacher if there is any homework the minute before the final bell on Friday afternoon, I kept my mouth shut. At least I got to go home puncture-free.

When I returned the following week, a nurse saw me. This nurse had the same first name as my mother, an uncommon if not unusual name. I registered this fact but thought little of it at the moment. She sat me down in the exam room and asked me what I needed to have done. I told her about my phobia. She told me she would be right back. "Oh shit," I thought, she's gone to fetch some brawny orderlies to restrain me while she needles me. When she returned a moment later, she had it in her hand. The needle. I immediately became nervous. She put it on the table where I could see it. Still more nervous. In a moment, the needle had become the absolute center of the room. Its terrible power radiated outward, its rays intersecting everything in the room, connecting everything to it. Everything reflected and magnified its terrible power.

The nurse observed that I had gone pale. She told me to sit on the floor lest I fall out of the chair I was sitting on. I did and was more comfortable. Surprisingly, she joined me on the floor. Then she did something I could never have expected. She asked me if I wanted to hold the needle. I didn't know what to say. I was sure that this was a ploy of some sort. After a moment, I assented. She placed the needle—with its safety cap still on, a condition sine qua non—in my hand. It was small and light, almost weightless. Its physical presence said nothing of its dominating power over me. Gradually, I began to grasp what she was doing. She was diminishing the power of the needle by letting me hold it. All of my experiences with needles up to that point involved someone coming at me with one. In this case, *I* was holding it. I was holding it and I *wasn't* being annihilated. This was a new experience.

What followed was one of the greatest surprises of my life. The nurse asked if I wanted to give her a shot. The prospect of giving her a shot filled me with nearly as much dread as that of her giving me one. Added to this dread was an unsettling amazement at the offer: What could she be thinking?

I did as she asked. I trusted her without knowing why. She handed me a small syringe filled with a harmless saline solution and guided my hand as I slowly punctured the skin of her outstretched arm with it. The puncture didn't annihilate her. She was unharmed and so was I. I had taken part in the act that terrified me the most and was not traumatized. A week later I returned and she gave me the TB shot. For the first time in my life, getting a shot wasn't a struggle. Afterward, I felt free. My terror had departed. I didn't know what made it leave, but I knew that I hadn't dispatched it through any power of my own.

My fear was transformed into an ecstatic release, but it wasn't like ecstasies I had known. It was more intimate and subtle. In fact, I wouldn't describe it as a "high." I was aware that an important change had taken place. It wasn't a dramatic breakthrough, as I had expected, an emotional event equal in magnitude to the intensity of the terror that I had felt. Instead, getting the shot was a quiet and sober affair. The feeling was unique. The only way I can describe it is to say that I had never felt freer or more exposed in anyone's presence, feelings that were thrown into sharp relief by the fact that the nurse and I were strangers.

I felt that that puncture was loving and caring rather than harmful. It hurt, but this hurt wasn't the negation of care or of love. Grace did not spare me the needle, did not magically make the needle go away; rather, grace chose it as its instrument.[5]

Defined simply, grace is a help, favor, or blessing given without regard to the recipient's merit or expectations (or even his understanding). In AA, grace is the key to recovery; it is the working of a higher power, higher in the sense of beyond our inabilities—our powerlessness over alcohol—and any ability to earn favor, aiding us in our recovery. Alcoholics who see themselves in the AA description of alcoholism view grace as necessary to their recovery. According to this view, unaided by grace, the alcoholic cannot break out of his addictive spiraling and the deep distortions of character that propel it. The spirituality of AA doesn't teach that the alcoholic strikes a bargain with his Higher Power—indeed, apart from its being a source of unmerited grace, AA makes no theological assertions about the nature of the Higher Power, because it defines this concept in terms of the alcoholic's own understanding of it, and even the theological idea of grace is presented in the AA literature as optional. (AA is humble in its assertions about the applicability of their program of recovery, insisting that the steps are only *suggestions* and only for those who see something they want in the AA program.)

But trusting grace, seeing the needle as an instrument of grace rather than simply as a threat of violence, enabled me to move beyond the fixed point to which my terror of needles reduced me. My fear of the needle focused everything that I was on its point. The gracing needle punctured that point, depriving me of the self that desperately huddled there. The needle left in its wake a puncture, an emptiness, an opening. It hadn't annihilated me as I had feared; rather, it did something unexpected. By depriving me of that point-self, the self that was a locus of so much fear, it freed me from the needle's power. The needle hadn't annihilated *me;* it had rid me of the illusion of myself that I was clinging to: a durable self that couldn't, *shouldn't,* be punctured. I came to realize that I had feared the needle because it had the power to perforate my illusory belief that I shouldn't be susceptible to annihilation, that I should be able to make myself unafraid of the needle, that I shouldn't be afraid of the needle because I should be an invulnerable being. The needle, I learned, wasn't aimed at *me,* wasn't a device that would poke a ruinous hole of contingency in my otherwise solid, assured presence, because my real being *wasn't* solid or self-assured. The needle's puncture hadn't been threatening my imminent destruction for twenty-five years; it had been prophetically signaling an imminent revelation that would destroy my illusions.

As long as I labored under my illusions of solidity and self-possession, I had to reject the help of grace. Only a being susceptible to annihilation, incapable of being divine, incapable of perfection, needs the help of grace. It was revealed to me that I was not who I thought I was. I was not an invulnerable god. I was a being who needed help. I was not a being who was hollowed out by the needle's perforation. I was always already the emptiness the perforation leaves in its wake.

Letting go of the illusion, accepting that I am the emptiness the perforation leaves in its wake, meant that I had to ask for help and, more important, to *let* help *help.* It meant not attempting to paper over or to fill in the hole. Whatever help would come, whatever grace was going to do, I could accede to it only by remaining open, only by accepting my emptiness, only by accepting my profound poverty.

## Lord, Make Me a Channel . . .

In the AA book *Twelve Steps and Twelve Traditions,* we find what AAs call the "Eleventh Step Prayer," better known as the Prayer of St. Francis.[6] It begins with "Lord, make me a channel" and goes on to entreat God to make the self a passage through which grace and love flow from God to others.

I find this image of the spiritual life—becoming a channel for grace—particularly apt. Here's why. Not long after the TB test and for related reasons, I had to get a blood test. The tiny needle used for the TB test was terrifying but it was nothing compared to the much larger needle used for drawing blood. Still more awful was the fact that this larger needle wasn't inserted and then withdrawn in the space of a few seconds like the TB needle but lingered in the vein for a seeming eternity of fifteen to twenty seconds while blood flowed through an attached tube and was captured in a vial. As before, I was terrified, but with the help of the same nurse, I was able to go through with it.

Medical professionals call this needle-cum-tube a *cannula*. *Cannula* is the diminutive of *canna*, Latin for "small reed." The device is so called because it resembles a hollow reed through which blood flows. *Canna* is also the Latin root of *channel*, a passage through which something flows.

The common etymology of *cannula* and *channel* is striking against the backdrop of my experience of grace. It is the perfect image for the spirituality I had discovered through this. Just as the needle punctured my vein and allowed my lifeblood to flow through the *cannula*, so also did the grace of the needle open me and allow what I had pent up inside me to flow. The perforation made it possible for me to become a channel of that grace. Grace flowed into and through me, but could do neither if the passage was blocked, fortified against puncture by terror. I had, in a sense, been made a channel.

A channel only works when open, unobstructed. To control the flow, as the white-knuckle grip of self-control would do, would collapse a channel as surely as a tourniquet would collapse an artery. To allow grace to work is to accept becoming a channel for it. It is to accept that God reaches down to you, in the depths, rather than raising you to a summit. Grace, in sobriety, doesn't raise you up to God, or get you high; it opens a channel that allows God to reach you in your lowliness and to flow through you.

NOTES

1. *Alcoholics Anonymous*, 62.

2. Many members of AA describe alcoholism as "the disease of more." Ernest Kurtz, in *Not-God*, 217, notes that the spiritual disease at the root of drug or alcohol addiction shares certain basic characteristics with what he identifies as the modern understanding of the self:

> In the modern demand for absolute independence [and] denial of absolutely all human dependence, Alcoholics Anonymous locates . . . its deeper diagnostic understanding of the dis-ease of modernity as illuminated by the metaphor of alcoholism in the demand for domination. . . . Frustration of this modern demand for absolute control is inevitable, for the quest for such rationalization and control is intrinsically insatiable — doomed by its very nature as absolute to an ever emptier and ever more destructive

craving for "more" and "again." A.A. points out that the "modern" quest is . . . the claim to infinity . . . the equation of the self with God.

In *Addiction and Virtue,* Kent Dunnington argues that "addiction is . . . a form of idolatry because it elevates some proximate good to the status of an ultimate good, a status which belongs to God alone" (191). However, idolatry is not simply a matter of pursuing a good as if it were a god; it is always a pursuit—through proxies—of the good of the self in which any other good is utilized only as a means to the end of exalting the self. Addiction is really a symptom of the core problem, which is the self's refusal to be anything less than god. Playing god begins with the self's refusal of its contingency, limitation, mortality, and powerlessness.

In *Addiction and Responsibility,* Francis Seeburger argues that addiction is actually iconoclastic because it enables the addict to see that every object s/he pursues as the absolute turns out not to be (113–16). I believe this is correct but would add that seeing this does not necessarily lead the addict to abandon self-exaltation.

Emmanuel Lévinas and Jean-Luc Marion, major figures in the Continental philosophy of religion, have explored the problem of idolatry in ways that happen to parallel the Twelve Step model of addiction and my discussion here. For Lévinas, egocentricity is intimately linked to idolatry; he calls for a thoroughgoing iconoclasm to combat both in many of his works. See, for example, "Reality and Its Shadow" in the *Levinas Reader.* Marion develops a critique of idolatry that is based on his distinction between an icon and an idol. See, for example *God without Being.* For a detailed exploration of these matters, see Danner, *Beyond the Either/Or.*

3. Mircea Eliade's theory about the human relation to the sacred, elaborated in works such as *Sacred and Profane,* helps illuminate the cycle of getting high and coming down. According to Eliade, the axis mundi—the center of the world—was the place where the divine manifested itself most intensely to humans. The summit of a mountain, for example, was one image of an *axis mundi,* the highest point in a landscape, closest to the heavenly abode of the gods. Humans, according to Eliade, long to live in proximity to such heights in order to escape the suffocating ordinariness of their everyday lives.

4. To use Dunnington's terms, sobriety, too, can be an idol. One can pursue it as an idol-like source of power over one's addiction. Such an approach to recovery misses the two essential and linked elements of Twelve Step recovery: powerlessness and grace. I might note that I have seldom—indeed, almost never—heard AA members speak of sobriety as a power they use to combat their addiction. Moreover, the trajectory of Twelve Step recovery is not toward sobriety as the final good; rather, sobriety is throughout described as preparation for service to others and the world. See Lewis Hyde's description of the Twelve Steps as a gift-economy in *The Gift.*

5. I viewed this experience through Flannery O'Connor's idea of grace as a violent interruption.

6. *Twelve Steps and Twelve Traditions,* 99.

# Paradoxes of Authenticity in
# Twelve Step Spirituality

Drawing upon thinkers as different as Socrates and Nietzsche, Nicholas Plants's essay challenges us to critically examine our commonsense assumptions about what is involved in "being oneself." By carefully examining the difference between Socrates and his fellow Athenians, Plants demonstrates that "being oneself" is not nearly as straightforward as it may initially seem. In fact, it requires us to embrace a number of paradoxes that are at the very heart of Twelve Step spirituality. An aphorism of Nietzsche's provides Plants the crucial clue he thinks we have to follow if we're to understand why one must not flee from but become the addicted self one is if one is to recover from addiction.

While a prisoner in a Nazi concentration camp, the distinguished psychiatrist Viktor Frankl had to make an agonizing decision. He was offered the chance to escape the camp and had to decide whether or not to leave. Frankl had already lost his family, his manuscript, and almost his mind. He had been tattooed, shorn, starved, beaten, and desensitized. The Nazis had done all they could to make him lose his self-respect, and at times it seemed to him that his dignity had been taken away. So when he was given the chance to escape, it was just what Frankl most wanted. But to do so would have meant leaving behind the group of prisoners suffering from typhus he had been caring for. Frankl had found ways to help other prisoners who were dying to suffer a little bit less. Doing so gave him a sense of purpose that was uniquely his. In the midst of the tortures and deprivations of the camp, he had begun to cultivate a spiritual life. So when faced with his decision, Frankl had to consider the fact that although he had almost nothing to live *on,* he did have something to live *for.* To leave would have been not just to abandon the camp but to abandon himself. Working in the typhus hut, he realized, he had found the purpose, and with it the meaning, that enabled him to live as an authentic self.

Frankl ultimately chose to remain in the horror because there was something uniquely his to do in the horror.[1]

Frankl's story teaches us something important about the concept of authenticity. Choosing to remain in a very difficult situation, making the choice to do the hard thing, can be the good, right, and appropriate thing to do if one is to be oneself. A provisional definition of authenticity, then, is that to be authentic one must simply be who one is. Had Frankl chosen to leave the camp, he may have increased his chance of survival but he would have ceased being true to himself. He may have continued to live but he would have done so inauthentically, or at least less authentically.

The concept of authenticity has a broader relevance. It has a bearing on our being as a whole. In every area of life, we have to make choices similar to the one Frankl made—a choice to be ourselves or not be ourselves, to be authentic or inauthentic. To do this, a person has to be able to distinguish one from the other. Distinguishing them can be extremely difficult. It's not just that the choice is difficult. Understanding whether a particular option is authentic or inauthentic can itself be as difficult as the choice one faces once the two have been identified.

Addiction is one kind of human experience that makes it especially difficult to discern what is involved in being oneself. The active alcoholic is liable to feel that being authentic means to continue to practice her addiction because the addiction has become such a dominant part of who she is. The addict may think that, in order to be herself, she needs to use what she is addicted to. In the mind of the addict, it may actually seem to be inauthentic to *stop* using. To her mind, being herself may mean being an active addict.

We have to consider the possibility that she may be right. If distinguishing the authentic from the inauthentic really is exceptionally difficult, we must not assume that the addict is necessarily mistaken. We have to think through these concepts in order to figure out whether an addict should practice her addiction, or renounce it, if she is to be herself. More generally, we have to consider the relationship of authenticity and inauthenticity to addiction.

Because it is a way of being rather than an aid to recovery like a particular Step, slogan, or virtue, authenticity is difficult to characterize without venturing into philosophy. Perhaps this difficulty accounts for its conspicuous absence from program literature, despite the crucial role it plays in Twelve Step recovery. In fact, recovering addicts seem to identify instances of their own *in*authenticity more easily than they can articulate the kind of authenticity that makes sobriety possible. This suggests that it may prove helpful to bring the contours of authenticity into greater relief.

In my attempt to relate authenticity to addiction, I will be drawing on two paradigmatic figures in Western philosophy—Socrates and Friedrich Nietzsche—although neither directly treats the issue. The story of the relationship between Socrates and Athens nicely illustrates the profound difference between authenticity and inauthenticity. After using this story to clarify authenticity by contrasting it with its opposite, I will try to deepen our appreciation of its positive but paradoxical character by turning to a much-discussed aphorism of Nietzsche's. Though he may seem an unlikely ally, Nietzsche is an intrepid explorer of different ways of being oneself. In the case of both Socrates and Nietzsche, my hope is that, by reflecting on them, we may better understand the kinds of authenticity that promotes, and the kind of inauthenticity that obstructs, the practice of Twelve Step spirituality.[2]

## Wisdom Lost, and Found, in Athens

According to what has become the standard interpretation of Plato's *Apology*, Socrates emerges as the wisest Athenian as a consequence of his being the only citizen who knows that he knows nothing.[3] However, when responding to Chaerophon's query of whether any Athenian is wiser than Socrates, the Oracle of Delphi does *not* say that Socrates is the wisest but rather that no one is wiser than he.[4] The difference may seem a mere trifle, to use the term Socrates employs to describe what distinguishes him from his fellow citizens.[5] But it is deeply significant. In fact, it fundamentally alters the meaning of the Oracle's utterance and helps explain why Socrates is put to death by his countrymen. The Oracle's statement, once carefully considered, should be taken to mean that the real reason none of the Athenians is wiser than Socrates is not because he has knowledge they lack, but because he uses knowledge everyone in Athens has more wisely than anyone else. This reading makes better sense of Socrates's claim that what differentiates him from others is comparable to a mere "trifle"—something apparently insignificant. It suggests that the crucial difference between authentic and inauthentic ways of living is small and yet profound. Like his wisdom, the "trifle" of Socratic authenticity is paradoxical.

The truth is that no one in the dialogue knows literally nothing because all persons in it, including Socrates, know that there are things they don't know. Athenians of every stripe are aware of the unknown, especially with regard to topics that take them beyond their range of expertise—for example, philosophical topics like truth, beauty, piety, and justice. Socrates himself knows something about these topics, but he also knows there is much about them he has yet to know. It is true that the men he questions do not know as much about philosophy as Socrates, but it is also true that they all know more about their respective professions than he does—a truth Socrates readily admits.[6] So the difference between Socrates and his fellow Athenians cannot be that they lack the knowledge of their ignorance that he possesses. Above and beyond their different professions, the difference between Socrates and everyone else in the city arises from what they *do* with the knowledge that they are ignorant.

The craftsmen, poets, and politicians already know they are ignorant, but *they pretend not to be ignorant* in an attempt to ensure that their reputations for wisdom remain intact. They fear having their ignorance revealed because they believe that being ignorant means they cannot possibly be wise or be regarded as wise by others. It is for both reasons that they fear the revelation of who they are. They would rather pretend not to be ignorant than lose their reputations for wisdom. And so rather than admitting they don't know how to answer the philosophical questions Socrates asks, they recoil from the knowledge they already have of their ignorance because they view it as a curse rather than as a blessing.

Socrates does not share their fear. He believes that his knowledge of his ignorance is just that—knowledge—and as such presents a golden opportunity for wise action. He can use his knowledge of his ignorance to learn more about the unknown, precisely by asking questions about what he already knows he does not know. It is true that his questions will reveal his ignorance but, far from this revelation troubling Socrates, he recognizes that his knowledge of his ignorance is a boon rather than a curse because it enables him to further his knowledge.

This positive response to ignorance, and more precisely to the knowledge one has of it, is the sign of wisdom that Socrates is searching for in his fellow citizens. Socrates is unable to find such wisdom, and with it the person who might prove the oracle wrong, because no one else in Athens ever embraces his knowledge of his ignorance sufficiently to realize that it is not in spite of it, or even only because of it, but precisely *in and through* knowledge of one's ignorance that further knowledge is to be gained. And so it is, paradoxically, Socrates's embrace of ignorance that renders him wise.[7] The oracle is right that no one in Athens is wiser than Socrates. However, this is not because he is the wisest, but because others don't use their knowledge of their ignorance as wisely. And so the real rub of *The Apology* is not that the Athenians are ignorant like Socrates but don't know it. They *do* know they are ignorant but pretend not to, and therefore lack his wisdom.

Whether one is wise depends, then, on one's inauthenticity or authenticity —whether one futilely pretends to be what one isn't or does not pretend. Because we are one and all ignorant, and know we are, we can be wise only if we embrace this knowledge instead of fleeing it. We tend to think of ignorance as a fatal, humiliating flaw, but the real flaw is our inauthenticity—our pretending not to be ignorant when we already know we are. The craftsmen, poets, and politicians of Athens deny that they are ignorant, not because they do not know they are, but because they know they are but are unwilling to expose this. To prevent this exposure, they are willing to place on trial, and even put to death, the person who challenges them with exposure. Socrates, on the other hand, proclaims his ignorance rather than renouncing it because he refuses to pretend not to be ignorant when he already knows he is. Such pretentiousness turns out to be one of the hallmarks of inauthenticity. The breakdown of it is a blessing rather than a disaster because it breaks one open to a philosophical exploration of the unknown. Obsessed as they are with avoiding breakdown, the Athenians remain tragically closed. The city flees the same self-exposure Socrates embraces—the embrace in and through which he lives authentically and faces death soberly. The "trifle" that differentiates him from his fellow citizens involves an authentic mode of self-relationship that they refuse.

What the example of Socrates shows us is that authenticity requires, first, becoming aware of, and then embracing, the very shortcomings and inadequacies in oneself (such as ignorance) that prevent one from being the person one most wants to be. But becoming aware of such inadequacies is made possible only in and through self-reflection. What this suggests is that authenticity cannot mean simply being oneself, as we provisionally supposed. Authenticity requires something more than immediacy, namely, a reflective relationship to and with oneself. There are, then, two decisive possibilities: one can relate to oneself truthfully or one can flee oneself by fleeing the relationship one ought to have with oneself. The addict who says one can be authentic just by being oneself—and practicing one's addiction—is mistaken. There can be no authenticity without self-reflection.

### Becoming More Than One's Addiction

Friedrich Nietzsche issues an imperative that *does* take into account the fact that authenticity requires us to have a certain kind of relationship with ourselves: "You must become who you are."[8] Like Socrates's wisdom, Nietzsche's imperative is paradoxical. Why do we have to become who we are when we already *are* who we are? Becoming who one is would seem at best redundant and at worst impossible. Why not just be who one is? Wouldn't being who one is be more authentic than becoming something else? The very logic of Nietzsche's imperative seems too contorted to be possible, let alone necessary.

Nietzsche's imperative cannot be taken to imply that he believes there is an ideal self who we are really meant to be. For there is, according to Nietzsche, no ideal self and thus no ideal we have to actualize in order to be true to ourselves.[9] So who, then, are we and why is it imperative that we become who we are?

When those in Twelve Step fellowships ask the first question, the program offers them an unambiguous answer, one that is sometimes viewed as overly harsh by both newcomers and people outside of recovery: Whether they are active or in recovery, addicts are addicts. They are, and will always remain, addicts, regardless of whether they get sober, relapse, or get sober again and again. The paradoxical wisdom of this seemingly harsh response is crucial because of the fact that those in recovery who no longer acknowledge themselves as addicts are likely to relapse. No matter how long a recovering addict's sobriety lasts, it is, and will remain, a conditional, and thus contingent, mode of being. It is true that, for as long as addicts stay sober, they are not only addicts, but addicts who have ceased the *practice* of their addiction. But recovering addicts remain authentically sober only in and through their proclamation of their addiction. Proclaiming one's addiction is how one embraces one's addicted self. *And it is only by embracing one's addicted self that one becomes the addict one is.* It seems on the surface that the recovering addict already *is* who she is, and so doesn't have to become it. But, in fact, relating *to* one's self is essential to being true to one's self.

The difference between the practicing and recovering addict is that the former pretends to be who she is *not* in an attempt to avoid becoming the addict she already is, whereas the latter becomes who she is by embracing what she already knows herself to be. The fact that the user avoids becoming the addict she is by means of her very addiction is a paradox of pivotal importance. The addictive experience is easy, effortless, soothing, pleasing, soporific, and, well, addictive, precisely because it is not reflective. The avoidance of reflection makes it impossible for one to relate to one's self truthfully. In fact, it does not just involve a tragic flight from becoming one's self; it can actually lead to the final destruction of this self. The Twelve Steps tell addicts starkly who they are—*addicts*—because of the fact that is perhaps best expressed by paraphrasing Bill W.: "We must face who we are, else we die."[10]

As difficult as it is to abandon it, the practice of one's addition becomes less and less likely the more one faces the truth by way of becoming the addict one is. Authenticity enables the recovering addict to stay alive because it is the mode of self-relationship that enables one to relate to the addict one already is without practicing one's addiction. One cannot be true to who one is in any other way than by first facing and then embracing this truth about one's self, and one cannot do this if one is not sober. A life of authenticity requires affirming that one is broken rather than rejecting this truth by relying on the object of one's addiction.

We are now able to give a fuller answer to the question that set these reflections in motion. The practicing addict may think that, to be authentically who she is, she should continue using. But, in fact, the addict who uses is being the addict she is in order to avoid *becoming,* that is, entering into relationship with, her addicted self. The unique logic of Twelve Step authenticity is circuitous, not contradictory, paradoxical, not absurd. It is not redundant but revolutionary to become the addict one is because, to do so, one has to abandon the practice of one's addiction.

Becoming authentic is not a feat that recovering addicts manage by way of a specific Step, slogan, or virtue, because it is not a single achievement but a mode of self-relationship. The Steps, slogans, traditions, and virtues, as well as the group conscience, approved Twelve Step literature, and other helpful resources that are available to newcomers and recovering addicts, all promote recovery because they encourage one to authentically connect with oneself. Authenticity is promoted in a special way by actual Twelve Step meetings because they provide the primary context within which addicts can proclaim their addiction. Such self-disclosure is one of the indispensable portals through which a recovering addict must pass on her way to sobriety. This is why I've emphasized "proclamation" throughout this essay. Although there are other important portals, self-proclamation—self-exposure—is what enables the addict to start becoming herself, instead of trying to escape it. As such, it is a singular breakthrough to what is and must remain an all-inclusive way of life. The truth is that there is much more to an addict than her addiction. But practicing one's addiction, since it turns one away from self-relationship, leads one to renounce everything one is besides one's addiction. So it is possible for one to find out what "more" there is to one's self only in and through the process of soberly embracing the truth about one's self.

It is with regard to the "more" that Nietzsche's own views on living authentically are helpful to us, even though there are numerous reasons why Nietzsche himself would likely find Twelve Step spirituality problematic.[11] According to him, authenticity is not a matter of being true to anything that already exists because the self *is* a dynamic process of becoming. Becoming who we are does not lead to becoming static. It leads to incessant energy. Nietzsche is therefore opposed to restraint. He doesn't want the self to hold back. He doesn't want the self to say "no" to life or its unfolding. He wants us to embrace life on its terms—to say "Yes!" to and unreservedly affirm the process of living and dying. Living openly, flowing, being in movement, expressing oneself, in short, exulting in life—these are what becoming is all about in Nietzsche's view. For the self to restrain itself is to not let life flow through it. The self is like a conduit through which life passes. But it is a conduit that is itself in process. The self must become if it is to be true to itself.

Nietzsche is, among other things, a philosopher of dancing. His Zarathustra proclaims, "Now I am light, now I fly, now I see myself beneath myself, now a god dances through me."[12] Much like Zarathustra, Nietzsche's dancing is unrestrained, sometimes to the point of seeming like madness. His dancing is extravagant because it's expressive of the energy that is flowing through him. Being true to himself means letting life force, energy, passion, and fervor discharge themselves, expend themselves, so as to reveal, show, and express their exuberance. "At my foot, frantic to dance, [life] cast a glance, a laughing, questioning, melting rocking-glance: twice only you stirred your rattle with your small hands, and my foot was already rocking with dancing frenzy."[13] Zarathustra claims that the best parables should speak of becoming because Nietzsche thinks that becoming is creation.[14] "Creation—that is the great redemption from suffering, and life's growing light. But that the creator may be, suffering is needed and much change. . . . . To be the child who is newly born, the creator must also want to be the mother who gives birth and the pangs of the birth-giver."[15]

Nietzsche expresses himself in dancing because he has been, and continues to be, affected by life. Dancing is how he expresses what has affected him most profoundly, especially what devastates him. The addict who becomes herself creates herself, rather than repressing or otherwise rejecting herself. Addiction profoundly affects addicts and so in order for her to become the addict she already is, the addict needs to proclaim rather than reject her addiction. She is thereby empowered to not practice it. What devastates the addict is the fact that she never feels more down than when she is closest to proclaiming her addiction. But Nietzsche would remind her that her devastation must be embraced. The paradox is that in the moment she proclaims her addiction, the addict finds she cannot simply be her addicted self because she is more than her addiction alone. Her lowest low becomes the first step toward becoming who she is.

## Wholeness in and through Brokenness

It is tempting to say that this Nietzschean vision of authenticity as becoming opens us up to a real fullness of being—a kind of wholeness that inauthenticity precludes. But Twelve Step spirituality insists that wholeness too has to be understood paradoxically.

Although addicts long for wholeness, their addiction reminds them of their undeniable brokenness. Indeed, it's likely that the more they strive to recover from their addiction, the more they are reminded of how broken they are. This "brokenness" refers not just to the life-threatening addiction itself but also to the mess of a life it creates and the defects of character that produce it. In fact, brokenness seems to be nothing but an endless series of flaws, shortcomings, and failings. The addict who becomes aware of all these inadequacies is inclined to flee because they reveal just how far away she is from wholeness. But the spirituality of imperfection that runs throughout Twelve Step programs strives to interrupt this flight.[16] According to this spirituality, it is not brokenness but the *rejection* of brokenness that obstructs recovery. For it leads the addict to practice her addiction, or the "white-knuckling" that culminates in the "dry-drunk," or some other mode of pretentiousness and/ or denial. Pursuing wholeness, the addict excludes brokenness from her self-conception. But the result is inauthenticity instead of wholeness.

To face one's brokenness instead of fleeing it is to "hit bottom." But the staggering truth at the basis of Twelve Step spirituality is that "hitting bottom" is at one and the same time what the addict most dreads *and* what she most needs to do. Paradoxically, wholeness is not possible until one's brokenness is embraced. On the surface, such an embrace would seem to make the wholeness the addict seeks inaccessible. But the irony is that brokenness obstructs recovery when it is rejected, not when it is affirmed. *Embracing brokenness transforms it from a potential trigger for relapse into an enabling condition of sobriety.*

This transformation can occur because of the fact that the addict's brokenness is also her being *broken-open-to* all that is beyond her, and especially to the power greater than herself that can restore her to sanity. Addicts are broken apart by their addictions. But the very admission that they are powerless over their brokenness enables them to see it not as an excuse to relapse but as a truth that exposes them to all that their flight from reality has hidden from them. The more one denies one's brokenness, the further one is from admitting one's powerlessness. The more one embraces one's brokenness, the more available one is to the possibility that there is something beyond one's self that has the power to do what one cannot do on one's own. Thus, any self-conception that does not include an acknowledgment of brokenness paradoxically blocks the path to wholeness. It leads one to pretend one is the whole person one wants to be, rather than the broken person one already is. The addict who makes the heartfelt proclamation, "I'm Jane, and I'm an alcoholic," includes brokenness at the very heart of her self-conception. To make this proclamation in a room full of strangers is terrifying for numerous reasons. But precisely by doing so, the addict inaugurates a way of relating to herself that enables her to recover from addiction. It is not the practice of addiction but admitting the naked truth of one's addiction that constitutes authenticity. Each and every meeting an addict attends presents another opportunity to relate to herself instead of fleeing herself.

The wisdom of authenticity lies in the fact that it is a mode of self-relationship that enables an addict to steer herself *into* her slide to the "bottom" of her inadequacy and failure. The problem is not what the practicing addict laments, namely, that inadequacies get in the way of her being the ideal self to which she aspires. The problem is that her pursuit of this ideal, this wholeness, itself derives from her desire to avoid the truth of who she actually is. Opening herself to this truth does not just create an authentic self-relationship. It is a mode of self-understanding that can become a way of life. For it makes one's very self into an opening. Recognizing one's inadequacy in all one's affairs, one is led to turn one's life over to a power greater than one's self.

This is a kind of wholeness that involves allowing yourself to be affected by life, by reality, by everything. You are not trying to repress, deny, evade, or escape anything. A wonderful example of this is provided by the recovering addict when she celebrates her first year of sobriety together with her fellow addicts at a meeting. This exemplifies wholeness in a number of ways. First, the recovering addict is not celebrating alone: the whole group of people that has supported her for the past year is taking delight in the fact that she has been authentically herself. Second, the event is the addict's celebration *of* her whole self: because she has not partitioned herself, she is embracing her intelligence, her passions, her imagination, her memories, and her vulnerabilities; she *becomes* her flaws and her strengths, her shortcomings and her gifts, her disappointments and her successes, her regrets and her joys. Third, the addict is celebrating *with* her whole self: she shares her story, her experience with the Steps; she laughs and perhaps cries; she hugs her sponsor and perhaps newcomers who are strangers. Fourth, the celebration gives witness to the fact that her life is whole in a way that it has never been. She is a wholly different person because she has authentically, and therefore wholly, become the addict she is. And, as if all of this is not enough, she is given a medallion to commemorate her year of sobriety that reads "To thine own self be true."[17]

## NOTES

1. Frankl, *Man's Search for Meaning*.

2. My aim in what follows is to explore the paradoxes inherent in Twelve Step spirituality's conception of recovery by reflecting on the paradoxical character of authenticity. This contrasts with the work of those philosophers, such as Richard Garrett, who examine the paradox inherent in addiction (namely, that addiction is in one sense voluntary and in another sense involuntary). See Richard Garrett, "Addiction, Paradox, and the Good I Would," in Poland and Graham, *Addiction and Responsibility*, 247–68.

3. See, for example, Potter, *Authenticity Hoax*, 17.

4. Plato, *Apology*, 21a.

5. Ibid., 21d.

6. Ibid., 22d.

7. The "strange experience" Socrates has when he cross-examines the politician results from the fact that Socrates is wiser than him by only the trifle that "what I do not know I don't think I do" (ibid., 21 c–d).

8. Nietzsche, *Gay Science,* section 270. The translation I use here is that of Alexander Nehamas, who notes that Kaufmann's translation—"You shall become the person you are"—misses the imperative force of the German. See Alexander Nehamas, "How One Becomes What One Is," in Guignon, *Existentialists,* 73–100. In his own historical inventory and defense of authenticity, Guignon further explores Nietzsche's imperative by articulating the role it plays in contemporary conceptions of authenticity. See Guignon, *Being Authentic,* especially 126–45.

9. See the section "On the Three Metamorphoses" in Nietzsche, *Zarathustra,* 25–28. Unlike the camel, which is the spirit burdened by the weight of the ideal, the child is the spirit as creator—as engaged in and by the process of becoming.

10. Bill W., personal correspondence, in Kurtz and Ketcham, *Spirituality of Imperfection,* 11. Bill W. originally wrote, "We must find some spiritual basis for living, else we die."

11. More specifically, Nietzsche would probably object to the claim that an addict is always an addict, as well as the claim that only a power higher than oneself can restore one to sanity.

12. Nietzsche, *Zarathustra,* 41.

13. Ibid., 224.

14. Ibid., 86–87.

15. Ibid., 87.

16. Kurtz and Ketcham, *Spirituality of Imperfection,* 61.

17. This essay is dedicated to Eddie W.

RUSSELL ANDERSON

# Is Twelve Step Spirituality Compatible with Autonomy?
Foucault, "Care of the Self," and
Spiritual Surrender

The concept of the autonomous self plays a pivotal role in much contemporary philosophizing, and Russell Anderson argues that autonomy is not only compatible with but essential to the authentic practice of Twelve Step spirituality. After arguing that addiction impairs autonomy, he draws on the late work of the twentieth-century French thinker Michel Foucault to contrast the Greco-Roman "care of the self" that enhances autonomy with those strains of the Christian tradition that, in Foucault's view, undermine it. Anderson's essay provides a provocative counter-position to the views espoused by Wamae Muriuki, Jason Danner, and, later on, Mary Riley.

It seems that some of the demands of Twelve Step spirituality are prima facie incompatible with a meaningful notion of personal autonomy, especially those steps in the Alcoholics Anonymous program for recovery that call for an admission of powerlessness and a surrender to God. In this essay I suggest, however, that these demands are better understood as benevolent and functionally oriented features of a program aimed at *restoring* the autonomy that alcoholism undermines. Much of the concern about these demands is due, I think, to a mistaken identification of Alcoholics Anonymous with a kind of Christian spirituality that is oppressive. However, the functional components of Twelve Step programs operate independently of this kind of spirituality and are important tools for those who struggle with addiction. To show how the powerlessness and surrender characteristic of Twelve Step spirituality may in fact be benevolent and necessary components of a program aiming at autonomy, I draw on Michel Foucault's distinction between the Christian spiritual tradition, on the one hand, and, on the other, a form of spirituality focused around the "care of the self" that is cultivated by certain Hellenistic practices and traditions.

## What Is Addiction?

It will be helpful to begin with a clear account of what addiction is and is not. According to Alcoholics Anonymous literature, the addict is someone who has lost the ability to control her drinking, has an "allergy" to alcohol, and is suffering from an "illness of self."[1] This view has a few important implications for how we understand addiction. First, it means that Alcoholics Anonymous provides a provisional set of strategies for managing the effects of alcoholism, and not a permanent "cure." Alcoholism is a lifelong battle and an incurable "allergy," but this does not mean that alcoholics cannot make progress. Secondly, we need to note that the powerlessness that is characteristic of addiction is not a literal powerlessness, of the type we might speak of when we say "it was impossible to do otherwise." This cannot be what Alcoholics Anonymous has in mind. If an addict is literally powerless over her addiction, we would expect abstention and recovery to be impossible, or at least anomalous. But people do abstain and recover, both inside and outside of Twelve Step programs.[2] And as we shall see in what follows, the Alcoholics Anonymous characterization of addiction involves a choice in a way that cases of "literal powerlessness" do not.

We can further reject two commonsense accounts of powerlessness in addiction. First, according to Alcoholics Anonymous, addiction is not strictly a physiological compulsion. It is a "social illness" and concerns an addict's relation to the world, to others, and to herself. It is not reducible to physiological states in the way that, say, tuberculosis or athlete's foot is. Rather, the Twelve Step account of addiction involves a psychological component that is the focus of its treatment process. Secondly, addiction is not simply an inescapable psychological compulsion, the kind that might lead us to say an addict is unable to choose to abstain. It is a commonly reported feature of addiction that even in their darkest moments many alcoholics retain the idea that they can abstain.[3]

A more accurate account of addiction is that it undermines our ability to live autonomously. Typically, we use the concept of autonomy to pick out some capacity to live our own lives and to ensure that our life is "a life worth living," or at least to guarantee that we have adopted a sufficiently caring and critical attitude toward our beliefs and decisions. A crucial component of an autonomous life is that we are able to develop and revise our ideas about the good life that we pursue, and that we are capable of integrating the many diverse pressures, relations, and desires that we experience into a coherent understanding of ourselves. But the fact is that we often encounter pressures and desires that tend to turn us away from our long-term goals, and we need to be able to avoid being sidetracked by these desires. It is true that sometimes these wayward motivations are benign—for example, a desire to travel or read fiction. But they can also be quite malevolent, as in cases of addiction. In malevolent cases, wayward desires undermine the strategies we employ to keep our motivations in line with our ideas about the good life we want to lead.

Reports of addiction support this autonomy-undermining model when they suggest that alcoholism generates an oscillation of preferences that may lead us to rationalize giving in to wayward desires. For one, alcoholics often emphasize the self-centeredness that is generated by alcoholism, as well as the internalization of a myth of self-control. Despite any evidence to the contrary, alcoholics oftentimes believe that they can control their drinking.[4] Their choices and relationships can become centered around preserving this myth, and in this way alcoholism often co-opts the strategies that alcoholics formerly employed to maintain their long-term commitments. Secondly, this myth of self-control often permits feelings of anger and resentment to run rampant through their lives and relationships, making it difficult for them to rank their preferences in a manner consistent with attempts to construct a unified, autonomous self.[5] As one philosopher has it, "Addiction impairs autonomy—when it does—because it fragments the agent, preventing her from extending her will across time. . . . *Addicts experience preference reversals which are sharper and less controllable than those to which non-addicts are subject.*"[6] Addiction is capable of undermining autonomy insofar as it is experienced as an obstacle to the life that we desire and identify with most of the time. Importantly, this implies that recovery involves equipping alcoholics with patterns of thought and action that will be helpful in rebuilding the relationships and self-understandings required to counteract the harmful effects of alcoholism. Hence the appeal to spiritual programs like the Twelve Steps to provide these important structures.

## What Is Autonomy?

Nevertheless, it still may be the case that such spiritual programs conflict with our attempts to develop autonomous selves insofar as they demand that we admit powerlessness and surrender to a "higher power." However, a careful consideration of the components of an autonomous life will show that this challenge misses the mark.

I noted above that autonomy involves a capacity to live according to our own determinations of the good life. Importantly, this means that autonomy is not reducible to the exercise of control over our desires and actions, or to independence from the wills or values of others. Such a model of autonomy is implausible for a number of reasons. For one, it too narrowly construes autonomy in that it fails to recognize our physical, emotional, and political/economic dependence on others. This model also overlooks the important fact that our desires and motivations often originate outside our control, and only later come to be integrated into our lives. Motivations such as familial relations, as well as socioeconomic, political, and historical factors, play an often under-recognized role in our capacity to develop and enjoy our lives. We are relational beings, and it is only by abstraction that we think of our lives outside this context. An independence-based model of autonomy is thus not suitable for discussions of real-life situations, which often involve many complex, sometimes conflicting motivations that are generated from any of a number of social or personal sources and that affect us in many different ways.

If our notion of autonomy is going to capture the complexity of life, it must include two features. First, it must refer to "the rich and complex social and historical contexts in which agents are embedded," and so require only that we make realistic demands of ourselves.[7] We cannot ignore the significant roles that relationships with other people play in our lives. Take for example an alcoholic's relationship with her spouse, which may be riddled with feelings of guilt, bad faith, denial, and even self-hatred. These feelings are likely to undermine her ability to stay sober insofar as they constantly increase the pressure to drink for relief, to "get away" or relax. Part of living autonomously, then, will be cultivating the right kinds of relationships, those which help us to develop and apply practices of critical inquiry and principles of right action. Secondly, our notion of autonomy must include an ability to critically form, revise, and act upon ideas about the good life. We can think of this as a feedback cycle in which our experiences provide practical wisdom about the kind of things that are good, and this wisdom in turn informs our selection of principles of action and reason. This feedback cycle allows us to make progress in our personal development in a critically informed and practically tested manner, and it connects our more lofty pursuits with the daily experiences and actions in which they are realized and tested.

## Spirituality and Autonomy

With this robust account of autonomy in hand, we can turn to a discussion of spirituality, paying special attention to its connection to autonomy.

In Michel Foucault's view, spirituality has three characteristics: it posits that we do not have access to the truth (for example, about ourselves or the divine) in a straightforward way; that we must undergo some set of changes if we are to discover this truth; and that when we do gain access to this truth in a spiritual manner, we experience it as enlightenment, and not merely as knowledge. The truth that is revealed through spiritual experience transforms one's mode of being in a way that, for instance, knowledge of scientific truths or logical maxims does not.[8] Take, for example, the young prince Alcibiades, who, having discovered how to care for himself under Socrates's guidance, comes to see how important being just is to good governance, and so alters his comportment to better serve this purpose.[9] Another example is the Christian monk who is supposed to gain beatitude as a result of his experience of the divine, after following a lifetime of prayer and service.

However, there are important differences between these two cases— between what we might label Foucault's Hellenistic and Christian images of spirituality. On the one hand, there is the Christian mode of spirituality, which Foucault traces to its origins in monastic ascetic practices, such as confession, in the early fifth century. In this tradition, spiritual practitioners must constantly compare themselves to God's will in order to discover how far their actual selves are from their ideal. This comparison is carried out by the examination of conscience and the confession of the practitioners' thoughts to a priest who tests their purity. Importantly, this confession demands that practitioners renounce their faults and replace their corrupted selves with versions more in line with God's will, and so become better suited to receive enlightenment.[10] Foucault's worry is that this type of spirituality involves surrendering one's actual self in an attempt to become more like some abstract other; it suggests that we have to renounce the values and practices we developed in the context of our concrete lives because they don't mesh with this ideal. The problem is that this type of comparative spirituality often leads us to include too dominant an image of another (God) in our lives and undermines the crucial relationship with our concrete selves that autonomy requires. This concern parallels the worry expressed by critics of Alcoholics Anonymous that the spiritual demands of the Twelve Steps undercut our ability to be autonomous.

On the other hand, we have Foucault's discussion of Hellenistic care of the self, a tradition characterized by the cultivation of an "attitude towards the self, others, and the world" aimed at securing a mode of being that is "stronger than, or not weaker than, whatever may occur" and that promises to help us act in a manner appropriate to the situation and consistent with our determinations of right action.[11] Care of the self is a *tekhne,* a matter of craftsmanship or artistic know-how, as opposed to *episteme,* which considers more abstract or contemplative forms of knowledge. In the Hellenistic context, there is a *tekhne* of building, of sculpture, of music composition and performance, of medicine, ship building, and so on, and also a *tekhne* of life. To "care for your self" is thus a matter of treating your life as something to be carefully crafted, to be produced. It is a matter of developing a "strong structure of existence" that is not reducible to any legal, social, or religious prescriptions.[12] We must acquire the relevant skills and knowledge, apply these to a material (our life), and continue to refine these practices by reflecting on the adequacy of the life that is produced. Importantly, the reflexive relationship that underscores this development of a *tekhne* is generated by a set of practices "exercised on the self by the self" through which "one changes, purifies, transforms, and transfigures oneself" in accordance with one's own critically informed understanding of the form one's life should take.[13] This spiritual-aesthetic production of a life requires that our passions, desires, knowledge, and practices are carefully critiqued and selected to ensure that they aim toward the ends we choose, and that they increase our ability to pursue these ends and avoid wayward influences. Insofar as it is aimed at increasing our capacity to manage our passions and actions, and does so by equipping us with concrete strategies likely to be successful in this regard, care of the self appears to avoid the criticisms directed against the Christian tradition.[14]

However, this Hellenistic form of spirituality consists of many of the same core practices we find worrisome in the Christian tradition—self-examination, exposure to truth, and obedience to a spiritual guide. Nevertheless, there are crucial differences in how these core practices operate, and what they aim to accomplish, in the traditions we are considering. Take for example the Stoic practice of daily self-interrogation, which involves both a recounting of one's actions and a criticism of one's mistakes, as does Christian confession. Unlike this juridical Christian mode, the Stoic investigation aims to discover how well our actions correspond to our own proper use of practical reasoning, and so concerns situations in which our actions exhibit a mistake, either in the means we take or the ends we desire. In addition, the Hellenistic mode does not seek penance or other punitive measures, but the adjustment of our reasoning in order to limit or eliminate further similar errors.[15] Hellenistic spirituality also differs from its Christian counterpart with respect to the type of individual it tries to foster. The Stoic examination, staying with this example of the Hellenistic tradition, produces what Foucault calls, following the Greek idiom, a "gnomic" notion of the self in which *one's will follows from and is one with her knowledge.*[16] A "gnomic" self is characterized by a close relationship between our actions and what we have discovered for ourselves to be good, very much in the way the feedback cycle I mentioned in the earlier discussion of autonomy works. Care of the self thus aims at equipping individuals with a set of attitudes and practices that help them to develop their lives autonomously.

A third important distinction between these two modes of spirituality is the different role played in each by the spiritual guide. In care of the self, practitioners are to seek a master who will provide practical advice and help them to make the relevant adjustments to their reasoning and behavior.[17] Unlike the Christian tradition, in the Hellenistic form "the obedience of the disciple was founded on the capacity of the master to lead him to a happy and autonomous life," and so was provisional and benevolent.[18] Nevertheless, this obedience is an essential component of care of the self. Foucault notes that practices of care of the self most often occur within a "background of errors and ignorance,"[19] and so the role of the master is "to free the young man from his ignorance" and to help him to pass "from ignorance to non-ignorance, from ignorance to knowledge," for "ignorance cannot escape from itself on its own."[20] The practices that make up care of the self must help individuals overcome an inability which, because of its extent and depth, they cannot move past on their own. In our state of ignorance we not only lack knowledge of the things we ought to know—how to conduct ourselves properly—but we fail to recognize that we lack this knowledge; we are unaware of our ignorance. The role of the spiritual master is to correct this, for "passing from the status of 'to be corrected' to the status of 'corrected' *a fortiori* presupposes a master. Ignorance cannot be the element that brings about knowledge; this was the point on which the need for a master was based in classical thought."[21]

The fact is that one cannot care for one's self on one's own. We need the support, guidance, and practical wisdom of those who have experience overcoming ignorance and bad habits in themselves and others, and this help is gained in the form of obedience to a spiritual master. In these cases, recognizing our powerlessness and surrendering to a spiritual guide are instrumental conditions for care of the self, and also for autonomy. Recall the earlier discussion in which I suggested that relationships with others are a central component of our lives, and so need to be taken into account when discussing our capacity for autonomy. We need to avoid poisonous relationships, but we also need to develop, express, and revise the practices, beliefs, and goals that constitute our lives *in* concrete relationships with others.[22]

What is at stake in care of the self is a mode of relating to oneself through which an individual closes the gap between what she knows to be true and good, and the kind of life she lives—the gap between her knowledge and her practices. This is quite different from the uncompromising self-mastery some critics suggest Foucault is endorsing, and which is clearly incompatible with Alcoholics Anonymous.[23] Moreover, care of the self marks a mode of spirituality in which surrendering to another and recognizing powerlessness are compatible with an autonomous life.

## Recovery and Spirituality

The remaining question is whether Twelve Step spirituality necessarily undermines our autonomy in the way the Christian mode of spirituality criticized by Foucault appears to do—by demanding that we substitute an idealized notion of what we ought to be for the pragmatic set of strategies and goals that are grounded in our concrete experiences and relationships. I think that considering two key themes of Twelve Step spirituality that may seem to make it autonomy-impairing—the admission of powerlessness and surrender to God—will actually help us see that it is autonomy-enhancing. My investigation will show that the goals of Alcoholics Anonymous can be understood as aiming at equipping participants with strategies and practices that are of great use in their everyday lives, despite the oppressive-sounding rhetoric.

In discussing these themes, we would do well to keep in mind the context of alcoholism as a pattern of behavior that undermines our future ability to form, revise, and act in accordance with our long-term goals. But we should also note that the Twelve Steps are set against a backdrop of a particularly difficult problem: self-willing. According to Alcoholics Anonymous literature, one of the central features of addiction is that an alcoholic is helpless in the face of the first drink because there is no means of defense against the addictive impulse; the alcoholic individual is "absolutely unable to stop drinking on the basis of self-knowledge."[24] The problem is that "the alcoholic is an extreme example of self-will run riot," and so is afflicted not only with the myth of self-control I discussed earlier, but also with an ignorance of the depths of the problem and the means that are needed to correct it.[25] An alcoholic's successful recovery requires that he or she overcome this lack of knowledge and problematic self-willing, much in the way that initiates to care of the self must overcome their ignorance.

According to literature from Alcoholics Anonymous, the admission (outlined mostly in Steps One and Five, but implicit in Six and Seven) that one is powerless over alcohol and unable to manage one's life on one's own serves three purposes. First, it requires that one recognize one's addiction, and hence forms "the firm bedrock upon which happy and purposeful lives may be built."[26] It helps one keep present in one's mind the dangers of symptomatic self-willing and ignorance, and so acts as a first defense where previously there was none. Secondly, the admission marks the beginning of one's struggle to overcome addiction, confirms in one's own mind the depth of the problem, and helps one adopt a sense of enlightened separation from past mistakes: "Now I know why I did those things!" To be sure, much more than this separation is required to overcome addiction. Regardless, when combined with the investigations of self called for in Steps Four, Eight, Nine, and Ten, this critical distance helps provide content for a mode of self-reflection uncontaminated by bad faith, old habits, and harmful self-will that serves as the basis of a positive project of self-development. Thirdly, the admission is supposed to motivate alcoholics to stick to the program. Without first admitting to oneself that one is no longer in control of one's life, one may have very little reason to carry out a program as challenging and rigorous as the Twelve Steps. The admission of powerlessness is thus not, as the critic would suggest, a worrisome statement of an alcoholic's helplessness, but is instead an important functional component of his or her recovery. The philosopher Owen Flanagan, remarking on his own experience with addiction, goes so far as to say that not only does the admission of powerlessness "seem true" insofar as addiction involves broken "motivational circuits" leading to the kind of irrational judgment shifts discussed above, but addicts have difficulty leveraging "the small zone of control between the addict and that first drug or drink" into sustained abstinence. This leads him to call the admission of powerlessness "a trick that works."[27] There is nothing inconsistent with living an autonomous life and admitting that some of our actions and desires are beyond our control, especially once we recognize that a capacity for autonomy is always embedded in a complex social context. What is important is the color we give these wayward motivations in the larger context of our lives and how we respond to their continued presence. Just as in care of the self—where the central question was not "Was I in control of that action?" but rather "Did I employ the correct principle in accordance with my goals?"—powerlessness in Alcoholics Anonymous is a matter of self-recognition and correction, not self-abdication.

The second key theme of the Twelve Steps I want to discuss is the notion that alcoholics must surrender their "will and lives" to God and ask Him to remove their "defects of character." This surrender appears to violate the requisite conditions of an autonomous life and so may be thought imprudent. But I don't think we have reason to believe this an accurate portrayal of Twelve Step spirituality. In fact, there is good evidence that Twelve Step spirituality offers the kind of practical program that secures, rather renounces, the self insofar as it helps prepare alcoholics for the concrete obstacles they are likely to encounter and the kind of struggles that may lead them to relapse. Consider the fact that the surrender involved in Twelve Step programs is enacted by following a set of practices and guidelines developed from careful introspection, from the experiences of others shared at meetings, from the one-on-one advice of sponsors and helpful others in the group, and from the wealth of narratives in Alcoholics Anonymous literature. All of these resources aim to secure and develop an autonomous self, rather than abdicate it. Moreover, the steps that seem to directly demand autonomy-undermining surrender—Steps Three, Six, and Seven—all target specific harmful characteristics of addicted psychology with an eye to concrete solutions. Steps Six and Seven portray the humility required for self-development in the context of the problematic self-willing I noted above, and Step Three gives advice for overcoming this self-willing characteristic of many experiences of alcoholism.

I am not suggesting that asking God to remove our faults will not result in becoming less self-indulgent and so more effective at overcoming addiction. My argument is the more modest one that this result can be obtained without divine intervention and the spiritual renunciation it requires, insofar as the practices through which recovering alcoholics seek a "higher power" provide many of the tools their recovery requires. Alcoholics Anonymous appears to allow for the possibility of such an agnostic reading when it wavers on just what type of figure a participant must recognize as a "higher power." Despite the overpowering rhetoric of Alcoholics Anonymous literature and many meetings, there is no reason to think it impossible to substitute for "God" the combined practical wisdom of the community of alcoholics that constitutes Alcoholics Anonymous.

If the critic's concern about Twelve Step spirituality is analogous to Foucault's worry about the oppressive tendencies of the Christian mode of spirituality, then it seems to be misplaced. Insofar as the powerlessness and surrender Alcoholics Anonymous asks its participants to acknowledge and practice are directed toward a future in which they are more capable of autonomy, and of resisting and making productive use of desires that do not correspond well with their long-term projects, we have little reason to expect the Twelve Steps to necessarily undermine autonomy.

We might ask, finally, what distinguishes spiritual demands that we ought to be concerned about from those likely to increase our capacity to live autonomous lives. One answer that I've suggested is that we can objectively determine whether a set of spiritual practices are connected to our own lives, struggles, and goals, or to some external ideal that may lead us away from this important context. But we also need to be aware that the attitude we bring to a spirituality can determine our experience: If we are seeking to renounce ourselves and our responsibilities, surely we will find just about any ideal adequate. If, at the other extreme, we are looking to develop self-mastery via assertion of our will, then we may overshoot and fall back into the problems of self-willing and indulgence. However, if our attitude is geared toward establishing a relationship with ourselves centered around being better equipped for the problems we are likely to encounter, the concerns about surrender and powerlessness are far less worrisome than critics suggest. Care of the self aims toward this spiritual equipping, and so may Alcoholics Anonymous.

NOTES

1. *Alcoholics Anonymous,* 30 and 64. See also Denzin, *Treating Alcoholism,* as well as Denzin, *Alcoholic Self,* 73.

2. See Bennett Foddy and Julian Savulescu, "A Liberal Account of Addiction," *Philosophy, Psychiatry, and Psychology* 17, no. 1 (2010): 13, for a discussion of current research and statistics regarding recovery.

3. For example, take one alcoholic's report that "I like what alcohol tells me. It tells me I can drink it and control it. . . . Alcohol tells me everything will be O.K. But it never is." See Denzin, *Alcoholic Self,* 126, for this and other similar reports.

4. Denzin, *Treating Alcoholism,* 25–26.

5. Ibid., 28.

6. Neil Levy, "Autonomy and Addiction," *Canadian Journal of Philosophy* 36, no. 3 (2006): 440; my emphasis. Levy continues, "We all discount future goods hyperbolically. . . . Addicts are a partial exception: their discount curves remain highly bowed, so that they experience preference reversals more easily than most of the rest of us. The very fact that addicts are subject to such reversals suggests that they are less unified than non-addicts." Levy elsewhere suggests that addicts are susceptible to such judgment shifts because self-control is a limited, depletable resource that "can be drawn down by a temptation of any strength, so long as it persists for a sufficient period of time." This explains, he thinks, the relative difficulty of long-term abstinence over short-term, as well as the apparent cue dependence of cravings and the shifts in judgment that he argues are characteristic of addiction. See Neil Levy, "Addiction, Responsibility, and Ego Depletion," in Poland and Graham, *Addiction and Responsibility,* 102.

7. Catriona Mackenzie and Natalie Stoljar, "Introduction: Autonomy Refigured," in Mackenzie and Stoljar, *Relational Autonomy,* 21.

8. See Foucault's distinction of "spirituality" from "philosophy" in Foucault, *Hermeneutics,* 15.

9. See Plato's *Symposium,* and Foucault's discussion of it in *Hermeneutics,* 31–38.

10. "A Christian is always supposed to be supported by the light of faith if he wants to explore himself, and, conversely, access to the truth of faith cannot be conceived of without the purification of the soul" (Foucault, "About the Beginning," 211).

11. Foucault, *Hermeneutics,* 321.

12. Michel Foucault, "On the Genealogy of Ethics," in Foucault, *Ethics,* 260.

13. Foucault, *Hermeneutics,* 11.

14. Richard Garrett also discusses spirituality in relation to addiction recovery. However, where I emphasize the strategic importance of autonomy to the self, Garrett stresses the value of internalizing the Christian-Buddhist golden principle. While Garrett's analysis touches on some of the same themes as mine, e.g., cultivation of strategies of

inquiry and the development of right action in accordance with self-understanding, we disagree with respect to the end of this caring attitude toward oneself. On my model, Twelve Step spirituality is about cultivating a self capable of maintaining itself over the course of a life, not aligning oneself with the golden rule. No matter how effective, such alignment always risks the kind of self-sacrifice found in the Christian tradition that my Foucauldian account criticizes. See Richard Garrett, "Addiction, Paradox, and the Good I Would," in Poland and Graham, *Addiction and Responsibility,* 247–68.

15. Foucault, "About the Beginning," 207.

16. See Foucault, "On the Genealogy of Ethics," in Foucault, *Ethics,* 209.

17. For more on the criteria of an effective guide and the appropriate selection process, see Foucault, *Hermeneutics,* chapters 8 and 20.

18. Foucault, "About the Beginnings," 216.

19. Foucault, *Hermeneutics,* 94.

20. Ibid., 128–29.

21. Ibid., 130.

22. Francis Seeburger makes a similar point when he distinguishes well-intentioned "caretaking," which is nevertheless disabling insofar as it "robs its recipients of their independence," from "caregiving," which "makes it possible for the care receiver to assume his or her own proper, personal care. See his *Addiction and Responsibility,* 98.

23. For an example of this critique, see Allen, *Politics of Ourselves.*

24. *Alcoholics Anonymous,* 37.

25. Ibid., 62.

26. Alcoholics Anonymous, *Twelve Steps and Twelve Traditions,* 21.

27. Flanagan suggests that this "useful trick" does not absolve the addict from responsibility: "Addicts speak of themselves as if they are and were responsible in all the normal ways other people speak about such matters." See Owen Flanagan, "What Is It Like to Be an Addict?," in Poland and Graham, *Addiction and Responsibility,* 291.

# PART FOUR

# "I Can't, We Can"

## The Role of Others in Recovering Selfhood

STUART GRANT

# Being-Together-Toward Recovery

In addition to requiring that one be honest with oneself, all the Twelve Steps at least implicitly require the practitioner to authentically engage with others. Stuart Grant finds support for this dimension of Twelve Step spirituality in an array of twentieth-century Continental thinkers including Martin Heidegger, Emmanuel Levinas, and Martin Buber. He argues that, because our selves are primordially constituted by intersubjectivity, and because one-on-one encounters are essential to human existence, it is impossible for recovery to occur in isolation. The profound self-transformation that Twelve Step spirituality promotes is made possible by our opening ourselves to other persons and to our ultimate source of value.

The Twelve Step program of recovery effects a transformation of relations with self, others and the divine. This essay offers a phenomenological analysis of how this transformation occurs. It tells the story of the journey from an isolated self, cut off from others, to a "responsible, productive member of society."[1] It is about the changes in the ways active and recovering addicts perceive, value, belong, and relate to themselves, to other people, and to an ultimate source of value, divine or worldly.

The essay is a phenomenology. Phenomenology is a very specific philosophical discipline that requires a new understanding of some everyday terms. The essay begins with a definition of some of these terms, in particular *intentionality* and *intersubjectivity*. It should be noted that when these terms are applied to an understanding of the processes of recovery, those processes are revealed as profoundly paradoxical. The transformation of the addict requires a surrender of self. Recovery begins with a radical passivity that opens the way to the creation of a renovated self held in new relationships with itself, others, and the divine.

The essay concentrates on the Twelve Steps themselves and the literature supporting the steps as practiced in Narcotics Anonymous (NA). NA is the only Twelve Step fellowship that does not refer to a specific substance or behavior in the First Step but to the general condition of addiction. According to the NA World Service Bulletin #13, this places the problem not in the substance but in the person of the sufferer, "in our thoughts and feelings."[2] NA claims not to discriminate between users of different drugs. This generality and inclusiveness foregrounds the basic condition of the disease of addiction that unites all addicts, whatever their drug of choice. For these reasons, this essay employs the NA version of the Steps as the most general and widely applicable variant.

## The Concept of Intentionality

This essay is a phenomenological-intentional analysis. Phenomenology studies the ways in which we apprehend and are constituted by the objects, people and values around us. We apprehend things through perception—touching, seeing, hearing, tasting—but also through valuing, willing, judging, using, producing and through emotional connection. So I apprehend myself (among other ways) through thinking, the experience of feeling my own body, self-valuing, and self-narration. Other people are apprehended through such phenomena as perception, language, social values, and emotions. I apprehend the divine through prayer, belief, revelation, cultural custom, and practice. The aim of phenomenological-intentional analysis is to describe and assess the structures of these relationships.

## Note on Intersubjectivity

Twelve Step recovery, as a process of changing relations with self, others, and the divine, is profoundly intersubjective. It is about what happens between and among people. The history of interpretations of intersubjectivity in phenomenology is characterized by a tension between two tendencies that appear to be in conflict but that are, in fact, mutually complementary. The first of these tendencies emphasizes the primordial intersubjectivity that affects us by virtue of our being born into a preexisting world of others, values and social and cultural practices. Examples of this theory can be found in the *open intersubjectivity* described by Husserl in his unpublished writings, Heidegger's *mitsein,* and Merleau-Ponty's *intercorporeality.*[3] We encounter this primordial intersubjectivity clearly in queues, families, audiences, clubs, and other situations where we belong to a common cause or purpose. The second tendency, exemplified by Husserl's *primordial reduction,* Sartre's *for-the-other,* and Levinas's *face-to-face,* treats the one-on-one encounter with the single other person as the fundamental relation.[4] According to this tendency, the structure of the self is dependent on looking into the face of the other person. It begins when the suckling infant stares into the eyes of its mother or another adult holding and comforting it. This develops into a sense that who we are is shaped by the way we think the other person sees us as we see ourselves reflected in his or her gaze.

Merleau-Ponty defines the first tendency through his concept of intercorporeality, "a primordial phenomenon of the body-for-us" through which "our perspective views . . . slip into each other and are brought together finally in the thing." He writes of "an anonymous existence" and says, "We are collaborators . . . in consummate reciprocity. . . . Perspectives merge into each other, and we co-exist through a common world."[5]

Sartre criticizes this position, likening it to a "crew" in "which the rhythm of the oars or the regular movement of the coxswain will . . . be made manifest to them by the common goal to be attained."[6] However, Sartre insists that this is no "real unification" of subjects. "It is I who produce this rhythm. But at the same time it melts into the general rhythm of the work or of the march of the concrete community which surrounds me."[7]

Despite Sartre and Merleau-Ponty's conflicting views on which position is primary, they share an important link. The key is in the world we share. For Sartre, it is the rhythm, the "concrete community"; for Merleau-Ponty, the "common world." Heidegger precedes both with his conception that being-with-others is being-in-the-world.[8] Whether or not the unity or the one-on-one encounter is primary, it is our intentional relationship to the world we share that brings us together.

This is the main premise of the possibility of Twelve Step recovery. The foundation of mutual objectivity of shared experience is the kernel of the intentional structure of recovery. Recovery is a dwelling-in, a revelation-of, an arising-from, a primary belonging that is not only a belonging together one-on-one but a mutual belonging to experiences that are there for all of us: a fundamentally intersubjective intentional phenomenon. In Husserlian terms, the belonging-together in recovery fellowships is a primary instance of "a single unity of intentionality with the reciprocal implication of life fluxes of the individual subjects."[9]

This is the structure that underlies the recovery slogan "I can't, we can."

Recovery institutes a radical belonging that has been lost by the solitary, self-obsessed addict. Twelve Step recovery is a continual process of intersubjective validation of a shared world and experience.

For the remainder of this essay, I will elaborate the structure of this intersubjective validation in Twelve Step recovery, in a description of the radical rearrangement of the ways in which self, other, and the divine constitute each other and are perceived, valued, and judged.

## Saying Recovery: Sharing and Admission

The Steps begin with an admission. "We admitted we were powerless . . . and our lives had become unmanageable." Recovery begins with an act of saying. Saying is an essential ongoing operation of recovery. Addicts are encouraged to "share" in meetings, to get a sponsor to whom they will reveal their deepest secrets, to speak regularly and honestly about what they are thinking and feeling. The utterance of such proclamations as "I am an addict" and "I am powerless" are continually reiterated in meetings and throughout the working of the steps with a sponsor. This continual reiteration, the very act of admission, brings forth and reinforces the awareness, belief, and orientation necessary to enter and sustain recovery. This utterance is an example of a Levinasian *Saying* that is not "simply a sign or expression of a meaning; it proclaims and establishes this as that."[10] In this regard, the admissions the Steps involve are related to J. L. Austin's concept of the *performative utterance*, a class of statement whose purpose "is not to *describe my doing* . . . or to state that I am doing it; it is to do it. . . . The issuing of the utterance is the performing of an action."[11] The admissions made in doing the Steps are not strictly performative in the sense of verbs such as "I swear" or "I apologize," in which the saying is the action that is performed, but they are performative in the sense that they institute and reinforce the state of affairs to which they refer. It is through the admission, the saying, the nomination of themselves, that addicts come forth *as addicts* in their own understanding and in the understanding of others. I am not an addict for myself until I admit it before others and my primary value source.

The act of admission, the performance of it, the saying as doing, recurs throughout the steps: through prayer in Steps Three, Seven, and Eleven; through the sharing of wrongs in Step Five; through the writing and sharing of the inventory in Steps Four and Ten. The efficacy of the performance of the admission serves to initiate and reaffirm the commitment to recovery. The admission of powerlessness and unmanageability in the First Step effects a passivity in the relationship with self, an abdication of agency. The addict is subject to the demands of the addiction, an uncontrollable interior foreign force. "We placed their use [drugs] ahead of the welfare of our families, our wives, husbands, and our children. We had to have drugs at all costs."[12]

Emmanuel Levinas figures the human being as fundamentally a response to the call of the other. What I am is the way I come forth in response to the demand of alterity. I emerge as responsibility to and for the other. The using addict forgoes this fundamental structure of the human, or rather replaces it with obedience to the demand of the drug or behavior. Levinas describes the demand of the other as a fundamental state of obsession at the core of self; an obsession or besieging by the responsibility to the other person.[13] "It is in the passivity of obsession, or incarnated passivity, that an identity individuates itself as unique."[14] Thus the individuated self is manifested as response to a preexistent "force of an alterity in me,"[15] a "restlessness,"[16] an anxiety through which I feel "uneasy in my own skin."[17] For the active addict, in isolation, the drug replaces the other person. This underlying anxiety is taken over and manifests as persecution by and obsession with the disease of addiction, the bad other within the self which wills its very destruction. To initiate and sustain recovery, the addict must will the abdication of the diseased will. In the "rock bottom" of recovery, the addict has no choice but to acknowledge that the destructive interior force has taken over the will completely. For recovery to begin, it is necessary not only that this state of indigence and depredation be reached but that the addict utters an acknowledgment of complete powerlessness. The utterance begins the road to recovery. The structure of self that had been given over to the insistent demand of the drug, the addiction, can now be re-attuned to hear the call of the other person. The admission, to self, others, and the divine, opens the way for the self to be restored.

## Apprehension of Self

This restoration deepens with the intense self-engagement of the Fourth Step. The addict writes an inventory of relationships, resentments, wrongs done to others, moral assets, emotional life, and drug use, leaving no stone unturned. The inventory challenges everything one holds true about who one is. Facing the past allows for the apprehension of the self in a new light and opens the possibility of new ways of being. Much of the Fourth Step pertains to relations with others but considered in such a way that a new relationship with self is forged. The inventory is a "moral" inventory. The primary aim is to reveal the actions that have determined who the addict has become as a product of the values espoused, transgressed, and betrayed. The intensity, depth, detail, and courage of the examination opens the possibility of a profound change in the values, attitudes, and actions of the addict based on a new level of self-awareness of destructive habitual responses and emotional states. The newly struck relationship with self, based on a previously unattained experience of self-honesty and courage, also becomes the foundation for the deepening of the relationships with the divine and with others.

However, the new relationship with the self can only reach fruition through attunement with a primary belonging. Recovery is a group process. The individual cannot recover alone. The first tradition states clearly: "personal recovery depends on NA unity."

## Apprehension of Others

The Steps begin with the word "We." According to Twelve Step fellowships, addiction is a disease of isolation. The NA Basic Text states that "our disease isolated us from people except when we were getting, using and finding ways and means to get more.... Our world shrank and isolation became our life."[18] The constant mission to find drugs and the perpetual nagging sense that something is wrong turn one's attention away from others and onto the needs of one's own body and state of mind and the endless incompletion and anguish of the obsession and compulsion.

Addiction is understood as "a disease of self-obsession" and self-centeredness.[19] As remedy to this complete obsession with self, it is necessary to begin a thoroughgoing reorientation toward others. The explicit statement of the "we" attests to and foregrounds the belonging that sustains the fellowship, opens the individual addict to recovery, and guides attunement to the needs of other people. The themes of service-to, recognition-of, amends-to, and care-for others are basic intentional attitudes that reoccur throughout the Steps. As has been previously noted, the slogan "I can't, we can" is a basic tenet of all Twelve Step programs. This dependent belonging to a we-subject reveals the primordial intersubjectivity, but the Steps themselves are also practiced in face-to-face partnership with a sponsor who becomes the site of a newfound trust, an initiating intersubjective relationship at the core of recovery, the first building block of a new way of life. In this way, the intersubjectivity of the steps is constituted according to both of the aforementioned intentional modes of intersubjectivity, the one-on-one and the belonging-to an underlying preexistent intersubjective ground that precedes self and society.

Steps Eight and Nine offer the most profound renovation of the ways in which we perceive, value, judge, and make relationships with others. Every harm done to others is recalled and noted, and an attempt at amends is made. The relationship with self is further articulated in the context of taking responsibility for the effects of addiction and its associated behaviors on others. These Steps operate at a most fundamental level of the formation of self.

Levinas is useful for understanding how these two Steps work. As mentioned earlier, the structure of self, which, according to Levinas, comes forth as a response to the ethical demand of the other person, was previously taken over by the drug, the addiction. In the Levinasian view, I *am* my obligation to the other. The active addict replaced this with obligation only to the addiction. Only through a deep reappraisal, a re-hearing of the call of the other person, can the self come forth in a more complete, fulfilled manner. In Steps Eight and Nine, this is achieved by the action of making amends. The paradox of recovery emerges here again. Through making amends and consequently taking up a position of the possibility of being forgiven by the other person, the addict also gains the ability for self-forgiveness and thus gains a greater capacity to forgive. This initiates an intense phase of establishing relations with others and self in a mode of forgiveness and acceptance of others as they are. If performed thoroughly, this grounds a shift to a sustainable mode of relation to others and self. "The main thing that Steps Eight and Nine do for us is to help build awareness that, little by little, we are gaining new attitudes about ourselves and how we deal with other people."[20]

This raises again the profoundly paradoxical core of the Twelve Steps. It is only through a complete giving over of self to the higher power in the Third Step, to the trust in the sponsor, to the becoming "entirely" ready of the Sixth Step, to the becoming willing to make amends to "all" of those we had harmed in the Ninth, that recovery is possible and a new self is given back. One of the oft-cited clichés of recovery is "half measures avail us nothing." Commitment to recovery must aim to be complete and unconditional. The more complete the giving of oneself over entirely to the needs of the other, the more profound the renovation of self. This can be understood through an application of Martin Buber's concept of the "I-Thou" relation. For Buber, all relations through which humans, worlds, and God are given to each other occur as the saying of two basic word pairs, "I-Thou" or "I-It." The I-It relation is the intentional realm of objects, goals, experience, and knowledge. It is depersonalized and objectifying. It elides the possibility of a human relation. The I-Thou relation, on the other hand, is pure founding relatedness: "Whoever says Thou does not have something for his object. . . . He stands in relation."[21] Moreover, "The I-Thou can only be spoken with one's whole being."[22] This is not an intentional relation of a subject apprehending preexistent objects but a simultaneous coexistence in which self, world, other, and the divine require each other to come into being. In the self-centeredness of active addiction, the other person is encountered as an object in the I-It relation, as more or less useful. In the Ninth Step, the other is apprehended through the I-Thou relation. The needs of self are suspended in full service to the other, dedicated entirely to making amends to the other, and yet, paradoxically, simultaneously, the self is remade anew in the relation.

This causes a shift in the basic disposition of the addict. The measure of the amends is in the ongoing change in the behavior of the addict. "Not only do we make amends to the person we've harmed, we follow upon those amends with a serious change in our behavior."[23] This "serious change" in behavior is rooted in a profound change in the way we perceive, value, and judge others and are consequently constituted by our engagement with them. "If we have been inconsiderate, always wrapped up in what we wanted and needed, we now begin to be sensitive to the needs of others. . . . We need to go on by making a concerted daily effort to stop hurting our loved ones."[24]

Our recovery is also a way of making amends to ourselves. The amends process drives home the knowledge that we are becoming truly different people. One of the most paradoxical aspects of our recovery is that by thinking of ourselves less, we learn to love ourselves more. We may not have expected our spiritual journey to lead to a fresh appreciation of ourselves, but it does. Because of the love we extend to others, we realize our own value.[25]

So again, it is precisely in the taking up of a new relationship with others that a new relation with self is forged. The new self has arisen precisely from and to the extent to which a complete as possible giving over to the other was attained. This new self/other structure is achieved, as was mentioned above, in the immersion in forgiveness, in making oneself available to being forgiven by others, and subsequently being able to forgive oneself and others.

The one-on-one encounter and the primordial intersubjectivity debated by phenomenologists are again revealed as different aspects of the same phenomenon, rather than radically different processes.

## Apprehension of the Divine

The Twelve Steps constitute the divine as an open and uncertain offer. The Second Step does not say "a power greater than ourselves restored us to sanity." Nor does it say that this power *will* restore us to sanity; it says it *could* restore us. It does not say we *know,* but that we *came to believe.* We are not in a pregiven state of belief; we are on the way in an indeterminate stage of an unfinished process. In order to enter this ongoing, uncertain process, it is necessary to establish a relationship with "a power greater than ourselves." This Step does not even offer the certainty of a specific named power, *the* power, but an unspecified power whose only quality is that it is greater than our own. The only certain thing in this step is its uncertainty. This relationship is never finished. It is an invitation to the beginning of a tenuous relationship with an unspecified, unknown, immeasurable, infinite divine.

Nevertheless, despite all this uncertainty, the step does offer hope of redemption and restoration. Hope is, in essence, an unfinished state. A hope is neither a fulfillment nor even an expectation, but a desiring openness to a belief in a possibility. This is, in itself, despite any specified possible goal, an improvement on the destitution and despair of the First Step. The Second Step offers the possibility of a restoration of sanity. The obsession, the compulsion, the lack of control, the persecution by the destructive enemy within, and the unmanageable wreckage of the life it has created, can be remedied. The addict has a foothold in the hope. The establishment of the relationship with the greater power also lays the ground for a new relationship with self. Through the belief in the new power, the addict can be restored to sanity.

In Step Three, the uncertainty of the power greater than ourselves moves toward greater but still not absolute certainty. The power becomes articulated as "God." Still, this is not a particular God, but "God as we understood him." This "as we understood him" is an important turning point. It is not merely the "complete personal choice and freedom"[26] as to the nature of the God underlying the "as we understood him" that is significant here, but the very fact that, after the powerlessness of the first two Steps, the addict is able to choose at all. Through the establishing of the relationship with the God, a new, more certain relationship with self is established. The self emerges as "making a decision." This is a key moment. In the first two Steps, agency was curtailed, abdicated. In powerlessness, unmanageability, and turning oneself over to the "power greater than ourselves," responsibility has been successively given over, first in destitution, then in hope. In the Third Step, a decision is made. The power of this moment cannot be underestimated. It is the birth of a new sovereignty and power to act.

However, this new sovereignty is born as a decision to "turn our will and our lives over to the God." In deciding to turn will and life over, an apparent further abdication, the addict, again paradoxically, arises as responsible, sovereign, and active. Just as the complete surrender of self to the process of making amends to the other had been the founding moment of the new self, here the abdication of power to the higher power is the moment of birth of a newly empowered self. The addict no longer merely believes, but acts, makes decisions; the actuating decision is the active willingness to surrender the will, which is reborn in the act of turning itself over. The turning over to the divine becomes a source of freedom and founds new ways in which the self perceives, values, judges, and becomes itself. These apparent contradictions, these paradoxes, constitute the irreducible, fundamental living moments of the recovery process.

Still, the question remains, what does it actually mean to "turn our life over"? In the simplest terms, the NA literature describes a transformation in the structure of the way the self perceives, values, judges, and understands itself, through a reflective practice of actions and attitudes toward others and the divine:

> Recovery is a process of discovery. We learn about ourselves, and we learn how to cope with the world around us. When we are sincere in our desire to allow our Higher Power to care for us, we begin to gain a sense of serenity. We notice a gradual change in our thinking. Our attitudes and ideas become more positive. Our world is no longer distorted by self-pity, denial, and resentment. We are beginning to replace those old attitudes with honesty, faith, and responsibility; as a result, we begin to see our world in a better light. Our lives are guided by our emerging integrity.... We learn to trust; as we do, we open the doors to intimacy and develop new relationships.[27]

In the Second Step, the addict comes to believe; in the Third, action is taken and a choice made. The belief manifests as a concrete practice of turning outward. This turning outward in a spirit of openness and care toward another is the fundamental gesture of prayer.

The Eleventh Step maintains and deepens the means by which the relationship with the divine is sustained through prayer and meditation. Prayer is a more or less willed action of direct address to something outside of oneself. To pray, even for the atheist, is to call upon something outside, for help, assistance, protection, guidance.

The first impulse of the addict is self-destructive and self-centered. The prayer and meditation of the Eleventh Step are aimed at maintaining a relationship with an exterior source of value in relation to which it is possible for one to see and assess one's behavior more clearly, more honestly, and more constructively. Whether this power is a traditional God, an undefined divine presence, or the counsel of a group of trusted friends, it is necessary to make admission, ask for guidance, listen openly, and act on it.

## Mutual Interdependency of Self, Others, and the Divine

The Twelve Steps forge new intentional relationships with self, others, and the divine through continued acts of admission in meetings, in working the Steps, and in practical engagement. These relationships underpin each other so as to constitute a mutually reinforcing intentional web. The admission of the Fifth Step, "to God, to ourselves, and to another human being," brings them all together. Before the divine value source and the other, the addict is reflected back in a new light. A greater level of acceptance of self is necessary in the face of the other. The one-on-one, face-to-face relationship with the sponsor becomes the site of a new intimacy and trust founded in a more honest, courageous view of self. The admission before the divine value exposes actions and self-valuations to an external source of an ultimate validation. Whether these values are attributed to a divine origin or a group of people committed to a life based on loving and caring for each other, this places the addict before a value context constituted as both a primordial intersubjectivity and an emergent web of one-on-one relationships.

Step Twelve embodies the ultimate goal of this new disposition. All three of the relations are again explicit: a spiritual awakening, carrying the message to others, and living by principles "in all our affairs." The journey that began with admitting powerlessness over the obsession and compulsion to continue a destructive behavior has resulted in a transformation of life rooted in a mutually dependent relationship with self, others, and the divine.

NOTES

1. Narcotics Anonymous, *Narcotics Anonymous,* 101.

2. Narcotics Anonymous, "World Service Board of Trustees Bulletin #13: Some Thoughts regarding Our Relationship to Alcoholics Anonymous," NA.org, http://www .na.org/?ID=bulletins-bull13–r.

3. See Husserl, *Zur Phänomenologie der Intersubjektivität;* Heidegger, *History of the Concept of Time,* 237–41; Merleau-Ponty, *Visible and Invisible,* 139–42.

4. Husserl, *Cartesian Meditations,* 92–99; Sartre, *Being and Nothingness,* 337 ff; 537 ff; Levinas, *Totality and Infinity.*

5. Merleau-Ponty, *Phenomenology of Perception,* 351–54.

6. Sartre, *Being and Nothingness,* 332.

7. Ibid., 549.

8. Heidegger, *History of the Concept of Time,* 238.

9. Husserl, *Crisis of European Sciences,* 257.

10. Levinas, *Otherwise Than Being,* 35–36.

11. Austin, *How to Do Things,* 6.

12. Narcotics Anonymous, *Information Pamphlet #1: Who, What, How, Why* (Van Nuys, CA: Narcotics Anonymous World Services, Inc., 1989), n.p.

13. Levinas, *Otherwise Than Being,* 87.

14. Ibid., 112.

15. Ibid., 114.

16. Ibid., 25.

17. Ibid., 118.

18. *Narcotics Anonymous,* 4.

19. Narcotics Anonymous, *Information Pamphlet #12: The Triangle of Self-Obsession* (Van Nuys, CA: Narcotics Anonymous World Services, Inc., 1983), n.p.

20. *Narcotics Anonymous,* 39.

21. Buber, *I and Thou,* 55.

22. Ibid., 54.

23. Narcotics Anonymous, *Narcotics Anonymous: It Works: How and Why* (Van Nuys, CA: World Service Conference, Literature Approval Committee, 1986), 62.

24. Ibid., 63.

25. Ibid., 67–68.

26. Ibid., 22.

27. Ibid., 25.

JOHN HOUSTON

# Friendship, Accountability, and Mutual Growth in Virtue

John Houston continues our examination of the role of others in the recovery process by offering a philosophical meditation on sponsorship, one of the cardinal practices of Twelve Step fellowships. Houston finds in Aristotle's account of friendship a philosophical framework that helps him to identify the distinctive characteristics of this unique relationship, and to explain the indispensable contribution it makes in the evolutionary process of transformation that the Steps set in motion. Like the best kind of friendship, the sponsor-sponsee relationship is an intrinsic good that enhances the virtues of those who participate in it.

Central to the philosophy of the Twelve Step tradition is the notion that the welfare of the individual is inseparable from the human community to which that individual belongs. The first of the Twelve Traditions states, "Our common welfare should come first; personal recovery depends on A.A. unity."[1] Solidarity is essential to Alcoholics Anonymous: "The unity of Alcoholics Anonymous is the most cherished quality our Society has. Our lives, the lives of all to come, depend squarely on it. *We* stay whole, or A.A. dies. Without unity, the heart of A.A. would cease to beat."[2] Foundational to Twelve Step organizations is the recognition that the good of one is the good of the many, and the good of many is the good of one. This philosophical principle finds strong support in the ethical thought of Aristotle. According to Aristotle, human beings are by nature political animals: it is only in and through community that we realize our flourishing. While this principle might initially strike us as abstract, Twelve Step recovery programs provide a unique and practical application of it in sponsorial relationships. In this essay I will draw on resources from the Aristotelian ethical tradition to illustrate the practical necessity of sponsorial relationships for growth in recovery, which I will argue constitutes a unique kind of growth toward virtue.[3]

## The Nature of Addiction

Before exploring what recovery looks like, we must first examine what it is recovery *from*. This requires attending to the nature of addiction. Substance addiction consists in a multidimensional and complex web of psychological and physiological variables relating to the continued reliance on or use of a substance.[4] Though some addictions arise with more immediacy than others, common to all of them is a personal history of the loss of freedom in relation to an appetite that is linked to a specific kind of behavior. In the case of the alcoholic, the appetite and behavior concern the consumption of alcohol. Through the repeated use and abuse of alcohol the alcoholic has lost the freedom to partake in the activity of drinking with moderation. Where at one time he or she likely possessed more freedom in relation to this behavior, that freedom is now gone.[5] The alcoholic does not consume alcohol; rather, alcohol consumes the alcoholic. The solution of Twelve Step recovery programs is not to attempt to will or work oneself back to one's original condition, where moderation becomes once again a possibility.[6] For the genuine alcoholic, such a solution is not in the cards. There is no such thing as drinking at the right times, for the right reasons, and in the right amount, as Aristotelian prudence would ordinarily enable one to do.[7] For such a person the activity of drinking is in itself an excess. Recognizing and acknowledging this fact is at the heart of Twelve Step spirituality. The principles of Twelve Step recovery programs are not designed for one who merely "fails to moderate" his or her behavior, but one who has lost the freedom to do so, and who therefore must now abstain altogether. "If anyone who is showing inability to control his drinking can do the right-about-face and drink like a gentleman, our hats are off to him. Heaven knows we have tried hard enough and long enough to drink like other people!"[8] But the wisdom that comes from experience reveals that in the case of the genuinely alcoholic person, such repeated "trying" is only met with repeated failure.

> Here are some of the methods we have tried: Drinking beer only, limiting the number of drinks, never drinking alone, never drinking in the morning, drinking only at home, never having it in the house, never drinking during business hours, drinking only at parties, switching from scotch to brandy, drinking only natural wines, agreeing to resign if ever drunk on the job, taking a trip, not taking a trip, swearing off forever (with and without

a solemn oath), taking more physical exercise, reading inspirational books, going to health farms and sanitariums, accepting voluntary commitment to asylums—we could increase the list ad infinitum.[9]

Notice that all of the proposed attempts at moderation here cited have ended in failure. This passage should be understood proleptically, that is, as an anticipation of the alcoholic's various attempts to substitute modified treatments in the place of abstinence. The problem with each of the proposed alternatives is invariably the same: it doesn't work. Yet the point of the passage is not to suggest that there is nothing to be done, or that one must be consigned to permanent helplessness in the face of the temptation to drink. As we shall see, the Twelve Step tradition offers hope for the seemingly hopeless. However, being prepared to receive this hope requires that one first fully face and acknowledge the state of his or her addiction and the behavior that engendered and exacerbates it.

Those who suffer from substance addiction, or know someone who has so suffered, are aware of its effects on one's ability to live with the freedom that is characteristic of a flourishing human being. It is precisely the enslavement to the substance that constitutes the tragedy of addiction. I believe the primary evil of substance addiction is the deterioration of an individual's agency.[10] By "agency" I mean to indicate the center of the person: that which decides and chooses. Substance abuse debilitates agency and impedes an individual's ability to deliberate, to choose, and to live intentionally. It replaces one's ability to pause and reflect before acting with an unreflective acquiescence in destructive impulse. When addiction is in full bloom, the individual's sense of self as one who freely thinks, feels, and chooses becomes eclipsed by the singular consuming appetite for the substance.

This erosion of agency is painful to observe, but for the one undergoing it, it is often imperceptible. As a young man, I had the misfortune of witnessing this process firsthand in a very close friend of mine. To protect his anonymity, I will refer to him as Merrick. Merrick had a number of admirable traits and talents. He was a principled and dependable person, enjoyable to be around, and a born athlete. He also possessed a formidable wit and an infamous sense of humor. He did well in school and was a hard worker. But during his junior year of high school he began a pattern of substance abuse, and it did not take long for the use and abuse of drugs and alcohol to effect a radical change in his life. Over a period of just a few months Merrick went from his sociable, candid, competitive, and life-loving self to a reclusive person with very little or no interest in any activity not involving the use of substances. The gleam and zest once observable in his eye came to be replaced with a continually blunted, dull expression that was interrupted by a smile only when he was drunk or high. His athletic performance plummeted, and he became increasingly indifferent to academics. Where previously one could take him at his word, he became manipulative and dishonest. The common factor in all of these changes was his consuming desire to abuse drugs and alcohol. The social circle in which he moved shrank to include only those who would drink or use substances with him. He avoided and lied to those outside his circle, and he became increasingly incapable of human intimacy. Those close to him reacted to his behavior with a combination of bewilderment, anger, and sadness.

As a young person, I didn't understand what was happening to Merrick, but I understand it now: his abuse of substances was erasing his agency. His entire psychological makeup was changing. His ability to choose a virtuous way of living was supplanted by the destructive impulse to use. His substance abuse began with selfish choices. But eventually his choices and actions were replaced by mere behavior—a behavior as predictable as that of Pavlov's dogs.[11] If confronted, he would respond in one of two ways: denial or further substance abuse. Curiously, these responses would often occur simultaneously. He would go out and get either high or drunk, all the while talking about how no one else really understood—that he did not have a problem, and that, contrary to the opinion of those who loved him, he remained wholly in control of his life and destiny. Frequently his episodes of drunkenness were spent reciting to himself and whoever would listen what I dub "alcoholic resolutions." Alcoholic resolutions are dreamy narratives of how one is going to accomplish grand things, and how one is going to begin doing so *first thing tomorrow*. For the alcoholic or addict, yes does not mean yes; no does not mean no; and "I will" is rarely followed by action. Those who were raised as children of alcoholics have experienced firsthand the painful effects of alcoholic resolution in their lives. We can never underestimate the potential for deception in the genuinely alcoholic person. Though it is difficult to be on the receiving end of such deception, the real tragedy of an alcoholic's situation lies foremost not in the propensity to deceive others, but in the propensity to deceive himself. With the diminishment of agency that accompanies addiction comes an increase in the tendency toward alcoholic resolution. If it is not interrupted, many persist in such behavior up to and including their very last breath. To this day my dreams are haunted by images of Merrick's premature funeral.

This is a dark picture, and yet all is not lost. What is inspiring about Twelve Step spirituality is its ability to recognize the personal helplessness of the addict without at the same time declaring him or her hopeless. Twelve Step recovery provides multiple forms of practical assistance and encouragement for the suffering addict. In what remains, I will touch upon only one of them, namely, sponsorship.

## Sponsorship as a Kind of Friendship

Though the desire to grow in virtue must begin with the individual, it is only in and through the life of the community that we are able to attain and sustain virtuous living. Substance addiction recovery constitutes a special kind of growth toward virtue. It occurs through the support of the community as a whole, and through the unique relationships between newly recovering addicts and their sponsors. I have suggested that the primary evil of substance abuse lies in the loss of agency. Now I want to address an aspect of the recovery of agency.

A key aspect of the alcoholic's recovery consists in surrendering foolish pride. By "foolish pride" I mean that tendency of an alcoholic to nurse a false sense of control over his or her addiction. For the addict, foolish pride consists in the assurance that one can handle one's addiction on one's own. A prerequisite to recovery is admitting that one cannot emerge from the labyrinth of addiction alone. Twelve Step spirituality has the practical wisdom to recognize our need for another, and it attempts to meet this need through the formal activity of sponsorship. Recovery means, in part, regaining oneself through learning (or relearning) to live with moral agency.[12] As an addict I am incapable of effecting this on my own, but where I am weak, another can give me strength. Twelve Step programs are not "self-help" programs in the literal sense of the term. Though they do insist that one take responsibility for one's actions, they do not advise or encourage one to simply "pull oneself up by one's bootstraps." Such advice is contrary to the spirit of Twelve Step spirituality, as it disregards the frailty and fragility of the human condition in general, and the plight of the addict in particular. The Twelve Step tradition demonstrates its commitment to the social dimension of recovery through the institution of sponsorship.

Though sponsorial relationships have not traditionally been characterized as "friendships," several principles justifying such a characterization can be culled from Aristotle's ethical thought. Aristotle highly prized friendship and valued it as preeminent among external goods.[13] For Aristotle, friendship requires mutually acknowledged and reciprocated affection and concern between persons of relevant equality.[14] He distinguishes different kinds of friendship, based on the different objects of love and concern upon which they focus. Some friendships are based on the recognition of mutual utility. Others arise from the enjoyment of shared activity or the pleasure of one another's company. Most choice-worthy, however, is friendship that is established on the basis of a mutual love of virtue, and nurtured through shared activities reflecting that end. Aristotle refers to such friendship as *teleia philia,* or "complete friendship."[15] Such friendship is rare. While I do not pretend that sponsorial relationships share a one-to-one correspondence with Aristotelian *teleia philia,* I think they share remarkable affinities, and so I would like to reflect on some of them.[16]

Sponsorial relationships arise out of a combination of utility and a desire for mutual growth in virtue. Fundamental to sponsorial relationships is the recognition that growth in virtue is not an autonomous enterprise. Such relationships are grounded in a mutual recognition of needed support for overcoming the temptation to substance abuse. As such they are based on acknowledged and reciprocated concern for one another's well-being. Yet, unlike Aristotle's complete friendship, sponsorial relationships are, to some extent, relationships of inequality. Like the sponsee, the sponsor too is in recovery. However, the sponsor has journeyed further toward recovery by progressing from incontinence and addiction to continence and sobriety. Thus, the sponsor's accomplishments are the sponsee's aspirations. Where the newly recovering addict or alcoholic has struggled and failed to resist the impulse to use substances or drink, the sponsor has found some level of success. The sponsor is one who has grown in self-knowledge and practical wisdom related to the impulse to abuse substances, and he or she seeks to share this and cultivate a similar growth in the sponsee.

Aristotle describes a friend as "another self." Complete friends in the Aristotelian sense recognize virtue in one another, and through sharing their lives they continue to cultivate and enjoy that virtue. Like complete friends, sponsors and sponsees psychologically identify with each other, and their focus is shared virtuous activity. Through their mutual resolution to say no to substance addiction and yes to life, the sponsor and sponsee restore and strengthen one another's agency, and, consequently, one another's identity.

At their inception, sponsorial relationships are typically asymmetrical, as newly recovering alcoholics tend to rely more heavily on their sponsors than vice versa. In paradigmatic cases of sponsorial relationships, the alcoholic's agency and sense of self comes to be restored through the presence, encouragement, and assistance of the sponsor. Through drawing on his or her experience of successfully struggling against destructive impulse, the sponsor offers empathy and practical wisdom to the newly recovering alcoholic. By forming a relationship in which the restoration of agency is the preeminent purpose, the sponsor and newly recovering alcoholic become mutual sources of strength, accountability, and growth toward virtue. Such relationships are at the very foundation of recovery, as it is through them that the recovering addict regains and develops the ability to think, feel, deliberate and choose. This is the recovery of one's very *self.* Such self-recovery is made possible by our social-political nature, and it is realized through living in fellowship with another.

Sponsorial relationships make possible a kind of recognition and resurrection of the self. The numbness that is characteristic of addiction stultifies the addict's ability to see fully both the world and herself. Part of regaining sobriety is reawakening to *reality,* both in relation to oneself and in relation to other persons. In the process of recovery, the fragmented and dissolute self comes to be replaced with a stronger, more resolute, and more integrated self. While Twelve Step spirituality is careful to avoid claims of "having arrived" or "attained final victory," it is undeniable that in the process of recovery the addict regains some level of moral agency and integrity as she learns to say no to alcohol and yes to herself. As we are reminded in *Alcoholics Anonymous,* "We are not saints. The point is we are willing to grow along spiritual lines."[17] Growing along spiritual lines constitutes a unique kind of growth toward virtue. It entails strengthening one's central core self, and strengthening one's central core self involves the fortification of one's intentional and deliberate progress in relation to one's power to abandon self-destructive desires.

Such growth does not occur suddenly. It takes time. The "spiritual awakening" that Twelve Step seeks to elicit is not the sudden mystical experience or theophany sometimes characteristic of religious conversion. It consists in a process of awakening to one's own condition, one's own selfishness, one's own limitations, one's own faults, and working to amend one's life.[18] It is not an immediate, dramatic change marked by brief and extreme alterations in behavior. In this respect, the recovery process accords with the developmental aspect of Aristotle's moral psychology. For Aristotle, character development takes time and is the result of a repeated concerted effort to forge virtuous dispositions through repeated virtuous actions. In Aristotelian language, recovery might be described as involving the alcoholic's journey from incontinence to continence. The incontinent person is one who struggles with appetite and succumbs to it, whereas the continent person still struggles but succeeds in not being overcome. In the recovery process, the alcoholic learns not merely to modify his or her behavior, but to cultivate deliberately those virtues of agency that addiction erodes. Sponsorship, therefore, assists the alcoholic's rehabilitation through re-habituation.[19] This is accomplished through the sponsor's serving as an example of progress in sobriety, and striving to cultivate a similar progress in the sponsee. Being a sponsor does not require moral perfection, but rather some history of personal success in overcoming destructive impulse. Thus, the sponsor stands in relation to the sponsee not as a moral exemplar of impeccability, but as one who has progressed toward continence.[20] The sponsor has learned through experience what is required to live with continence in the face of temptation, and has worked to cultivate mindfully the habits that make this possible.

## The Unique Role of Sponsorship in Recovery

The purpose of Twelve Step recovery programs is not theoretical, but practical. They aim not at merely gaining our intellectual assent, but at our learning how to live in a particular way. Consequently, I would like to conclude by reflecting briefly on the practical role of sponsorship in the recovery process. Common to each of the Twelve Steps is the language of mutual participation. The first person plural—"We"—that appears in each of the original Twelve Steps characterizes the participatory nature of recovery in general, and sponsorial relationships in particular. Through its use of the plural pronoun, the Twelve Step tradition encourages a dialogue of mutual identification among its members. "We" is not the language of analysis and observation, but of participation. It is not the language of isolation, but of community. "We" necessarily includes the recognition of both "I" and "Thou." As such, this participatory language of the Twelve Step tradition engenders a context of mutual identification and solidarity among its members.

Three of the Twelve Steps are especially relevant to the personal growth of the recovering alcoholic within the context of sponsorial relationships. They are as follows:

1. We admitted we were powerless over alcohol—that our lives had become unmanageable.
5. [We] admitted to God, ourselves, *and to another human being* the exact nature of our wrongs.
10. [We] continued to take personal inventory and when we were wrong promptly admitted it.[21]

We can discern a natural order of progression within these respective steps.

Step One consists in our acknowledging the problem of our addiction, especially to ourselves. This disarms foolish pride and self-deception. This is necessary if recovery is to become possible. One must acknowledge there is a problem before one can seek to address it, and insofar as foolish pride and self-deception are present, this is impossible.

Step Five requires that we acknowledge our wrongs to another. This entails recognizing that the effects of our actions extend beyond ourselves, and admitting this fact to a person or persons other than ourselves.[22] Furthermore, Step Five does not merely require that we admit wrongdoing; it also explicitly requires that we acknowledge "the *exact* nature of our wrongs" (emphasis added). The requirement of exact admission ensures that the addict will come to terms in detail with his or her offenses, as opposed to vaguely hand-waving at his or her guilt. This forces the addict to acknowledge in detail precisely where he or she was wrong. This in turn makes it possible to add explicit content to the resolution toward personal improvement.

Finally, Step Ten requires not that we acknowledge our faults once and for all, but that we commit ourselves to doing this whenever we err. Implicit in this Step is the recognition of our fallible nature, that we are creatures who not only have erred, but will likely err again. Thus, Step Ten makes explicit the recovering alcoholic's resolution to act in a way that is in keeping with continued acknowledgment of his or her condition.

A common feature of Steps One, Five, and Ten is that their practical application requires the presence of another. Each requires from the addict an act of admission. Acts of admission are acts of confession. Confessions of wrongdoing are directed not to one's self, but to another party. Though one might point out that an act of confession can be accomplished through addressing a group of persons, or even God, sponsorship provides something that neither of these does, namely, a specific, perceivable individual with whom one can enter directly into a mutual dialogue. Unlike God or groups of people, a sponsor is a concrete individual who provides an opportunity for immediate interpersonal dialogue.[23] Further, unlike a group of persons, a sponsor can serve as a kind of personal confessor. Confessions offered to groups are directed to the many, and therefore to no one in particular. Unlike a group, an individual sponsor provides the opportunity for the ongoing activity of mutual personal accountability.

By "activity of mutual personal accountability," I mean to indicate the practice of voluntarily interacting with another fallible individual for the purpose of reflectively acknowledging our faults and limitations, seeking to amend those faults, and fortifying our resolve toward mutual growth in virtue. Contexts of accountability are contexts of self-disclosure; and contexts of self-disclosure make self-discovery possible. In sponsorial relationships both the sponsor and the sponsee are encouraged to share their experiences and struggles as fallible individuals seeking personal growth in virtue. Unlike the asymmetry of the traditional confessional, the sponsor is free to acknowledge his or her own faults in turn.[24] This mutuality of sharing is a distinguishing mark of the sponsorial relationship, making it less like a doctor/patient relationship and more like a friendship. As we have seen, an Aristotelian friend is "another self," and the mutual accountability that structures sponsorial relationships makes self-discovery possible through the discovery of "another self." A sponsor is another self not in the sense of being metaphysically identical with the sponsee, but in the sense of having in common with the sponsee a shared history of struggle in relation to a particular appetite, and a firm resolution toward personal growth in relation to that appetite. Like Aristotelian friends of virtue who share a mutual interest in one another's growth and development, sponsors and sponsees listen to, admonish, and encourage one another as together they strive to fortify their resolve to live full and meaningful lives that transcend the enslavement of addiction.

NOTES

1. *Twelve Steps and Traditions,* 129. The Twelve Traditions are the governing guidelines of AA that accompany the Twelve Steps.

2. Ibid., 129 (italics mine).

3. This is not to suggest that Aristotle's ethical thought is perfectly compatible with Twelve Step spirituality. It is not. To try to synthesize the two would be to place either or both on a procrustean bed. Aristotle presents us with an idealized or "perfectionist" ethical framework, whereas Twelve Step does not. Further, while both frameworks would regard arrogance as a vice, Twelve Step, unlike Aristotle, recognizes humility as a virtue. My purpose in this essay is not to syncretize Aristotle with Twelve Step, but to employ certain fundamental Aristotelian concepts to reflect on the practical aspects of the Twelve Step recovery process.

4. This characterization of addiction stands in contrast to what Kent Dunnington refers to as the "disease" and "choice" models of addiction. The disease model characterizes addiction exclusively in terms of deterministic biochemical processes of the body, while the choice model ignores the physiological aspects of addiction, treating it as something fully chosen by the addict. Dunnington argues that both models fail to capture fully the phenomenology of addiction. The disease model, he argues, is too reductionist, as it ignores important voluntary aspects of addiction. The choice model is naive, as it ignores the complexity of biochemical processes and their relation to human behavior and action. See Dunnington, *Addiction and Virtue,* especially chapters 1 and 2.

Though in this essay I focus more explicitly on alcoholism than other forms of addiction, the principles of my discussion apply to the multiple forms of addiction that are addressed in the various fellowships that follow the Twelve Step tradition.

5. *Alcoholics Anonymous,* 30.

6. For Aristotle, morally virtuous activities lie in a "mean" or "middle ground" between excess and deficiency. This middle ground exists relative to the individual. Thus, what constitutes excess for one person might not be excessive for another. Gluttony, for example, will not be the same for a Sumo wrestler and a horse jockey. But for the alcoholic, who is no longer able to operate as a free agent in relation to his or her appetite, moderation is not an option, as the activity of drinking just *is* an excess.

7. See *Nicomachean Ethics,* 2.9.

8. *Alcoholics Anonymous,* 31.

9. Ibid.

10. This is not to diminish or ignore the manifold effects that substance addiction has on third parties, but to recognize that these are consequent to and resultant from the bondage of addiction, which diminishes the addict's ability to make wise and unselfish choices. We must never forget that alcoholism affects the lives of many beyond the alcoholic. This is poignantly captured in *Alcoholics Anonymous:* "The alcoholic is like a

tornado roaring his way through the lives of others. Hearts are broken. Sweet relationships are dead. Affections have been uprooted. Selfish and inconsiderate habits have kept the home in turmoil" (82).

11. Dunnington characterizes the person who suffers from addiction to this extreme degree as a "morbid addict." He likens the condition of the morbid addict to that of a person suffering from epilepsy or madness. The morbid addict is "rendered ineffectual, thereby removing the agent's behavior from the category of human action altogether" (*Addiction and Virtue*, 39). In what follows I address how AA provides a context for the addict's recovery of agency through the activity of sponsorial relationships.

12. Were this not the case, Twelve Step spirituality would lose its practical application for the purpose of recovery.

13. Aristotle devotes more time to a discussion of friendship than any single subject in his ethical treatises. Approximately 20 percent of the *Nicomachean Ethics* and the *Eudemian Ethics* was devoted to the subject of friendship (*philia*). For Aristotle, friendship is an aspect of what makes a life choice-worthy: "No one would choose to live without friends, even if he had all the other good things" (*Nicomachean Ethics*, 1155a5–6).

14. See *Nicomachean Ethics*, 8.1–5.

15. An alternative translation of this phrase is "perfect friendship." For Aristotle's discussion of the different kinds of friendship, see *Nicomachean Ethics*, 8–9.

16. Dunnington too acknowledges that the principles undergirding sponsorial relationships are "ancient and deeply Aristotelian" (*Addiction and Virtue*, 188). He seeks to address why AA communities have succeeded in providing a context amenable to Aristotelian friendship while the modern institutional church has failed to do so. My analysis explores how the process of recovery illustrates the affinities between Aristotelian friendship and sponsorial relationships.

17. *Alcoholics Anonymous*, 60 (my emphasis).

18. See *Alcoholics Anonymous*, appendix 2, "Spiritual Experience."

19. Dunnington points out the conspicuous absence of the concept of "habit" in recent discussions of addiction, and argues that its reintroduction is indispensable for understanding addiction and recovery (*Addiction and Virtue*, chapter 3).

20. The emphasis of Twelve Step Recovery is not on perfection but progress: "The principles we have set down are guides to progress. We claim spiritual progress rather than spiritual perfection" (*Alcoholics Anonymous*, 60).

21. *Alcoholics Anonymous*, 59–60.

22. Often this means seeking out and addressing those whom one has wronged when doing so is possible and will not cause further harm. But when this is not possible, one's sponsor can serve as a surrogate for the wronged party.

23. I am not suggesting that we cannot speak of entering into "dialogue" or "conversation" with God. However, what is meant by conversing with God and conversing with

my brother is clearly qualitatively distinct. I can sit down and converse with my brother about the details of my life over a cup of coffee. I cannot do this with God.

24. While the mutual confessional model of sponsorial relationships differs from the Christian sacrament, there is a biblical precedent for the model of mutual confession. The author of James, for example, admonishes believers to confess their sins "to each other" in order that they might be healed (James 5:16 NIV).

MARY K. RILEY

# Get Over Yourself

## Self-Transformation in the Confucian
## and Twelve Step Traditions

While John Houston focuses on the one-to-one sponsorial relationship unique to
Twelve Step fellowships, Mary Riley considers the crucial role that tradition and
community play in the recovery process. She broadens our understanding of this
aspect of Twelve Step spirituality by explaining how the Confucian concept of *li*
and *yi* can enhance our appreciation of it. Riley shows that even as the Confucian
and Twelve Step traditions emphasize the profound importance of belonging
to a community and following traditional practices, they encourage one to be a
unique, individual self and to make a unique, harmonizing contribution to social
accord.

Alcoholics Anonymous is most prevalent in the United States, where the
Twelve Step tradition began. While extant in China and other Asian countries, AA has not thrived in the same way in Asia as it has in Western cultures,
such as the United States, Great Britain, and Australia. In Beijing, a city of
around twenty million, there are thirty-four meetings of Alcoholics Anonymous a week.[1] This can be compared with the approximately 3,100 weekly AA
meetings that take place in the Los Angeles metropolitan area (an area with
a population of around 16.3 million).[2] While there are certainly many factors
preventing the growth of Alcoholics Anonymous and other Twelve Step Programs in China and Asia, we can also see the gap in demographics within the
United States, where only 1 percent of AA members were reported as Asian.[3]
These statistics raise the possibility that cultural differences play a role in the
apparent divide that separates AA and Asian traditions of spirituality. Making connections between aspects of Chinese thought and Alcoholics Anonymous can help to bridge this apparent divide and broaden the cultural relevance of Twelve Step spirituality. Because of the enormous influence exerted

by the Confucian tradition in China and much of Asia, it is a good resource on which to draw in making comparisons with AA.

In keeping with the goal of opening channels between Twelve Step and Asian traditions of spirituality, this essay will compare the Twelve Step and Confucian projects of moral self-transformation. But before proceeding with a comparison, it is important to note some relevant dissimilarities. The Twelve Step tradition of Alcoholics Anonymous had its beginnings in the Oxford Group, a religious movement that styled itself after what it perceived as first-century Christianity. The movement operated somewhat informally through small group discussions, which emphasized confession, honesty, unselfishness, and prayer.[4] Bill Wilson, cofounder of Alcoholics Anonymous, was able to achieve and maintain sobriety after having had a "spiritual awakening" through his involvement with Oxford Group members. As Alcoholics Anonymous grew and split from the Oxford Group, its founders outlined six principles they adapted from the latter that had guided their recovery. These principles were later expanded and codified by Wilson into their present form as the Twelve Steps. Wilson attempted to evangelize other alcoholics, but he only found success after heeding the advice of his physician to avoid preaching and instead focus on convincing the alcoholic that he suffered from a physical allergy and mental obsession.[5]

While the absence of religious doctrine makes the program of AA (and other similarly styled Twelve Step programs) accommodating to believers of many different faiths and even some agnostics and atheists, there is an underlying assumption about a transcendent entity. In fact, six out of twelve Steps include references to "God" or a "power greater than ourselves." While every member may not adopt the notion of a transcendent entity or "God" wholesale, it is an important concept within the Twelve Step tradition. The primary text of Alcoholics Anonymous, the "Big Book," notes, "When we became alcoholics, crushed by a self-imposed crisis we could not postpone or evade, we had to fearlessly face the proposition that either God is everything or else He is nothing. God either is, or He isn't. What was our choice to be?"[6] The text beseeches its audience to accept spiritual aid, in the form of a transcendent power greater than oneself, in overcoming alcoholism. While the text often uses the term "God" to denote this power, it does maintain that precisely how one chooses to conceive of "God" is an individual endeavor.[7]

In contrast, the *Analects of Confucius* lack emphasis on any sort of transcendent power. Confucianism has its roots in the literati class of the late spring and autumn period (546–221 BCE), which was concerned with cultural heritage. Confucius himself modestly claimed, "I transmit rather than innovate. I trust in and love the ancient ways."[8] Confucianism was but one among several schools of thought that developed during this time. Increasing chaos and violence marked this period as the centralized authority of the Zhou dynasty disintegrated. The philosophic thought of early China was in large part a response to this political instability. Various schools of thought responded by calling for impartial love, retreat to a life of eremitism, or, in the case of the Confucians, the installation of a virtuous ruler. Generally speaking, early Chinese thought was more concerned with *how* things should be organized rather than with *what* things exist; as a result, there is less of a concern with the origins of the world and thus the God question.[9]

Several contrasts between the Confucian and Twelve Step traditions should be apparent. One goal of the early Confucian tradition, and Confucius himself, was sociopolitical stability. Moral development or self-transformation is therefore inextricably bound up with fostering sociopolitical order. This does not mean that the Confucians were not concerned with the problems of the individual, but that the problems of the individual were not considered distinct from the problems of the social realm. The Twelve Step tradition, on the other hand, is ultimately concerned with effecting individual recovery. In AA, self-transformation is part and parcel of achieving recovery, which entails the maintenance of sobriety. Confucian emphasis on the *how* question also means that there is a lack of religiousness in the Judeo-Christian sense in the Confucian tradition.[10] Instead of drawing on the strength of a higher power, Confucius was interested in drawing upon resources in his cultural heritage to meet the demands of the chaotic world in which he lived.

Despite these and certainly other differences, we can find important and interesting resonances in the Confucian and Twelve Step traditions' visions of moral self-transformation. In order to do so, we now turn to an account of the Twelve Step tradition's program for recovery.

## The Twelve Step Approach

Twelve Step literature links the problem of addiction with the problem of self—that is, it gives us good reason to consider alcoholism and addiction as symptoms of an underlying disorder of the self. Jerome Levin notes, "Alcoholism is, by definition, a form of self-destruction by self-poisoning, of suicide on the installment plan—a fact which strongly implies that alcoholism is a form of self-pathology."[11] Indeed, the Big Book claims, "So our troubles, we think, are basically of our own making. They arise out of ourselves, and the alcoholic is an extreme example of self-will run riot, though he usually doesn't think so. Above everything, we alcoholics must be rid of this selfishness. We must, or it kills us!"[12] The alcoholic problem is thus linked to a certain conception of self, which adheres to the value of "looking out for number one," and the belief that self-will is the solution to one's problems. Such a self is separate from other individuals and its environment—it is autonomous. In this conception of self, a person is self-actualizing; everything an individual needs is already contained in the self. This leads to the view that anything can be achieved by further exertion of one's will and exercise of one's autonomy.

According to the Twelve Step literature, solving the alcoholic problem is inextricably linked with the transformation of the self-centered individual. The Big Book reads, "The first requirement is that we be convinced that any life run on self-will can hardly be a success."[13] Egocentrism as an ideal inevitably leads to conflict; when others do not acquiesce to the alcoholic's will, she becomes angry and resentful, often attempting to solve this problem by exerting herself more, which leads to further conflict, fear, and anxiety for the alcoholic. The lesson that self-concern is self-limiting is summed up in a prayer that asks God to "Relieve me from the bondage of self."[14] Underlying the alcoholic's drinking problem are problematic thought processes that urge one to run one's life by sheer exertion of one's will, egoism, and selfishness.

Part of the solution to the problematic self is found in the Twelve Steps. While the alcoholic begins with an acknowledgment of powerlessness over alcohol and the futility of a life run on self-will, he or she is led to a deep concern for others and for spiritual matters and acquires peace of mind. One must see that, in considering only one's own needs and wants, one causes oneself great difficulty and discomfort. To be rid of these difficulties one must consider one's relationships with other people and with a higher power. In serving their interests (variously through making amends, carrying the message to other alcoholics, and praying for the will of God rather than one's own), one overcomes one's selfish tendencies and maintains sobriety.

## Confucianism and the Relational Self

The Confucian tradition sees the problem of self in a somewhat similar manner as it is cast in Twelve Step literature. Confucius says, "Exemplary persons seek harmony not sameness; petty persons, then, are the opposite."[15] The petty persons are variously characterized as being concerned with profit or personal advantage, their own lands, and gains. The petty person makes demands of others, rather than assessing her own conduct.[16] In short, the petty person is selfish and self-seeking. This selfish conduct is disintegrative: we don't usually think of self-centered people as having good relationships with those around them; the petty person is disharmonious with her context. She is at odds with her environment and thus she is always agitated.[17] In Confucian terms, we might say that, being arrogant but undistinguished, the petty person becomes engulfed when facing adversity.[18] This account of the Confucian petty person gives us insight into the Confucian program for moral or self-transformation. If moral development means the overcoming of selfish pursuits and desires, which put a person at odds with her cultural context and other human beings, then the development of a relational self means integration into a context by becoming continuous with or harmonizing with a cultural tradition and the individuals that constitute a person's environment. How this occurs becomes clearer when looking at the Confucian notions of *li* and *yi*.[19]

"*Li*" (禮) has been variously translated as "rites," "rituals," "customs," and more. *Li* began as the set of ritualized procedures, rites, and sacrifices enacted by a ruler in order to maintain good relations with the spirits. These procedures were then extended to govern the relationships of other members of the court and community, and thus increased in social significance.[20] *Li* came to function as the norms that governed ceremonial behavior and social interaction and were an important part of Chinese cultural heritage. *Li* do not simply refer to general behavior, but govern the interactions involved in specific roles and relationships, for example, father and son, or ruler and subject. Although they are concerned with governing social conduct, *li* retained their religious significance.[21] Herbert Fingarette's interpretation points to this religiosity: "The examples of handshaking and of making a request are humble; the moral is profound. These complex but familiar gestures are characteristic of human relationships at their most human.... Looking at these 'ceremonies' through the image of *li*, we realize that explicitly sacred rite can be seen as an emphatic, intensified and sharply elaborated extension of everyday *civilized* intercourse."²² *Li* recognize spirituality in human interactions, and in a sense sanctifies them.

Confucius, being heavily influenced by the literati tradition of which he was a part, placed a great deal of importance on culture and tradition. One of his contributions to early Chinese philosophic thought was to conceive of *li* as the vehicle for transmitting these. In drawing on *li* to regulate one's relationships, one draws on an inherited cultural tradition. Confucius said, "Reviewing the old as a means of realizing the new—such a person can be considered a teacher."²³ The tradition itself, which gives a historical dimension to one's context and community, serves a normative function insofar as its standards are taken up in ritual practice. Confucius indicates that we can trace a tradition's cultural attitudes through knowledge of *li*.²⁴ Practicing *li* means becoming intimately a part of one's cultural context and a community of shared attitudes. *Li* ground us in a community by serving as guidelines, which reflect that community's ethos.

However, this does not mean that Confucius was merely interested in re-establishing the traditions of his ancestors. While *li* give us understanding of traditional cultural attitudes, they should be thought of neither as empty physical forms nor as fixed, immutable rules. In his discussion of *li*, Fingarette writes, "The ceremony may have a surface slickness but yet be dull, mechanical for lack of serious purpose and commitment. Beautiful and effective ceremony requires the personal 'presence' to be fused with learned ceremonial skill."²⁵ *Li*, if they are to be carried out effectively, require a personal investment. We are told that Confucius "did not claim or demand certainty" and that he "was not inflexible."²⁶ In *Analects* 9.3, "The Master said, 'The use of a hemp cap is prescribed in the observance of ritual propriety [*li*]. Nowadays, that a silk cap is used instead is a matter of frugality. I would follow accepted practice on this.'" Here, Confucius makes the pragmatic decision to depart from the ritual prescription. This indicates that there is a personal element in addition to the cultural prescription in determining the proper course of conduct. One is not subsumed by one's cultural tradition, but has a creative role to play in determining how one ought to proceed.

An individual's unique contribution to *li* is *yi*, or appropriateness. This understanding of appropriateness is not about conforming to a rule or standard. Rather, it is "appropriate" in the sense that one is able to determine the best course of action in a given situation. For example, there is no rule that says I must help this little old lady across the street. But since I am in no hurry and she is carrying a big bag of groceries, I find it appropriate to do so. Because I find it appropriate to do so, I carry out the task of helping her across the street in a more meaningful way.[27] What is appropriate or fitting is determined from the particular facts of each novel situation; as such, *yi* is flexible and responsive to the particularities of each unique circumstance.[28] Benjamin Schwartz holds that *yi* requires thought, and that such thought or knowledge "begin[s] with empirical cumulative knowledge of masses of particulars . . . and then includes the ability to link these particulars first to one's own experiences and ultimately with the underlying 'unity' that binds this thought together."[29] *Yi* has to do with continuity of all relevant aspects of a situation; it brings together the context with personal judgment.[30]

This aspect of *yi*, the individual's creative contribution to effecting harmony with a context, is reflected in the concept of *shu*. Confucius tells Zigong, "There is *shu*: do not impose on others what you yourself do not want."[31] At a basic level, *shu* means extending oneself by taking in the concerns of others.[32] But in taking others into consideration (or extending oneself to the circumstances of another), one must retain one's own judgment. Although one is "standing in the shoes of another," one does not dispense with one's own unique sense of appropriateness. In taking on the concerns of others, it is not as though the self is overcome or subjugated; rather, the exemplary person strikes a balance between self and others. The morally developed, harmonious individual effects continuity with the other individuals that constitute her context by drawing on a cultural tradition and acting in accordance with what she deems appropriate (*yi*) with respect to another's concerns.[33]

*Li* are passed down from the previous generations as the guidelines for appropriate conduct. But insofar as they require an investment of *yi*, they involve a creative dimension—they are revised with the unique contribution of *yi* and these refined ritual actions are passed on to the next generation. Since *yi* brings together disparate components of a situation with one's own experience, the disclosing of *yi* is a realizing of the self as contextual. Confucius tells us that he has never seen anyone act appropriately (*yi*) and extend the tradition in seclusion—moral development is a social and contextual endeavor.[34] *Li* are a resource on which an individual draws in making a unique judgment; rather than constraining *yi*, they condition *yi*. It is not the case that *li* or *yi* means the subjugation of an individual to the community tradition. That *li* conditions *yi* means the individual becomes continuous with a context, but with room for creative contribution and alteration of that context. One draws on one's environment and tradition to meet novel problems and in so doing extends the body of that tradition. In this way one becomes integrated into one's community.

The interplay of *li* and *yi*, qua the community and the individual, gives rise to the morally developed self that is continuous with her social and cultural context. Her environment is characterized by a state of harmony; as Confucius notes, "The exemplary person is calm and unperturbed."[35] *Analects* 14.13 illustrates such a harmonious situation in giving an account of Gongshu Wenzi:

> The Master asked Gongming Jia about Gonshu Wenzi, "Are we to believe that your master never spoke, never laughed, and never took anything?"
>
> Gongming Jia replied, "Whoever told you that is exaggerating. Because my master only spoke at the proper time, no one grew tired of what he had to say; because he only laughed when he was happy, no one grew tired of his laughter; because he only took what was appropriate for him to take, no one ever grew tired of his taking."

Gongshu Wenzi operates with ease in any situation by virtue of his consideration and attention to his relationships with others and the situation as a whole. The integrated person is a sort of moral artist who uses received ritual guidelines and her own unique judgment to weave together various attitudes and perspectives into a consummate experience. She defers to the cultural attitudes of the past, while at the same time contributing her own understanding of the tradition by appropriating those guidelines and attitudes to meet novel situations. In so doing, the morally developed individual effects harmony. In contrast, the petty person has a narrow understanding of herself on account of her selfish attitude, and consequently finds herself at odds with her environment. But as one begins to pay deference to one's cultural context and to consider others' perspectives, one realizes that one's self is deeply relational and finds equanimity in harmonizing with one's environment.

## Self-Transformation through Harmony with One's Context

We have already cautioned against making a wholesale comparison between the Twelve Step Recovery tradition and the thought of Confucius. There are important aspects of these two traditions that are simply not compatible. However, the above account of each tradition makes clear that they both view the moral self as relational. A salient feature of both the Twelve Step and

Confucian traditions is the recognition that the problems of addiction and conflict are tied to conceiving of one's self as distinct and separate from others and one's environment. Both traditions stress moving away from egocentrism and an isolated, individualistic understanding of self. Both see the self as interrelated with other individuals, tied to a community, and continuous with a cultural context. However, the Twelve Step literature focuses primarily on moral development as moving away from an egocentric model of self; it speaks less explicitly about the positive, relational self that emerges. The Confucian tradition's program of self-transformation through *li* and *yi* helps us to understand in positive terms the self that Twelve Step programs try to foster.

The belief that the Confucian tradition can add depth to our understanding of the Steps is confirmed when we look more closely at how the Confucian understanding of *li* and *yi* relates to them. The Twelve Steps bear resemblance to a Confucian understanding of ritual *li*. The exemplary Confucian embodies *li;* in practicing these rituals, she internalizes their meaning and thus the cultural attitudes that gave rise to them. *Li* facilitate integration of an individual into a cultural context, which includes a history. She no longer stands at odds with her environment but becomes a dynamic part of it. The Twelve Steps have a similar historical dimension insofar as they emerged from the Oxford Group as the most effective principles early members found as a means to recovery. Through the expansion of the original six principles into the Twelve Steps, we can see that the steps embody a cumulative history of perspectives, attitudes, and beliefs, which inform a culture. The Twelve Steps, like ritual *li,* are the concrete means of transmitting these cultural attitudes, which provide normative force in the form of conditioning the alcoholic's personal judgment.

Just as the Confucian understanding of *li* requires *yi,* the Twelve Steps also require a personal investment and element of appropriateness. Imitating the bare form of the Steps is not enough for moral development. The issue of appropriateness with respect to the Steps is evident in Step Nine: "Made direct amends to such people wherever possible, except when to do so would injure them or others." The literature cautions against hasty righteousness and emphasizes deliberation on all relevant aspects of a situation before acting. Too much frankness in admitting one's wrongs may compromise the alcoholic's usefulness to others or even directly harm those around her. For this reason, the Big Book warns, "We are not to be the hasty and foolish martyr who would needlessly sacrifice others to save himself from the alcoholic pit."[36] In righting her wrongs, the alcoholic must consider the effect her actions will have on her family or loved ones and the individual wronged. Simply imitating the form of the Steps is not enough to effect change in a person. The alcoholic must make them meaningful by tailoring them to meet the demands of each novel situation. Perhaps in my drinking I have said something unkind about Smith, of which he is unaware. Amends for my poor behavior would be less meaningful were I to go to Smith and apologize for saying unkind things about him when he was unaware that he had been the target of my gossiping. In all likelihood, his feelings would now be hurt, whereas he had felt fine before. In addition to the prescription of Step Nine, I ought to consider the particular facts of the situation, including Smith's perspective, in figuring out how to make an appropriate and meaningful amends.

While there is no explicit doctrine of taking up the perspective of another in the Twelve Step tradition, the Big Book does urge its audience to view those who have wronged the alcoholic as "sick" people, in perhaps the same way as the alcoholic herself is sick: "We avoid retaliation or argument. We wouldn't treat sick people that way."[37] Instead, the alcoholic, under guidance of the Steps, makes amends and restitution for her own poor conduct. In rectifying her conduct and reaching out to those she has harmed, regardless of their transgressions against her, the alcoholic seeks to effect harmonious relationships with those around her; but this is always done according to one's unique sense of appropriateness, conditioned by a community culture.

In comparing the Twelve Step and Confucian traditions by talking about the Twelve Steps in terms of *li* and *yi,* I have tried to illuminate the role of the Steps in effecting a relational self that is continuous with its context. Such cross-cultural comparisons are important and interesting if we look at the world climate for Twelve Step groups today. My hope is that highlighting relevant similarities will foster greater cross-cultural understanding and communication and enrich our understanding of Twelve Step and Chinese spiritual traditions. The Steps are a procedure for the transformation of the problematic, isolated, and individual self into a relational being. They, like Confucian ritual action, ground a person in a cultural and community context, which conditions and refines her unique sense of appropriateness. They serve as a resource upon which the recovering alcoholic can draw to effect a harmonious environment and harmonious relationships. This harmonizing or continuity with a context results in a sense of equanimity for the recovering alcoholic, and, most important, the removal of the obsession to drink.

## NOTES

1. Alcoholics Anonymous Beijing, "Welcome to Beijing AA; English Language Meetings at AA Club House," www.aabeijing.com; Alcoholics Anonymous [嗜酒者互诚协会], "Contact [联系方式]," www.aa-china.org.

2. May Wilkerson, "10 Best Sober Living Cities," *The Fix,* May 12, 2012, http://www.thefix.com/content/10-best-sober-living-cities.

3. AA World Services, "Alcoholics Anonymous 2011 Membership Survey," n.d., http://aa.org/pdf/products/p-48_membershipsurvey.pdf.

4. Harrison Trice, "Alcoholics Anonymous," *Annals of the American Academy of Political and Social Science* 315 (January 1958): 110.

5. Ibid.

6. *Alcoholics Anonymous,* 53.

7. Ibid., 93.

8. Confucius, *Essential Analects* 7.1.

9. This is not to say that these questions are mutually exclusive, only that Chinese philosophical thought tended toward the "how" question. For a more in-depth explanation of the differences between the kinds of questions that the dominant Western and Chinese philosophic traditions entertained, see Hall and Ames, *Thinking Through Confucius,* 199–200.

10. The claim here is that Confucianism is not religious in the Judeo-Christian sense, but this should not preclude us from thinking of Confucianism as broadly religious in some sense.

11. Levin, *Treatment of Alcoholism,* 3.

12. *Alcoholics Anonymous,* 62.

13. Ibid., 61.

14. Ibid., 63.

15. *Analects* 12.23. This and subsequent passages were translated by Ames and Rosemont, *Analects of Confucius: A Philosophical Translation.*

16. *Analects* 4.11, 4.16, 15.21, and 19.8.

17. *Analects* 7.37.

18. *Analects* 13.26 and 15.2.

19. In my discussion of the Confucian exemplary moral agent and the contrasting petty person, I make use of the feminine pronoun. While I do believe that the Confucian program for moral training is not intrinsically sexist, we should note that Confucius was specifically talking about the moral cultivation of men.

20. Hall and Ames, *Thinking Through Confucius,* 85–86.

21. Fingarette maintains that Confucianism is characterized by a kind of humanistic religiousness.

22. Fingarette, *Confucius,* 10.

23. *Analects* 2.11.

24. *Analects* 2.23, 3.9, and 6.27.

25. Fingarette, *Confucius,* 8.

26. *Analects* 9.4.

27. The notion that appropriateness is bound up with a personal investment of meaning leads Hall and Ames to talk about *yi* as "personal disclosure of significance" (*Thinking Through Confucius,* 93).

28. *Analects* 4.10, 7.3, 12.20, and 16.19.

29. Schwartz, *World of Thought,* 89.

30. While "appropriateness" or "fittingness" seems to capture best what the early Confucians meant by *yi,* it should be noted that during the warring states period in China, there was a robust discussion about the proper meaning of *yi.* So while most classical thinkers supposed *yi* meant some variation of "moral rightness," the ways in which they interpreted "moral rightness" differed. Hence, "appropriateness" is not always the best translation of *yi* outside of an early Confucian context.

31. *Analects* 15.24.

32. Graham explains, "Shu is not a virtue but a form of analogical thinking" (*Disputers,* 21).

33. Hall and Ames, *Thinking Through Confucius,* 117.

34. *Analects* 16.11.

35. *Analects* 7.37.

36. *Alcoholics Anonymous,* 79.

37. Ibid., 67.

# PART FIVE

# Transforming Virtue

Taking a Moral Inventory of
Twelve Step Spirituality

# The Virtues of the Twelve Steps

While Twelve Step spirituality requires the participant to perform a series of discrete actions, the process of doing so is supposed to lead to a profound moral transformation and a new way of living. Here, in the last section of this anthology, we do a kind of "moral inventory" of the Twelve Steps themselves in an effort to assess the kind of overall effect it can have on our lives as a whole. We begin with the essay of Matthew Pianalto, who discusses some of the specific virtues that one has to practice to perform the Steps and which thereby become part of one's moral identity. He finds that we have to rethink our usual idea of courage to appreciate the kind needed to take the Steps. Humility and patience, virtues usually not highly prized in contemporary culture, turn out to be equally indispensable. By drawing upon a wide array of philosophers from a variety of epochs, Pianalto shows that the virtues essential to practicing the Steps have been of perennial concern to philosophers.

In her memoir *Drinking: A Love Story,* Caroline Knapp describes a moment of insight in which she came to see the Twelve Steps as something more than a path to sobriety:

> I was astonished to discover that only one of the twelve steps, the first one, mentions the word *alcohol* (specifically, the admission of powerlessness over drink). The other eleven all have to do with getting by, with learning to be honest and responsible and humble, to own up to your mistakes when you make them, to ask for help when you need it. I remember sitting in on one of many lectures that described the twelve steps and thinking, *Oh! So* that's *how you're supposed to live.*[1]

Knapp's insight is telling. She does not think, "Oh! So that's how you're supposed to stop drinking," but rather "that's *how you're supposed to live.*" Following Knapp's lead, I suggest that the Twelve Steps can be understood as a comprehensive virtue ethic for living well, beyond the explicit quest for sobriety.

To read the Twelve Steps as a virtue ethic does not require one to take a position on whether alcoholism (or any other addiction) is itself a "character failing" or a physiological disease, or to reject the validity of medical treatments. No matter how we construe alcoholism or other debilitating addictions, those dealing with such problems face many challenges in seeking to adhere to a program of recovery and sobriety, in mending relationships, and in coming to better understand themselves. Meeting such challenges requires an ability to act and think with courage, humility, patience, and honesty. The Steps call upon a person to perform actions, and to repeat actions, that exhibit such virtues. Importantly, the value of such virtues is not limited to the struggles of those in AA or other such support groups, since the challenges such virtues enable an individual to meet arise, in one form or another, in every person's life. In that respect, we *all* have something to learn, and to gain, from the Twelve Steps.

## Courage

"We admitted we were powerless over alcohol—that our lives had become unmanageable." Courage is often thought of as a "manly" virtue. Indeed, the ancient Greek term translated as "courage"—*andreia*—literally means "manliness." What could be *less* manly than the First Step, the admission of powerlessness? A "real man" is a hero; he controls his fate. Courage involves assertion, domination, and nobly risking one's own life as the brave soldier does. On this picture, powerlessness and weakness are the opposite of manliness.

However, even though these ideas continue to influence our thinking about courage, William Ian Miller notes that courage has become considerably "democratized" since the Homeric age, and we now recognize courage, without strain, in many places beyond the battlefield.[2] This is in part because we are willing to extend the language of the fight, the noble struggle, to other areas of life. We recognize that fear and danger come in many forms, and that there is something admirable in the overcoming of such fears and dangers whenever one's aim is noble. And, of course, we recognize that women, such as Knapp, can be courageous too!

But alongside the *physical courage* of the soldier and the *moral courage* of those who risk social censure and punishment in order to take a stand for their convictions, Daniel Putman identifies a third kind of courage that he calls *psychological courage*.[3] These forms of courage can overlap in any particular courageous act, but what distinguishes psychological courage is that it involves overcoming the fear and threat of a loss of "psychological stability." The admission of powerlessness in the First Step poses just this sort of threat because admitting one's powerlessness threatens to undermine various other beliefs that one has about oneself, and thus poses a threat to one's own self-conception. We may fear that not only our self-conception, but our *very self*, will be destroyed (or otherwise shown to be a sham) through the admission of powerlessness, dependency, weakness, or error.

One key element of one's self-conception that is challenged by the First Step is the belief that one is in control of one's life and (in the case of alcoholics) one's drinking. Alcoholics such as Caroline Knapp often describe the rationalizations by which the alcoholic attempts to preserve this illusory sense of control: everything is okay because one does not fit "the popular definition of a 'real' drunk," or one will have a drink, "Just today. Bad day. I deserve a reward. I'll deal with it tomorrow."[4] As long as we believe we are in control, we will be able to convince ourselves that we do not need help, that we can manage just fine on our own. But there *are* times when each of us needs the help of another, and admitting this need may require (psychological) courage when such an admission threatens to undermine our own self-conception.

Another way to put this point is to emphasize that it may take courage in order to be *honest* with ourselves, as well as with others. The Fourth Step involves making "a searching and fearless moral inventory of ourselves." Although virtue theorists going back to Aristotle would suggest that fearlessness is different from courage (and that utter fearlessness is actually a vice), the point of the Fourth Step is clear enough: we must have the courage to make honest evaluations of ourselves, to look back at those embarrassing and dreadful moments of failure, at the problems we are now facing, and consider the extent to which this mess is precisely the one *we* have made. Assuming responsibility for failure is not fun—most of us will happily wait for someone else to bear the weight or to excuse us.

In the context of following the Steps, assuming responsibility may have an air of paradox since one is also supposed to admit one's powerlessness—one's lack of control. How can a person assume responsibility for those things—such as one's addiction—over which one is powerless? I would suggest here that taking responsibility be understood in terms of *owning up* to the facts of one's life and situation. Thus, taking responsibility for one's alcoholism would involve owning up to the fact that one is an alcoholic rather than engaging in rationalization. Being honest with oneself about this is itself a way of taking responsibility, even if coming to terms with one's alcoholism, and making necessary changes in one's life, is not something that can be done *by oneself.* This means that taking responsibility for one's alcoholism (and the effect it has had on others), as well as one's other limitations, failures, or flaws, is not inconsistent with acknowledging that changing oneself cannot be done alone. Taking responsibility means taking on a commitment to doing what is necessary to bring about positive change, and thus being *willing* to change, and willing to be changed through the help of others. The fear many of us have of change—the worry that our identity will be lost if we change too much, give up old habits, and so forth—indicates the necessity of courage here.

Just as the Steps call for courage in facing up to ourselves, they also call for courage in facing others. The Fifth Step requires that we admit our mistakes to another, and the Ninth Step calls for the making of amends with those we have harmed (except when attempting to do so would do more harm than good), and these are both cases where the Steps challenge the traditional militarized understanding of courage. Specifically, in admitting wrongs and making amends, we have to face others as our peers and equals, rather than as adversaries (or obstacles) to be bravely overcome. But we need courage in these endeavors because they put us in a potentially vulnerable position; we place ourselves at the mercy of others who might give us an (often well-deserved) earful of criticism (now that we are sober and can hear them), and who may or may not forgive us. However, if it takes some courage to initiate these interactions with others, it may take considerable *humility* to listen to what others have to say, and to accept the forgiveness they are able to give.

## Humility

In *Twelve Steps and Twelve Traditions,* Bill Wilson remarks that "the attainment of greater humility is the foundation principle of each of A.A.'s Twelve Steps," and that "all of A.A.'s Twelve Steps ask us to go contrary to our natural desires. . . . They all deflate our egos."[5] As he recognizes, some would reject the idea that humility is a virtue: "Humility, as a word and as an ideal, has a very bad time of it in our world."[6] The Greeks, including Aristotle, praised "greatness of soul," heroism, and taking pride in one's greatness; humility, as Hume later noted, seems rather "monkish" and life-denying by contrast.[7] Monkish or not, however, humility recommends itself as a virtue when it is situated in contrast with vices such as arrogance on the one hand and undue self-deprecation and a failure of self-respect on the other. Both of these attitudes are obstacles to embarking upon the process of development inherent in the Twelve Steps.

Bernard of Clairvaux defined humility thus: "Humility is a virtue by which a man has a low opinion of himself because he knows himself well."[8] Instead of dismissing humility as Hume does, we might ask, a low opinion compared to what? One contemporary answer suggested by Owen Flanagan is that most people (presumably, not counting those suffering from major depression) tend to *overrate* themselves and their abilities.[9] Thus humility could be understood as not *over*estimating ourselves, given that this is an all-too-human tendency. J. L. A. Garcia further suggests that humble people are "unimpressed with themselves"—that is, humble people do not overblow the significance of their achievements.[10] Similarly, Norvin Richards and Nancy Snow both suggest that the humble person keeps his or her own life and achievements (and failures) "in perspective."[11] The world is much larger than our own successes or failures. Perhaps the simplest definition of humility has been offered by Iris Murdoch, who characterizes it as "selfless respect for reality."[12] Her definition shares with the descriptions presented above the idea that a humble person is realistic, and also suggests that one's own desires, preconceptions, and rationalizations can prevent one from seeing both oneself and others as they truly are. Although the overt aim of humility is "ego-deflation," the *point* of humility is to open the individual up to a healthier life with others as well as herself. Acknowledging one's powerlessness over certain aspects of life takes both courage and humility, and this humble admission opens one up to the possibility of receiving help from others—help without which one will be unable to change, let alone flourish.

Some may wonder whether it makes sense for an ethic directed in the first instance at recovery from addiction to focus so much on *humbling* those who would embark upon this path. Addiction is often comorbid with depression, and it could be argued that, to the extent that one's addiction is reinforced by depression, a person does not need to be encouraged to be more humble. However, the attitudes that characterize humility are not to be confused with depressive thinking. In one respect, it is true that the depressed person does not need to be "more humble"—that is, such a person needs to have a *stronger* sense of self-worth. However, if we think of humility as an Aristotelian *mean* between two extremes, then we can say that the depressed person does need to be "more humble" in the sense of coming to *properly* value his or her own life and potential. One thing that happens in depression is that individuals tend to overgeneralize *failure* rather than success—to take specific mistakes or shortcomings to imply a general lack of individual worth. Thus, failing an exam (or falling off the wagon) leads one to conclude, "I'm a terrible person." Both depressed and arrogant individuals engage in bad reasoning that leads to unreasonable attitudes toward themselves (and often others, too): in depression or despair, we overgeneralize the significance of failure, and in pride or arrogance, we overgeneralize the significance of our successes.

Another way in which depressive thinking can be distinguished from proper humility is to note how depression can lead to a single-minded focus upon oneself and one's problems and failures. Here, humility contrasts with self-absorption. This is the point of acknowledging the role a "higher power" plays in one's life and in one's recovery (Steps Two, Three, Five, Seven, and Eleven), of seeking to admit errors to others and make amends with them (Steps Five, Eight, Nine, and Ten), and of carrying the message of the Steps to others (Step Twelve). All of these Steps direct one's attention to something or someone beyond oneself; they encourage one to acknowledge one's dependency upon, and interconnections with, others, and thus to adopt a broadened perspective so that one's own life, interests, successes, and problems are not placed at the center of the universe.

So far, I have put off discussing the notion of a "higher power" in the Twelve Steps. However, the particular form humility takes in the Steps depends crucially upon this idea, for it is this "higher power"—God *as one understands this notion*—to which one ultimately humbles oneself in following the Steps. It is the "higher power" to which one *turns over one's life* and which ultimately *removes* the defects in oneself that had prevented one from overcoming addiction.

It is tempting to misread these ideas as mere passivity. They certainly seem mysterious. However, we can diffuse some of the apparent mystery by noticing that the humble *acknowledgment* of powerlessness, and the *initiation* of a process that includes seeking out support and help, is both an active process and one that is not mysterious at all when we are seeking help from other people. The person who is clinging to some destructive or disabling pattern of thought or behavior must work toward acknowledging and accepting the necessity of change—if she is to flourish rather than crash and burn—and of doing what she can in order to set in motion the process of positive change. What the Steps imply is that one cannot bring about the *entire* change by oneself. Some might be inclined to deny this, to invoke grit, determination, and willpower as all one needs. But every achievement requires *some* amount of cooperation from the world. And many of our achievements would not be possible without much more specific forms of assistance and cooperation from others. So we can also come to admit that passivity—in the sense of allowing others to act upon us—is also not always bad.

Those who believe in a loving, involved God will believe that our own efforts to make positive changes do not go unnoticed by God, and that what we cannot do ourselves, God will help us achieve. But what about those who do not believe in such a God, and who find this talk of a "higher power" *too* mysterious and simply unbelievable? The difficulty here is that, if humility for a Christian, a Muslim, or a Hindu is fundamentally a matter of being humble before the Divine, the nonbeliever does not have available that way of orienting his or her humility. One might then wonder whether a nonbeliever can cultivate the kind of humility advocated in the Twelve Steps. It is noteworthy, however, that the Steps are inherently open-ended on this issue. The "God" to which one turns over one's life in the Third Step can only be God *as understood by that individual.* But what of the person who takes issue with the very concept of God? Here, we can consider the possibility of dispensing with the term "God" altogether in exchange for any notion of "a power greater than ourselves." As Wilson suggests, "You can, if you wish, make A.A. itself your 'higher power.'"[13] The point here is not to deify AA, or any other such program, but rather to draw attention to the fact that by committing oneself to such a program, by seeking outside help—whether it be from other people or from God (or from nature, etc.)—one *humbles* oneself by acknowledging the need for help in overcoming one's own problems. In this way, the humility called for in the Twelve Steps can be understood in secularized terms, and this includes the Eleventh Step, which calls for a deepening of one's "contact with God" through prayer and meditation. Here, the nonbeliever can substitute meditation on the Steps themselves and discussions about the Steps with others, and humbly seek a deeper understanding of their significance, and new ways of thinking about their message and their aims.

## Patience

Like humility, patience is often misunderstood by those who cannot be bothered to have any. From a superficial point of view, patience, too, might seem needlessly passive: don't wait, *act*! But patience is much more than waiting. The *Oxford English Dictionary,* which reflects a richer, older understanding of patience, characterizes it alternatively as "the calm, uncomplaining endurance of pain, affliction, or inconvenience"; "forbearance or long-suffering under provocation, especially tolerance of the faults or limitations of other people"; "self-possessed waiting"; and "constancy or diligence in work, exertion, or effort—perseverance." It becomes evident that patience requires strength of character when we bear in mind that pain, suffering, annoyance, frustration, and so forth cannot always be avoided—either because there is simply no getting away from them under the circumstances or because the goal we are pursuing cannot be realized without confronting these various forms of adversity.

Adhering to our deeply held moral and personal ideals requires patience at times—understood both as a virtue of restraint and endurance and as a strength that enables and reflects constancy of commitment—and so it should not be surprising that the aim of sobriety and recovery for the addict is one that will require great patience. Changes in our habits of thought and behavior are rarely, if ever, instantaneous. For that very reason, there is a case to be made for patience as one of the fundamental virtues, since the development of any other virtue (such as courage or humility) takes time, experience, and repetition. Of course, it might be thought that time, experience, and repetition are all that are needed—why insist upon adding patience to the mix?

One reason is simply that we can grow bored and distracted when confronted with repetitive activities. Our attention can wander from the task at hand, and one of the ways in which patience reveals itself to be an active virtue, and not only a virtue of restraint, is that patience with a task enables our attention to remain focused. Similarly, in the face of obstacles, interruptions, and failure, we can lapse into anger or despair—both of which are states in which we may deviate from our goals and our principles. Like the humble person, the patient person understands his or her own limitations and vulnerabilities and acknowledges that human control over events is itself limited. Things will sometimes go wrong. Our expectations and desires will sometimes be frustrated. The patient person possesses the strength to endure such disappointments and setbacks and, when necessary, the strength to begin anew.

The implicit need for patience in practicing the Twelve Steps is brought to our attention by what might at first seem like their unnecessary repetition. But this repetition—as in the Tenth Step's call for a continuation in taking a personal inventory of oneself—reminds us that in any difficult, ongoing task, it is often essential to the task that we take stock of things, measure our progress, and look to see whether we are indeed *making* progress. These inward, reflective tasks call for patient attention to our own activity. The mindfulness required here can prevent us from growing complacent or becoming lost in the distractions of everyday life (which may not seem to leave us time to engage in such reflection and inventory-taking). Such activities may take patience, but it might also be thought that such reflection and attention is itself a kind of training in patience. This is not only because self-examination requires time and honest, mindful attention, but also because when we find that we are still far off from realizing our long-term goals, or have to admit that we have failed to keep promises to ourselves or others, then we are presented with the further task of learning to be patient with ourselves.

To be patient with oneself is not to make excuses for mistakes and failures, but to understand that we are imperfect. A mistake can be borne with patience and humility rather than despair, and perhaps it is patience combined with courage and humility that enables us to avoid the temptation to despair in the face of adversity and setbacks. In the case of the recovering addict, the development of these strengths can thus be seen as essential for responding well to a relapse, which may otherwise threaten to undermine the progress one has made. But this will be true in many other contexts as well, which is why these virtues, and the ways in which the Steps require the development and exercise of them, offer a picture of individual development that extends far beyond the context of recovery. Patience in particular is central to such development because moral growth requires time, attention, endurance, and constancy to the task. This is why Gregory the Great claimed that "patience is the root and guardian of all the virtues."[14]

## Beyond Recovery and Restraint

The reflections above are intended to show how the Twelve Steps embody a substantive, virtue-oriented ethic. My method has been to argue by way of illustration, rather than to attempt to give a comprehensive account of the various virtues implicit in the Steps.[15] However, my attention to courage, humility, and patience is not accidental, for reflection on these virtues may also shed further light on Reinhold Niebuhr's "Serenity Prayer": "God grant me the serenity to accept the things I cannot change, courage to change the things I can, and wisdom to know the difference." That kind of serenity is made possible, in part, by both humility and patience. The form of the Serenity Prayer (in seeking Divine grace) is a reminder, of course, that our own efforts are only part of the story. (Again, the secularist may have a different story to tell here.) Furthermore, a humbled, patient attitude would seem to be conducive to, if not essential to, the task of growing in wisdom—to know the difference between what can and cannot be changed.[16] And while courage is essential to undertaking efforts to change what can be changed, there is also a kind of intellectual courage—implicit, for example, in the idea of making a "searching and fearless moral inventory" of oneself—that also promotes wisdom.

The main contention in this essay is that these virtues are virtues for all, not simply for the addict seeking recovery and sobriety, and so the Twelve Steps can fruitfully be employed by non-addicts too. At this point, however, we might ask, Where do we go from here? I have reflected upon how courage, humility, and patience figure into a commitment to following the Steps, and the relevance of such virtues for life in general should be clear enough. But it may seem that courage, humility, and patience leave a great many questions about how we should live unaddressed. Suppose we grow in these virtues, master or correct our shortcomings (with the help of others), and become better able to endure obstacles and adversity in our lives. What are we to do after that point? What *should* we do?

In raising these questions, I first want to draw attention to the explicit aim of the Steps: a return to normality or, as in the Second Step, "sanity." As long as recovery is one's primary goal, the Steps and their virtues have a clearly defined aim. But it may seem that an ethic such as the one promoted by the Steps, which appears to be largely directed toward recovery and restraint (and repairing past wrongs when possible), does not have enough to say about what the *next* goal, beyond sobriety or recovery, ought to be. Of course, for the addict, sobriety itself is a lifelong goal, and even the sober addict knows that he or she cannot take sobriety for granted. But sober living is not the whole of life. It is, we might say, a precondition for living well and flourishing (at least for those who are unable to enjoy an occasional drink or two without losing control). But an ethic that only counsels us back to normality (or sanity) might seem to be only half an ethic. In this respect the Twelve Steps would appear to be only part of the story about "how you're supposed to live."

However, the Twelve Steps end by calling upon the person committed to them both to share them with others who are suffering from addiction and "to practice these principles in all our affairs." Given the nature of the Steps, it is worth noting that carrying the message of the Steps to others is something that must be done in a spirit of tolerance. The Steps recognize and allow for a plurality of conceptions of God and/or a "higher power," and so in sharing the Steps with others, in bearing witness to their potential, one must be able to accept that others may not share one's own theological and metaphysical beliefs.

As for the call "to practice these principles in all our affairs," this provides at least a partial answer to the question I posed above: How should we live once we have found our way back to "sanity"? In my view, exercising virtues such as courage, humility, and patience (as well as honesty, tolerance, and the other virtues that can be related to the Steps) in all of our affairs will tend to make what we do good, and such virtues will, to the extent that we have them, prevent us from engaging in patently wrong actions and from choosing morally questionable goals (or questionable means to attaining our goals). There are many things we can do that will be improved by the virtues of the Steps. Patience will make us a better parent, humility and honesty a better friend and colleague, courage a better voice for justice and fairness in our communities. In this respect, the call to cultivate these virtues and exercise them in all of our affairs—by applying the ideals of the Twelve Steps throughout our lives—is much more than "half an ethic." To bring the virtues to bear upon all the areas of our lives, to achieve that kind of harmony within ourselves and through time, is itself a lifelong task.

NOTES

1. Knapp, *Drinking*, 253.
2. Miller, *Mystery of Courage*, 11–12, 260.
3. Putman, *Psychological Courage*, 2.
4. Knapp, *Drinking*, 12, 5.
5. Wilson, *Twelve Steps and Twelve Traditions*, 70, 55.
6. Ibid., 70.
7. Hume, *Enquiry*, 10.1.
8. Bernard of Clairvaux, *Steps of Humility*, 30.

9. Owen Flanagan, "Virtue and Ignorance," *Journal of Philosophy* 87, no. 8 (1990): 420–28.

10. J. L. A. Garcia, "Being Unimpressed with Ourselves: Reconceiving Humility," *Philosophia* 34, no. 4 (2006): 417–35.

11. Richards, *Humility;* Nancy Snow, "Humility," *Journal of Value Inquiry* 29 (1995): 203–16.

12. Murdoch, *Sovereignty of Good,* 93.

13. Wilson, *Twelve Steps and Twelve Traditions,* 27. Julian Taber has developed a "Universal Secular Twelve Steps," which articulates a version of the Steps that does not refer to God. See Taber's *Addictions Anonymous.*

14. Gregory the Great, *Forty Gospel Homilies,* 305.

15. See also the discussion of virtues in the Twelve Steps by Jennings in *Little Red Book,* as well as Dunnington's discussion of the significance of the virtue of friendship in Twelve Step programs in *Addiction and Virtue,* 184–91. (Dunnington's book focuses primarily on examining addiction itself from a traditional virtue perspective, whereas my essay is concerned with the role virtues play specifically within the Twelve Steps.)

16. See Valerie Tiberius and John D. Walker, "Arrogance," *American Philosophical Quarterly* 35, no. 4 (1998): 379–90.

# Stoic Philosophy and AA
## The Enduring Wisdom of the Serenity Prayer

The philosopher's school is a doctor's clinic.
—Epictetus

Morgan Rempel's essay provides a valuable "moral inventory" of Twelve Step spirituality by comparing its principle insights, expressed in the Serenity Prayer, to those offered us by the ancient proponents and practitioners of Stoicism. Rempel argues that both the Twelve Steps and Stoicism summon us to face very difficult, painful truths about what we can and cannot control. But doing so can creatively transform our most fundamental attitudes and hence our way of responding to life as a whole.

Every day, millions of people all over the world begin a Twelve Step recovery meeting with the Serenity Prayer: *"God, grant us the serenity to accept the things we cannot change; Courage to change the things we can; And wisdom to know the difference."*[1] Alcoholics Anonymous cofounder Bill W. wrote of the prayer: "Never had we seen so much A.A. in so few words."[2] While this particular form of the prayer is generally attributed to theologian Reinhold Niebuhr (1892–1971), those familiar with ancient philosophy may hear in the Serenity Prayer echoes of a much older wisdom tradition. More specifically, the prayer seems to resonate with insights of the ancient Greco-Roman therapeutic philosophy known as Stoicism. And as we see below, its goal of serenity turns out to be one of Stoic philosophy's raisons d'être.

Closer examination reveals that there are a number of aspects of this eminently practical, tonic ancient philosophy that find resonance in twentieth-century Twelve Step programs. In the following pages, several such connections are examined.

(1) The cardinal theme of promoting serenity by distinguishing those matters over which we *have* control from those we *haven't*.

(2) *Self-examination.* This basic philosophical goal, it turns out, is facilitated in both Twelve Step recovery programs and Stoic philosophy by a staunch emphasis on ongoing *personal inventories.* Classicist A. A. Long, for example, characterizes the Stoic philosopher Epictetus's lectures as "invitations to his audience to examine themselves."[3] Key to both traditions is the notion that before one can improve one's inner condition, there must be thorough self-examination.

(3) *Self-improvement.* The theme of self-improvement—and the related matter of the inevitable setbacks in one's transformative journey—also figure prominently in both traditions. At the heart of both Stoic philosophy and Alcoholics Anonymous one finds a series of practical, straightforward—though by no means *easy*—psychotherapeutic exercises focusing on gradual self-improvement.

Indeed, one of the things that recommends the comparison of AA and Stoicism is that, unlike much of contemporary philosophy, which is often highly theoretical and seemingly detached from everyday life, Stoicism offers real-world guidance for the art of living. More precisely, it provides practical guidance for living a flourishing life of enduring serenity. As we see below, a version of AA's goal of "peace, patience, and contentment"[4] was articulated by Stoic philosophers centuries ago. My hope is that the parallel examination of several key aspects of these two wisdom traditions will serve as both a helpful introduction to a routinely neglected ancient philosophy of personal transformation and empowerment, and a reminder of the enduring, therapeutic wisdom at the heart of Alcoholics Anonymous and the Serenity Prayer.

Introduction to Stoicism

Stoicism was founded in the third century BC by the Greek philosopher Zeno of Citium (c. 336–264 BC). As Zeno sometimes taught at the Painted Stoa, a covered colonnade in Athens, his followers came to be known as "Stoics." In addition to lectures on logic and physics, Zeno's teaching promoted an attitude of indifference toward external circumstances (wealth, status, honors, and reputation) and instead emphasized the importance of one's inner condition. After Zeno, the most influential Greek Stoic was the prolific Chrysippus (c. 282–206 BC), under whose tutelage the school experienced a period of significant growth. Historically speaking, one of the more important leaders of the school was Panaetius (c. 185–109 BC), who traveled to Rome around 140 BC and brought the gospel of Stoicism with him.

This journey proved to be the spark that would lead to a renaissance in Stoic philosophy, culminating in the figure of Roman emperor Marcus Aurelius (121–180 AD), at once the most powerful man in the Western world and a practicing Stoic. During the Roman period, Stoicism's interest in logic and physics diminished, while its emphasis on attaining tranquility increased.[5] Marcus's oft-cited *Meditations* contains hundreds of short, practical exercises in serenity and self-improvement developed by the emperor, sometimes while away on military campaigns.[6]

Among Roman Stoics, the most skillful writer was undoubtedly Seneca (c. 4 BC–65 AD), philosopher, statesman, dramatist, and tutor to the boy who would become Emperor Nero. Later, as advisor to the notorious emperor, Seneca wielded such power that some observers considered him "the real master of the world."[7] The Stoic mentioned most frequently by Marcus was Epictetus (c. 55–135 AD), a lame onetime slave of a member of Nero's court who gained his freedom and became an influential philosopher. Like Socrates, Epictetus did not commit his philosophy to writing, but his pupil Arrian brought many of his master's teachings to print. The most famous, the *Handbook,* is a short compendium of Epictetus's central teachings. Epictetus casts Stoicism, above all else, as a practical, therapeutic philosophy of life through which serenity and well-being can be achieved. The fact that both a lame slave and an emperor found life-changing inspiration in Stoicism says much about the character of the wisdom at the core of this ancient philosophy.

## In Our Power to Control/Not in Our Power to Control

Tellingly, the *Handbook* begins with what we might call Epictetus's "serenity meditation."

> Of things, some are in our power and some things are not in our power. In our power are our judgments, our pursuits, our desires, aversions, and our mental faculties in general. Not in our power are our bodies, material possessions, our reputations, status—in a word, anything not in our power to control. Now, the things in our power are naturally free, unrestrained and unimpeded, but those not in our power are frail, inferior, subject to restraint—and none of our affair.

Remember that if you mistake what is naturally inferior for what is sovereign and free, and what is not your business for your own, you'll meet with disappointment, grief and worry and be at odds with God and man. But if you have the right idea about what really belongs to you and what does not, you will never be subject to force or hindrance, you will never blame or criticize anyone, and everything you do will be done willingly.[8]

At first glance it may appear—particularly to our money-, status-, and fitness-focused society—that Epictetus wrongly places "our bodies, . . . material possessions . . . [, and] status" on his "not in our power to control" list. But I think most would be willing to grant Epictetus that we do not have *any* control over whether we are born male or female; whether we are six feet or five feet tall; white or black; born to an impoverished third-world family or the wealthiest noble family in Rome, and so on. Likewise, I think most would agree that our "power to control" things such as what other people say or think about us ("our reputations"), or whether we attain all the "material possessions" and "status" we hoped for, is limited indeed.[9]

Elsewhere, Epictetus offers more straightforward examples of the *in my power to control/not in my power to control* dichotomy. He points to the cold fact that all our loved ones will eventually die as a clear example of something not in our power to control. Cautions Epictetus, "You are a fool to want your children, wife or friends to be immortal; it calls for powers beyond you, and gifts not yours to either own or give."[10] Since, as Seneca reminds us, "All things human are short-lived and perishable,"[11] it is not only foolish but entirely unproductive to resent or be angered by something as inescapable and beyond our power of control as the inevitability of death. Far better to focus on those few things over which one *can* exert control and effect change than squander one's energies on the myriad of things over which one can do neither. Stoics from Athens to Rome argue that the former is the rational path to effective living and serenity. The latter, they consistently warn us, is but an invitation to anxiety, blighted hope, and sorrow. Sounding not unlike the Buddha, Epictetus cautions, "So direct aversion only towards things that are under your control and alien to your nature, and you will not fall victim to any of the things you dislike. But if your resentment is directed at illness, death or poverty, you are headed for disappointment."[12] Nicely summing up this practical, therapeutic theme in Stoic philosophy, Connolly notes, "Toward those unfortunate things that are not within our power which we cannot avoid (for example, death and the actions and opinions of others) the proper attitude is one of apathy. . . . It is absurd to become distraught over externals for the same reason that it is absurd to become distressed over the past; both are beyond our power. The Stoic is simply adopting toward all things [beyond our power to control] the only logical attitude appropriate to the past—indifference."[13]

While my *past* is fixed, unchangeable, and therefore, for the Stoics, a matter of "indifference," my *future* is another matter altogether.[14] Despite its association with determinism, fate, and even fatalism, Stoicism, as we see below, is a philosophy that *allows for* freedom of choice and indeed *calls for* the shaping and improving of oneself and one's future.[15] Writing of Stoicism, the Roman historian Tacitus notes that though "things happen according to fate . . . this school concedes to us the freedom to choose our own lives."[16] "Not even God," Epictetus insists triumphantly, "has the power of coercion over us."[17] And for the Stoics, the principal way we can (simultaneously) exercise our freedom, improve ourselves, and increase our serenity is by changing our judgments, attitudes, and overall mental outlook.

It is no accident that Arrian places "our judgments" at the top of Epictetus's deliberately short list of things "in our power."[18] Indeed, one cannot overestimate the importance Stoic philosophy assigns to recognizing that our "judgments" (sometimes translated as "opinions") are "in our power." And for the Stoics, our judgments, opinions, and attitudes have very real consequences for our psychological well-being. Asserting that "anxieties can only come from your internal judgment," Marcus succinctly underscores this all-important insight when he insists, "Life is judgment."[19]

In a well-known aphorism, Epictetus's *Handbook* emphasizes that "it is not events that disturb people, it is their judgments concerning them. Death, for example, is nothing frightening, otherwise it would have frightened Socrates. But the judgment that death is frightening—now that is something to be afraid of. So when we are frustrated, angry or unhappy, never hold anyone except ourselves—that is, our judgments—accountable. An ignorant person is inclined to blame others for his own misfortune."[20] In the *Discourses,* Epictetus again discusses the manner in which we face our inevitable mortality in order to underscore the importance of one's attitude and judgments. "I must die. But must I die bawling? I must be put in chains—but moaning and groaning too? I must be exiled; but is there anything to keep me from going with a smile, calm and self-composed?"[21] Elsewhere, he offers this equally therapeutic (and equally difficult) advice: "Remember, it is not enough to be hit or insulted to be harmed, you must believe that you are being harmed. If someone succeeds in provoking you, realize that your mind is complicit in the provocation. Which is why it is essential that we not respond impulsively to impressions; take a moment before reacting, and you will find it easier to maintain control."[22]

According to Stoic philosophy, by changing the way one thinks, one changes the person one is (and will be). And by learning to think like a Stoic— particularly vis-à-vis one's attitude toward those things in, and not in, our power of control—we wrest control of our mental well-being from other people and the vicissitudes of life and place it firmly in our own hands. Put into practice, this straightforward (but by no means easy) message is at once liberating and empowering. No longer are one's happiness and serenity dependent upon "externals" (things outside one's sphere of control). Our happiness and serenity, to a remarkable degree, really are "up to us." Stoic philosophy, declares Seneca, builds "an impregnable wall" around the individual. "Though it be assaulted by many engines, Fortune can find no passage into it. The soul stands on unassailable ground, if it has abandoned external things; it is independent in its own fortress; and every weapon that is hurled falls short of the mark."[23]

## AA/Power/Powerlessness

AA's emphasis on personal "powerlessness" is well known. Indeed, the first and likely most famous of AA's Twelve Steps reads: "We admitted we were powerless over alcohol—that our lives had become unmanageable."[24] But this well-known Step turns out to be only one side of the issue of personal power in the AA tradition. As with Stoic philosophy, much of the good news of Alcoholics Anonymous lies with its treatment of the *other* side of this issue—those things squarely *in* our power to change and control.

After quoting Step One, an AA reflection on powerlessness continues:

> It is no coincidence that the very first step mentions powerlessness: an admission of personal powerlessness over alcohol is a cornerstone of the foundation of recovery. I've learned that I do not have the power and control I once thought I had. I am powerless over what people think about me. I am powerless over having just missed the bus. . . . But I've also learned I am

*not* powerless over some things. I am *not* powerless over my attitudes. I am *not* powerless over negativity. I am *not* powerless over assuming responsibility for my own recovery.[25]

From the perspective of Stoic philosophy, AA passages such as this are interesting indeed. Like the Serenity Prayer, it shares with Stoicism an emphasis on the therapeutic value of distinguishing those things that *are* in my power to control from those things that are not. Among the latter are such familiar things as what other people think about me; the past ("having just missed the bus"); and, of course, alcohol. Among the former is the all-important matter of my attitudes (with particular emphasis on doing something about negative attitudes) and my ability to freely choose to be a positive force of change in my life. Another AA reflection, "The Past Is Over," employs similar examples to illustrate this familiar dichotomy of control: "Whatever is done is over. It cannot be changed. But my attitude about it can be changed.... I won't have to wish the past away. I can change my feelings and attitudes."[26]

Interestingly, with respect to the past, Twelve Step thinking at once reiterates and parts company with Stoic philosophy. As we have seen, Stoicism recommends treating the past—like all matters over which we have no power of control—with indifference. Alcoholics Anonymous, however, while recognizing that the past is indeed something we cannot change, strongly emphasizes that we learn from it. For example, AA literature suggests that when recovering alcoholics are tempted by an offer of a drink, "we now try to remember the *whole* train of consequences of starting with just 'a drink.' We think the drink all the way through, down to our last miserable drunk and hangover.... We are careful to recall the full suffering of our last drinking episode."[27]

What is more, a significant component of the Twelve Step recovery strategy, from AA's modest beginnings in the 1930s to meetings being held all over the world this very day, is that *others* can learn from your past, no matter how troubled. The tellingly titled reflection "The Treasure of the Past" begins by quoting *Alcoholics Anonymous:* "Cling to the thought that, in God's hands, the dark past is the greatest possession you have—the key to life and happiness for others. With it you can avert death and misery for them." It then goes on to observe, "What a gift it is for me to realize that all those seemingly useless years were not wasted. The most degrading and humiliating experiences turn out to be the most powerful tools in helping others to recover."[28] The past, in the AA tradition, then, is a more complex matter than for the Stoics. For Twelve Steppers, the same past that I am *powerless* to change can be *empowering* both to myself and to other sufferers.

## Self-Examination/Self-Improvement

Not surprisingly, the ancient philosophical themes of self-examination and self-knowledge figure prominently in both Stoic philosophy and Twelve Step recovery programs. And in both traditions, self-examination and self-knowledge are regarded as necessary steps in one's journey of self-improvement. AA's emphasis on regular personal "inventories"—what *Alcoholics Anonymous* characterizes as "drastic self-appraisals"[29]—is well known. Indeed, two of AA's Twelve Steps, and much of its therapeutic methodology, rest on the importance of ongoing "searching and fearless personal inventories" (Step Four).

In a passage that seems to reverberate with Stoic wisdom, AA's *Twelve Steps and Twelve Traditions* notes, "A continuous look at our assets and liabilities, and a real desire to learn and grow by this means, are necessities for us. We alcoholics have learned this the hard way. More experienced people, of course, in all times and places have practiced unsparing self-survey and criticism. For the wise have always known that no one can make much of his life until self-searching becomes a regular habit, until he is able to admit and accept what he finds, and until he patiently and persistently tries to correct what is wrong."[30]

Reviewing different ways to conduct such inner inventories, this volume advises, "There's the one we take at day's end. . . . Here we cast up a balance sheet, crediting ourselves with things well done, and chalking up debits where due."[31] *Alcoholics Anonymous* is even more specific: "When we retire at night, we constructively review our day. Were we resentful, selfish, dishonest or afraid? Do we owe an apology? . . . What could we have done better?"[32] The strategy is straightforward (though by no means easy): one scrutinizes one's day and one's self and makes note of, and reflects upon, both "things well done" and areas in need of improvement ("debits"). Over time, through trial and error, success and failure, one endeavors to gradually decrease the debits in subsequent "balance sheets" (inventories) as one moves in the direction of the *better* person one wishes to be. By emphasizing "inner" matters of opinion and attitude—resentfulness, selfishness, fears, and the like—AA, like Stoic philosophy, wisely focuses one's self-improvement efforts on those things truly "in our power" to change.

Despite its positive approach to self-examination and self-improvement, there is nothing Pollyannaish about AA's attitude to these matters. Firstly, AA recognizes that self-awareness and self-improvement are not short-term projects but *lifelong endeavors*. "It is not an overnight matter. It should continue for our lifetime."[33] Self-knowledge and improvement are not things one fully *achieves,* but rather things one continually strives for. This realistic insight informs the movement's famous claim that "the principles we have set down are guides to progress. We claim spiritual progress rather than spiritual perfection."[34] So it is that many in the recovery community characterize themselves as "recovering" rather than "recovered."

And secondly, as a movement contending with something as pernicious as alcoholism, AA is well aware of the likelihood of setbacks in one's journey (sometimes called "backsliding" by Twelve Steppers): "No one among us has been able to maintain anything like perfect adherence to these principles. We are not saints."[35] AA is realistic and open about this: "Maybe we have fallen short somehow, backslid a bit in our thinking or actions, despite knowing better. So what? We are not perfect creatures. . . . Some of us go back to drinking a time or so before we get a real foothold on sobriety. If that happens, don't despair. . . . Recovery can still follow."[36] The reason why the alcoholic need not despair and why recovery can still follow (even repeated) setbacks is that the process of self-improvement can begin again at any time. On the topic of the famous slogan "one day at a time," AA astutely points out, "I can start my day over again anytime I choose; a hundred times, if necessary."[37]

The extent to which the teachings of Stoic philosophy align with those of Alcoholics Anonymous vis-à-vis the allied matters of self-examination and self-improvement is impressive. Long, for example, characterizes Epictetus's lectures as "invitations to his audience to examine themselves."[38] Seneca, likewise, in a letter on the topic of attaining serenity, advises, "Our first duty will be to examine ourselves."[39] Sounding not unlike a Twelve Stepper taking his moral inventory, Seneca's teacher, Sextius, would ask himself each night, "What ailment of yours have you cured today? What failings have you resisted? Where can you show improvement?"[40] Anticipating the AA theme of "progress" rather than "perfection," Seneca insists his own goal is simply to "every day reduce the number of my vices."[41]

Like AA, Stoicism emphasizes that while one's quest for self-improvement is never over, the time to begin the journey is always *now*. Asks Epictetus:

> How long will you wait before you demand the best of yourself[?] . . . What kind of teacher are you waiting for that you delay putting these principles into practice until he comes? You're a grown man already, not a child any more. . . . Finally decide that you are an adult who is going to devote the rest of your life to making progress. . . . Realize that the crisis is now: that the Olympics have started, and waiting is no longer an option. . . . That's how Socrates got to be the person he was, by depending on reason to meet his every challenge. You're not yet Socrates, but you can still live as if you want to be him.[42]

Stoicism acknowledges that the task of self-improvement—of endeavoring to become a Socrates—is no easy matter. But one needs to establish a goal, begin moving toward it, and stick with it. Epictetus advises, "Settle on the type of person you want to be and stick to it, whether alone or in company."[43]

Stoic philosophy, like AA, recognizes the likelihood of setbacks in one's journey and offers similar counsel to the frustrated. Marcus Aurelius—no stranger to difficulties (both inner and on the world stage)—wryly observes that "the art of living is more like wrestling than dancing."[44] He also advises, "Do not give up in disgust or impatience if you do not find action on the right principles consolidated into a habit in all that you do. No: if you have taken a fall, come back again."[45] Recommending that we "take example from the wrestling-masters," Epictetus remarks, "Has the boy fallen down? Get up again, they say; wrestle again, till you have acquired strength."[46] Whether reading Epictetus's *Handbook* or *Alcoholics Anonymous,* the advice for those who "have taken a fall" is the same: Don't despair; get up; keep trying; tomorrow is another day.

## Mutually Illuminating Wisdom

Considering the fact that both Stoic philosophy and Alcoholics Anonymous devote considerable attention to explicating and emphasizing our *powerlessness* in certain matters, it is well to note the equally important attention both traditions pay to the tremendous *power* each of us has. As noted, this lessknown celebration of personal power—the power to control our judgments, attitudes, and mental outlook; the power to exercise personal choice, and in so doing, change and improve the person one is; the power to achieve happiness and serenity despite numerous challenges and obstacles—really is the good news of both these wisdom traditions.

"If a strong inner core of peace, patience, and contentment looks at all desirable to you, it can be had."[47] That this specific AA claim could just as easily have been made by Epictetus testifies to just how similar certain aspects of these two traditions are. The fact that Stoicism and AA arrive at comparable conclusions and offer similar therapeutic counsel on a number of topics is not necessarily evidence of any direct, heretofore undiscovered indebtedness to or even knowledge of the former by the latter. I am merely suggesting that both traditions appear to be tapping into the same empowering, tranquility-promoting wisdom—the enduring wisdom articulated in the Serenity Prayer.

## NOTES

1. *Twelve Steps and Traditions,* 125.

2. Bill W., *As Bill Sees It,* 108.

3. Long, *Epictetus,* 91.

4. Alcoholics Anonymous World Service, *Living Sober,* 46.

5. It is important to point out that Stoicism was a fluid, evolving intellectual tradition with different emphases and even significant variance in various Stoic thinkers. Dobbin notes in his introduction to *Discourses* that "the Stoics' openness to revision was a particular strength of their school" (xiii).

6. For centuries, Marcus's *Meditations* has been cited by thinkers and statesmen as an invaluable source of guidance and wisdom. Leaders from Frederick the Great to Bill Clinton have sung its praises, the latter apparently rereading it every year or two.

7. Robin Campbell's introduction to Seneca's *Letters,* 10.

8. Epictetus, *Handbook,* 1. This quotation combines Robert Dobbin's and Elizabeth Carter's translations of Epictetus's *Handbook,* which are contained in their translations of the *Discourses.* Unless noted, subsequent quotations are from the Dobbin translation. As many editions of the *Handbook* are available, I refer to it by using the chapter numbers and sometimes also the section numbers of Epictetus's text, not the page numbers of a particular edition. I follow a similar procedure when referring to Epictetus's *Discourses* and the texts of Marcus Aurelius and Seneca.

9. Marcus offers a more nuanced reflection on this matter when he writes, "Someone despises me? That is his concern. But I will see to it that I am not found guilty of any word or action deserving contempt" (*Meditations,* 11, 13).

10. Epictetus, *Handbook,* 14.

11. Seneca, "On the Happy Life," 3.4, in *Moral Essays.*

12. Epictetus, *Handbook*, 2.

13. William Connolly, http://ecole.evansville.edu/articles/stoicism.html.

14. See Epictetus, *Discourses*, 2.19.1–5.

15. The topic of Stoicism, determinism, and fatalism is a rich one and will not be settled here. Some scholars see in Stoic philosophy fatalism concerning our past, present, and future, while others (Irvine, *Guide*) emphasize Stoicism's fatalism concerning the past. For a more in-depth examination of the matter, see Bobzien's *Determinism and Freedom*.

16. Tacitus, quoted in Dobbin's introduction to Epictetus's *Discourses*, xii. This "freedom to choose our own lives" is crucial, particularly to Epictetus's brand of Stoicism. In the words of Dobbin, "the upshot" of Epictetus's emphasis on freedom of choice is "that it is 'up to us' how we act, and that we are responsible for determining the character and content of our lives" (xiii).

17. Dobbin's Introduction to *Discourses*, xiv.

18. The Stoics did indeed teach that *all* mental states, including such seemingly spontaneous, reactive emotions as desire and aversion, are, in fact, conditioned by our judgments. As Long writes in *Epictetus*, 27, "On this model of mind, there is no such thing as a purely reactive emotion or at least a reaction that we cannot, on reflection, control."

I think we can recognize that there are various *degrees* of control without doing disservice to Epictetus. In *Guide*, 89, Irvine introduces a *middle* category—"things over which we have *some* but not complete control"—and makes a convincing case that many things the Stoics characterize as "in our power" actually fall into this category.

19. Marcus Aurelius, *Meditations*, 4, 4.

20. Epictetus, *Handbook*, 5. Socrates's calm, cheerful demeanor at his trial and execution has served as a paradigmatic example of a "good death" for millennia. See the *Apology, Crito*, and *Phaedo* by Plato.

21. Epictetus, *Discourses*, 1, 1, 21.

22. Epictetus, *Handbook*, 20. Marcus emphasizes our "complicity" with respect to negative judgments and mental states: "Who is not himself the cause of his own unrest? Reflect how no one is hampered by any other; and that all is as thinking makes it so" (*Meditations*, 12, 8).

23. Seneca, *Letters*, 82.5.

24. *Twelve Steps and Traditions*, 21.

25. Alcoholics Anonymous World Services, *Daily Reflections*, 11.

26. Ibid., 141.

27. Alcoholics Anonymous, *Living Soberly*, 51–52.

28. *Daily Reflections*, 36.

29. *Alcoholics Anonymous*, 76.

30. *Twelve Steps and Traditions*, 88.

31. Ibid., 89.

32. *Alcoholics Anonymous,* 86.

33. Ibid., 84.

34. Ibid., 60.

35. Ibid.

36. *Living Sober,* 42, 86.

37. *Daily Reflections,* 80.

38. Long, *Epictetus,* 91.

39. Seneca, *Stoic Philosophy,* 87.

40. Irvine, *Guide,* 119.

41. Ibid., 124.

42. Epictetus, *Handbook,* 51.

43. Ibid., 33.

44. Marcus, *Meditations,* 7, 61.

45. Ibid., 5, 9.

46. Epictetus, *Moral Discourses,* trans. Elizabeth Carter, 4.9.

47. *Living Sober,* 46.

# Realizing Gratitude

We end, as we began, with an intensely personal essay. S. E. West's meditation, at once autobiographical and philosophical, describes how she has grappled with the virtue of gratitude that Twelve Step spirituality encourages practitioners to cultivate. With Friedrich Nietzsche as her companion, West explores some of the dark crannies of addicted subjectivity—and comes back from the exploration with an enriched understanding of why it makes sense to be glad for the journey. Her essay provides an appropriate conclusion to this anthology because it brings into play so many of the themes that have been pivotal in it. Readers who find the quotations in the essay singularly apropos may be inclined to suppose that many of them come from the official literature of Alcoholics Anonymous. In fact, all but the first two come from Nietzsche.

In retrospect, my personal experience of "hitting bottom," however acutely felt, was not, in the end, very different from that of so many others who are experienced in recovery: fear and desperation at the life destruction of years of rampant alcoholism; a flood of shame and despair; addiction's devious dissembling that made the words "I am powerless over alcohol" and "my life had become unmanageable" unspeakable; and acute anguish at what appeared to be equally horrendous choices—to continue to drink myself to death, or somehow to live without alcohol. My diametrically divided desires—to become sober and to flee back into drink—and the overwhelming intensity of the emotions that they caused are common to those who struggle to recover from addiction. But common, too, for those capable of the courage to risk sobriety and able to hold on to the support of others, is that the abyss of isolation and hopelessness begins to ease. Gradually it becomes easier to accept the first of the Twelve Steps, then slowly, very slowly, to embrace the other eleven.

The Twelve Promises,[1] however, long remained inaccessible. Perhaps they could be fulfilled for others, but, for me, they stood as cruelly seductive goads toward an impossibility, above all the Second Promise: "We will not regret the past nor wish to shut the door on it."[2] In my experience, the drive to drink was precisely the desire to disavow a devastating past, as if intoxication could eradicate or at least blunt an agony that continued to poison the present and all possible futures. Long embedded in me was the conviction that no true goodness could ever be attained unless that blighted past was obliterated. My entire life up to now must be *redone* from its very inception. Even as I was forced by intellect to accept the impossibility of this desire, I clung to it in feeling. How could such a debased past be allowed to coexist with a fledgling present sobriety? How could the burden of one's worthlessness be continuous with the First Promise that "we are going to know a new freedom and a new happiness"?[3] How was it conceivable that anyone so damaged could accept that past and want to keep the door open to it? It thus astounded me each time those veterans of recovery who most held me to and through early sobriety would not only say that they were grateful to be a recovering alcoholic, but grateful for having been an alcoholic in the first place. *Grateful to be an alcoholic?* I could understand gratitude for the capacity to continue to live soberly, but it was inconceivable that I would be grateful for the self-destruction and work-destruction and love-destruction of alcoholism itself. Or rather, it was theoretically possible but affectively unfathomable, a notion viscerally repellent and vehemently rejected, for my life had been stolen by the need to drink. Perhaps those who are grateful for being an alcoholic were better and stronger than I. Perhaps their hope for such a promised happiness, based on embracing their past, could be realized. But it was unimaginable that I could ever be grateful for my past, grateful for the incapacity to ward off the early despoiling of my life, grateful for those long alcoholic years seeking to escape it, grateful for decades of life wreckage. Yet in those first fragile years of sobriety, held by the love of others in recovery, I tentatively gleaned from their life stories that one's past, however deeply imprinted by trauma and suffering, cannot be severed from the growing goodness of the present. Most strangely, entrenched bitter despair and the first budding of hope seem to coexist; even more mysteriously, the "black root"[4] at the source of our spiritual illness seemed to be the very means for transformations into greater health.[5]

As I grappled with this paradox and the seeming impossibility of attaining such gratitude, my recovery expanded and deepened in other unexpected ways. I began to experience, in both affect and action, what had long been so conceptually meaningful to me in the academic study of philosophy: personal experience informed my philosophical reading; in turn, philosophy helped form my ongoing overcoming of addiction. This mutual *reforming*—of thinking through affect and of affect through thinking—constitutes what I came to understand as a spiritual awakening. By "spirit" I mean one's inner life, what is psychological, intellectual, and affective, what is at once mentally self-conscious yet intertwined with what is most often unconscious to us, our bodily processes and our animal drives. Spirit, as mind's feeling-thinking, is neither separate from nor opposed to our material selves. It is not a discrete "thing" we possess, but a capacity and its activity, the ever reflective and affective expression of our being and of our being in the world. It was through such an experiential, psychological, and philosophical spiritual awakening that I began to grasp what had long eluded me as to what it really is to be grateful for being an alcoholic. In this respect, Nietzsche's ideas are most salient to my experience, due to the fact that his insights into the inseparability of spiritual illness and spiritual health, and the vicissitudes of self-overcoming that lead to either end, are at the heart of his work. It is true that the problem of addiction, per se, is not central to Nietzsche. But if we read his work with addiction in mind, his penetrating diagnosis of many other forms of human spiritual illness makes evident its exceptional relevance to our experiences with addiction—and in my case, to what is specific to alcoholism.

### "This Supreme Sobering-Up through Pain"

Nietzsche has much to say about suffering, that which is particular to his own life and that which belongs to each of us by virtue of being human.[6] The problem arises as a result of our fateful self-transforming of physical suffering into spiritual suffering: we become human through the process of becoming socialized and civilized, but only at the cost of our instinctual "animal soul" falling ill, above all when *creature*-pain transmutes into distinctly *human*-pain, such as shame, self-pity, resentment, and nihilism. Through this transmutation, our "animal soul" turns "against itself," creating a new depth of misery, "man's suffering *of man, of himself,*" and this "*will* to misunderstand suffering [is] made the content of life"—so that suffering is made into "a matter of conscience and a reproach against the whole of existence."[7]

Addicts are by no means the exception in embodying spiritual illness, though we may be among those whose spiritual suffering is most obviously self-inflicted. In my experience, the spiritual illness of addiction was the unwittingly disastrous "cure" for the deep spiritual afflictions that I had absorbed when too young to comprehend them, much less cope with them. Surely many of us in recovery have in common that seemingly magnificent day when we first experienced the intoxicating deliverance of alcohol, however ephemeral, however deluded, from our suffering of worthlessness and despair. From that moment on we were exemplary practitioners of what Nietzsche calls "the objective of all human arrangements . . . to cease *to be aware* of life," desperately "wishing *not* to see something that one does *see;* wishing not to see something *as* one sees it," yearning to be "no longer conscious of what is without or within," and "fearing only one thing: *regaining consciousness.*"[8]

When we first get sober and tentatively gain self-consciousness, we may know that we have harmed ourselves and others, but we are often unable to understand why we drank, much less to see that we had been "living in some perilous world of fantasy."[9] If we remain blind to this essential next step toward self-insight, yet manage to stay sober over time, we remain fundamentally unchanged in spirit: we are merely dry drunk, healthier in body but still infested with the same ill needs, ill affects, ill convictions, and the deeply ill habituation that drove us to become alcoholics in the first place. If our craving for "self-forgetting" remains, our mindless suffering continues; there can be no new freedom, no new happiness.

If, on the other hand, we are fortunate when we hit bottom, we begin to have the courage to see that we have been living under a treacherous illusion that drunkenness freed us from suffering, as if making us "happy," as if making us "better." And if we are able to stand the grief of fully grasping what we have done to ourselves and to others, we undergo a profound disillusionment, *"this supreme sobering-up through pain,"* the very "means of extricating" ourselves from the delusional abyss of addiction.[10] If we can bear seeing ourselves in this "new light" without relapsing, its spiritual illumination allows us to overcome the "temptation to self-destruction," and with it comes "the first glimmering of relief, of convalescence," the first yield of *"the knowledge acquired through suffering."*[11]

With *this* knowledge came the first outpouring of gratitude for the help of those who held me, gratitude for the capacity to be held as I slowly pulled back from the life-destruction of alcoholism. This gratitude has sustained me, as it does all those in recovery as we undertake the long schooling in a sober-wholeness, creating the counter-habituation to addiction's uncontrolled cravings. This new habituation, which has slowly grown stronger and steadfast through spiritual cultivation, gives rise to a readily apparent gratitude that increases as I realize how much more I could have lost and imposed on others had I continued to drink. It is this past of coming to sobriety that I gladly hold open the door to, and can never regret.

## Spiritual Relapse and "The Great Health"

After having been sober for some time, I came to see that the "black root" of spiritual illness ran deeper in me than the reactive attempts to flee the cruelty of early life.[12] There is a far more unsettling insight to be gleaned from our "need" to be "no longer conscious of what is without or within."[13] Drinking is not simply self-administering palliatives, it is a self-infliction of further anguish that goes beyond the physiological and social ravages of alcoholism. For some of us, drinking becomes a disguised and displaced repetition of the very evil we sought to escape. In my case, I came to see that drinking was the playing out of a deeply felt but inchoate will that, with desperate triumph, I would rather be the first to shove an abusive substance into myself than to wait, stricken in despair, for someone else to do it. In confronting this insidious drama—my unwitting determination to be, simultaneously, the sufferer, the perpetrator, and the one who keeps the blighted past alive and active in the present—my *"knowledge acquired through suffering"* intensified. Grasping the abysmal ugliness in human spiritual illness was, and remains, frighteningly sobering. Yet it is also liberating; for if it is *I* who repeats that devastating past—and not, as I had thought for so many years, some impersonal, cruelly capricious cosmic force—then it is *I* who have the capacity to stop it, I who can turn away from it and turn toward "a new freedom."

Yet even after understanding how grotesquely I had transformed and misconstrued my own suffering, conflating past with present, confusing external and internal sources, all too often I still lose hold of this understanding, and fall back into that old condition of incoherent fear and desolation. Even when I am able to recall and re-grasp this understanding, all too often it remains only on intellect's surface, disavowed in affect, rendering it an empty knowledge that I fail to live. Such "letting oneself go and letting oneself drop" is the resurgence of an oblivious *"cowardice before reality,"* a regression to "the *will* to misunderstand suffering," though at least without drinking again.[14] This constitutes what I call a *spiritual relapse,* akin to what Nietzsche terms the inability to "get over" one's lived experience and "have done with it," and with this corrosive inability, gratitude disappears.[15]

In this form of spiritual relapse, an altered, frightening "perilous world of fantasy" descends. On one hand, we can plunge back into perpetuating the past in the present, where excessive fear reenacts those earlier confusions, where external terrors once experienced return, internally, with all their old force. The very thought of gratitude for such a life is, at least at that moment, incomprehensible. On the other hand, we can disavow the past, regressing as a dry drunk into alternative, albeit shorter-lived and hopefully less pernicious addictions in order to again blur the past and its pain away, engaging in obsessions such as sex or burying oneself in the myriad labyrinths of the Internet; this too obliterates any possibility of gratitude. Or, as a third version of the pernicious descent back into fantasy, we can try to shut the door on our past by, simultaneously, trying to undo it, as if by virtue of the force of our fervent will we can effect the impossible—make our past not be our past. But when we refuse to accept the past as it was, it neither disappears nor is it ever worked through. Gratitude for having been an alcoholic, for having been driven to be an alcoholic, and for forever being an alcoholic, utterly disappears, and with it, in my experience, a nearly unbearable spiritual pain arises: despair for all that was lost too early in life, despair for all that I continued to lose as a result of my more or less unconsciously adamant determination, decade after decade, to eradicate my past and be entirely *reborn*. Having gratitude for *that* past of wasting years of my life by being unable to get over my past is still, so often, reactively repellent to me. It demands a capacity of spirit that I must struggle for, and rediscover, against that resurgence of bitter regret sucking it away. It is the gratitude that I risk losing every day, and all too often do lose, relapsing into the spiritual illness where all that flourishes through sobriety suddenly seems to disappear.

Yet "strange and at the same time terrible," Nietzsche tells us, a "return to health" and "the way to 'myself', to my task," comes precisely through losing one's self.[16] If we have changed enough in our sober rehabilitation of habituation, spiritual relapse, henceforth, carries within it the drive and the means to convalescence again. Spiritual relapse is the spur to its own self-overcoming through the force of an alliance of the virtues we have forged from out of our vices: our "daring honesty" and "the *courage* to be healthy," the necessary constituents of a wholesome self-mastery that enable us to become "healthy again."[17] In spiritual relapse, there comes a great "*pressure* of sickness," an internal tension that compels spirit "to descend" again to its "ultimate depths," urging us to continue seeing what we do not want to see, self-overcoming our craving "to cease *to be aware* of life."[18] In this reacceptance of the past as it was, there develops a greater embrace of it, a deeper reconceiving of it. There is an extraordinary good that our years of vicious addiction have given us, for a most illuminating perspective takes root and flourishes precisely because of the seemingly barren soil of our earlier lives that led us to drink. It is from out of the "black root" within my past that gratitude revives, growing because I have been, and still am, a recovering alcoholic, growing because of what I have understood about myself, and even more, about the human, from the inside out. I could not have experienced gratitude for such *"knowledge acquired through suffering"* if not for the healthy self-mastery that being an alcoholic required that I learn.[19]

For Nietzsche, this self-mastery is the capacity "to have and not to have one's affects . . . at will"; this means there is an "order of rank" among "the authority of active forces" where a single dominant affect, or affective-cluster (such as earnest courageousness), ascends from out of the "whole economy of the soul," using the other affects by way of, and for the sake of, its overpowering interpretive presence.[20] Healthy self-mastery is always active in this way, incorporating even the reactive affects (such as groveling cowardice) that proliferate in our intemperance and dominate our lives when we are drinking or dry drunk. The aim in this healthy "struggle *against* the reactive feelings" is not to destroy them but to employ and reform them, to "impose measure and bounds upon the excesses of the reactive pathos and to compel it to come to terms."[21] In this coming to terms, the reactive affects, however currently weak and latent, are still engaged in the "whole economy of our soul": "to have" an affect means that it is fully present, its interpretive power becomes active and commands; "not to have" an affect means that it is more or less dormant, its power deactivated and subsumed. Both healthy and ill self-mastery rule by way of this activation and deactivation of the affects; the difference lies in the fact that healthy self-mastery is dominated by the active affects, such as gratitude, and ill self-mastery is dominated by the reactive affects, such as resentment, and in the degree to which each kind of mastery consciously grasps—or unconsciously resists and fails to grasp—the most fundamental kind of self-knowledge. When we are ill spiritually, we lose sight of, and worse, disavow, the entire affective complex. The drive of ill self-mastery demands that it must and, even more hubristically, believes that it can eradicate our past, and thereby eliminate our suffering once and for all. But healthy self-mastery does not lose, or wish to lose, the necessary existence of the whole complex of affective-tensions within us, nor does it lose sight of the potential traumatic upsurge of all the latent reactive-affects that may erupt. Spiritual health is inseparable from the very illnesses that have been overcome but still lie dormant. The self-mastery needed for active sobriety requires accepting that these addictions still lie dormant.

Even further, for Nietzsche, being spiritually healthy requires that our "whole affective system" be "excited and intensified," that each of our affects, no matter how terrible and problematic, be enhanced. The most vibrantly alive self *wants more* life, wants to feel all of it more deeply, to know from one's "own most authentic experience" the entire affective span of the human, possessing the "strength to withstand tension, the width of the tensions between extremes" and every gradation of suffering and joy in between—from zealous hope to embittered despair, from abased shame to ennobling *"second innocence,"*[22] from rampant desire to caustic repulsion, from the most terrifying evisceration of meaning to the most ecstatic overflow of meaning. For Nietzsche, health is constructed through our acute "self-observation" of our cyclical self-overcomings:[23] with spiritual relapse we descend into illness, then ascend into greater health, descend again and then ascend again, each time arising with an expanded experiential understanding of what it is to be human. The kinds of experience we addicts have had—our addiction in body and spirit, our ongoing recovering from addiction, our spiritual relapse and its overcoming—are thus to be embraced: "precisely because we seek knowledge, let us not be ungrateful to such resolute reversals of accustomed perspectives"; for it is by virtue of our living between conditions of illness and health that we come to learn "how to employ a *variety* of perspectives and affective interpretations in the service of knowledge."[24] In this way, we forge our "new health," which is "more seasoned, tougher, more audacious and more joyous than any previous health" precisely because it is constantly tested and tempered each time we fall ill.[25] Thus, all past experience, however demeaned and demeaning, and all past belief of false-truths (such as intoxication is necessary for us to be able to live) are never to be repudiated. Quite the contrary. They are to be embraced precisely because they illuminate the driving needs and desires at work within human being that granted us relief, however fleeting, however toxic, in addiction's delusions. Through grasping such ill drives and desires we learn to work with them, working through them, becoming able to master them and use them. Integrating our past, rather than cutting ourselves off from it, and embracing our illness, rather than disavowing it and its destructive effects, are necessary to overcoming that very past's ill repetitions. Not forgetting our past is essential in order not to relapse fully back into it by drinking again. Embracing our experience of addiction and its repeated overcoming, along with this doubled-consciousness of debased destruction and restoration from its ruins, constitutes the "spiritual awakening" that blossoms because we have been active alcoholics and remain ever susceptible to relapsing. We grasp a new way of being and flourishing, because of what we have learned from our illness. It is *this* capacity to bear one's past, and to hold the door open to it, that allows the recovering alcoholic to fulfill the Second Promise. Like Nietzsche, we ought to speak of our illness with gratitude; for we have returned to a renewed health precisely by having been ill again. Even more important, we attain *"the great health."* "Whoever has a soul that craves to have experienced the whole range of values and desiderata to date . . . needs one thing above everything else: *the great health*—that one does not merely have but also acquires continually, and must acquire because one gives it up again and again, and must give it up."[26]

## On Embodying the Human

Nietzsche asks himself, and asks us, "Shall my experience—the history of an illness and recovery . . . have been my personal experience alone? And only my 'human-all-too-human'?"[27] His answer, as ours ought to be, is *no*. If we are to fulfill the Fifth Promise, understanding that even our most abysmal experiences can be a benefit to others, we can no longer conceal our past and present experience from ourselves and others; we must be willing to reveal what we have known for far too long as addicts: the sickness of shame, resentment, alienation, nihilism, craving to be "no longer conscious of what is without or within." If we are to fulfill the Twelfth Step, we must share, not just in speech, but in action, what we have undergone and overcome, offering to others what we have gained in our spiritual awakening.

In this respect, Nietzsche exhorts us to a most challenging task. If we seek the most out of our recovery for ourselves and for others, we must undertake a "tremendous self-contemplation: becoming conscious of oneself, not as individuals but as humankind," seeking to encompass "the total consciousness of humankind," wanting "to bring back the whole past," refusing to "lose anything that [we] could possibly possess" of the human, as if to experience the lives of a multitude of "individuals, as though to see through *their* eyes, as though to grasp with *their* hands."[28] And if we are to cultivate and enrich our *"knowledge acquired through suffering"*—vital to us all, but particularly to those who are philosophers—then we must possess "the great *passion* of the seeker after knowledge," where *nothing* of the entire affective and spiritual spectrum of the human is to be lost, not even when we face "the highest problems and the heaviest responsibilities."[29] And so we must extend the "range and multiplicity" of our experiences and perspectives, wanting to see "how much and how many things one could bear and take upon oneself, how *far* one could extend one's responsibility" in embracing humanity, and grasp that all such seemingly disparate states of being are in fact "intertwined and interlaced."[30]

This capacity for a deepened and expanded subjectivity where nothing of the entire experiential spectrum of the human is to be lost is no dissolution into a streaming fragmentation of feeling and thinking, no anarchy of passions and desires. In recovery we are able to bear within us "a tremendous variety that is nevertheless the opposite of chaos," being strong enough to actively hold ourselves together as a *"totality,"* being strong enough to be the embodiment of "wholeness in manifoldness."[31] This capacity to cultivate and maintain ourselves as such a *whole* from out of our affective tensions and conflicting interpretive perspectives requires that we know and know how to practice "the art of separating" such differences "without setting [them] against one another," maintaining these tensions without mixing or "reconciling" them.[32] This capacity constitutes "that *mature* freedom of spirit" which requires equal shares of the virtues of "self-mastery and discipline of the heart," and which enables us to practice with virtuosity "many and contradictory modes of thought."[33] In this way, we become able "to pass through the whole range of human values and value feelings, *able* to see with many different eyes and consciences, from a height and into every distance, from the depths into every height, from a nook into every expanse" of what it is to be human.[34]

By virtue of embodying such "wholeness in manifoldness," we have earned the philosophical capacity to see "from the perspective of the sick toward *healthier* concepts and values and, conversely, the capacity to look again from the fullness and self-assurance of a *rich* life down into the secret work of the instinct of decadence."[35] Above all, because we have cultivated from the inside out how to use such *"difference* in perspectives and affective interpretations for the sake of knowledge," we now have the "the know-how to *reverse perspectives.*"[36] This is at the heart of our *"knowledge acquired through suffering,"* this is what allows us to come into our *"great health."* No longer needing to live through the perspective of dissembling cowardice with its toxic isolation and bitterness against the past, we activate and realize the perspective of courageous honesty that takes our vicious past as it was, while embracing our humanity as a *"totality,"* being strong enough to include within it even such dishonesty, cowardice, isolation, and bitterness. It is *this* capacity for sober self-transformation, sober health, sober choice, to which I owe the deepest gratitude.

## Gratitude

As it is for so many of us striving for recovery, I did not know when I first became sober whether I could stand to emerge from rampant alcoholism. I did not know whether I could self-overcome that long-embedded habituation in despair and self-destruction. Having started drinking at the age of fifteen, I had little grasp of what a thriving sobriety was, or even could be. In my case, but I think for each of us in recovery, rehabilitation must begin with a radical re-habituation: we must first learn to *act* differently so that we may *"learn to think differently,"* and with this new thinking learn to comprehend and to experience differently, "in order at last . . . to attain even more: *to feel differently."*[37] Above all else, it has been this transformation of *feeling* that most enables me to embody and express the flowing of gratitude that Nietzsche speaks of, and to share what those old-timers in recovery meant when they said that they were grateful to be an alcoholic. With learning *"to feel differently"* came a profoundly different desire, and will, than I had ever experienced before. For years as a child, before discovering the magical poison of alcohol, I yearned not to have a body, but rather to possess some form of consciousness while existing as if two-dimensionally between the walls of my parents' homes. Even in adulthood, when fortified with alcohol, I often joked that what I really wanted was to be a stone, or a tree, or merely a brain atop a pole. But through recovery, I came to accept being fully human, and I now want to become an even "more *whole* human being," at last embodying health's *"greatness,"* extending the "range and multiplicity" of my spiritual and perspectival understanding of the full spectrum of the human, "'being capable of being as manifold as whole, as ample as full."[38] It is *this* feeling-thinking that constitutes the very heart of my spiritual awakening. It is *this* feeling-thinking that, when I am at my best, informs and transfuses how I live and how I work, both in teaching and in writing. It is this *transformation* for which I am most grateful. I now know that I am deeply indebted to my alcoholism; grasping Nietzsche's words from the inside out—this "*higher* health" is "one which is made stronger by whatever does not kill it. *I also owe my philosophy to it.*"[39]

## NOTES

1. What I refer to here as the "Twelve Promises," specifically noting the First, Second, and Fifth, appear on pages 83–84 of *Alcoholics Anonymous,* where they are not called as such or numbered. However, individual groups often do refer to the Twelve Promises, and the meetings in which I found my sobriety regularly made use of them, listed and numbered on the backside of the Twelve Steps handout we used.

2. *Alcoholics Anonymous,* 83.

3. Ibid.

4. Nietzsche, *Human, All Too Human,* II.26. All references to Nietzsche's texts use his form of intra-textual demarcation: Roman numerals indicate his chapter or book divisions; Arabic numerals indicate his section numbers. I have slightly emended some translations based on my reading of the original German.

5. See Seeburger's *Addiction and Responsibility,* 112–13, for a brief account of "the 'grateful alcoholic.'"

6. The quote in the heading above is from Nietzsche, *Daybreak,* 114. Emphasis, in this and following quotes from Nietzsche, is his.

7. Nietzsche, "Schopenhauer as Educator," *Untimely Meditations,* section 4; *Genealogy,* II.16, III.20; *Gay Science,* 48. In brief, there is no inherent meaning to physical suffering, for Nietzsche: suffering is simply a necessary condition of being a creature. It is the *human* creature alone who needs to know the meaning of such suffering; for Nietzsche, this fateful creation of meaning, where otherwise there is none, constitutes our misunderstanding of suffering.

8. Nietzsche, *Gay Science,* preface.3; *Antichrist,* 55; *Genealogy,* III.17, 23. In brief, for Nietzsche, with our need to know the meaning of our suffering, we in turn invent all manner of ways to justify and to redeem it, that is, *to escape* from the horror of our suffering. All such inventions constitute our distinctly human spiritual illnesses because they involve blindly craving release from suffering through idealism, nihilism, etc.

9. Nietzsche, *Daybreak,* 114.

10. Ibid.

11. Ibid.

12. The quote in the heading above is from Nietzsche, *Gay Science,* 382.

13. Nietzsche, *Genealogy,* III.17.

14. Nietzsche, *Beyond Good and Evil,* 212; "The Case of Wagner," 2, in *Ecce Homo,* section III.

15. Nietzsche, *Genealogy,* III.16. In an extended parenthetical remark in this section of the *Genealogy,* Nietzsche speaks of physiological digestion or indigestion *as* psychological digestion or indigestion. In my view, he means this both metaphorically and literally.

16. Nietzsche, *Human, All Too Human,* II; preface, 4.

17. Nietzsche, *Beyond Good and Evil,* 295; *Antichrist,* 51; *Ecce Homo,* I.2.

18. Nietzsche, *Gay Science,* preface, 2, 3.

19. This is akin to what Richard Garrett calls "third level wisdom," which "enables us to live truly good and meaningful lives." Garrett emphasizes that such wisdom is a life "work forever in progress." But he also says that working through one's "awareness of and subsequent struggles with" one's addiction is "a blessing." See "Addiction, Paradox, and the Good I Would" in Poland and Graham, *Addiction and Responsibility,* 267.

20. Nietzsche, *Beyond Good and Evil,* 284, 224.

21. Nietzsche, *Genealogy,* II.11.

22. Nietzsche, *Twilight,* IX.10; *Gay Science,* 382; *Twilight,* IX.37; *Genealogy,* II.20.

23. Nietzsche, *Human, All Too Human,* I, preface, 6; *Gay Science,* 335.

24. Nietzsche, *Genealogy,* III.12.

25. Nietzsche, *Gay Science,* 382.

26. Ibid.

27. Nietzsche, *Human, All Too Human,* II, preface, 6.

28. Nietzsche, *Will to Power,* 585; *Science,* 249.

29. Nietzsche, *Gay Science,* 351.

30. Nietzsche, *Beyond Good and Evil,* 212; *Genealogy,* preface, 2.

31. Nietzsche, *Ecce Homo,* II.9; *Twilight,* IX.49; *Beyond Good and Evil,* 212.

32. Nietzsche, *Ecce Homo,* II.9.

33. Nietzsche, *Human, All Too Human,* I, preface, 4.

34. Nietzsche, *Beyond Good and Evil,* 211.

35. Nietzsche, *Ecce Homo,* I.1.

36. Nietzsche, *Genealogy,* III.12; *Ecce Homo,* I.1.

37. Nietzsche, *Daybreak,* 103.

38. Nietzsche, *Beyond Good and Evil,* 257, 212.

39. Nietzsche, "Nietzsche Contra Wagner," in *Portable Nietzsche,* epilogue, 1.

# Bibliography

Alcoholics Anonymous Australia. *Twelve Steps and Twelve Traditions*. Australia: Alcoholics Anonymous Australia, 2002.

Alcoholics Anonymous World Services. *Alcoholics Anonymous*. 4th ed. New York: Alcoholics Anonymous World Services, Inc., 2001.

———. *Alcoholics Anonymous Comes of Age*. New York: Alcoholics Anonymous World Services, Inc., 1985.

———. *Alcoholics Anonymous: The Story of How Many Thousands of Men and Women Have Recovered from Alcoholism*. 4th ed. New York: Alcoholics Anonymous World Services, Inc., 2002.

———. *Alcoholics Anonymous 2011 Membership Survey*. A.A. World Services, Inc., n.d. http://aa.org/pdf/products/p-48_membershipsurvey.pdf.

———. *Daily Reflections: A Book of Reflections by A.A. Members for A.A. Members*. 1990; New York: Alcoholics Anonymous World Services, Inc., 2011.

———. *Living Sober*. New York: Alcoholics Anonymous World Services, Inc., 1998.

———. *Twelve Steps and Twelve Traditions*. New York: Alcoholics Anonymous World Services, Inc., 1981.

Allen, Amy. *The Politics of Ourselves*. New York: Columbia University Press, 2008.

Ames, Roger T., and Henry Rosemont. *The Analects of Confucius: A Philosophical Translation*. New York: Ballantine, 1998.

Aristotle. *Nicomachean Ethics*. Translated by Christopher Rowe. New York: Oxford University Press, 2002.

Austin, J. L. *How to Do Things with Words*. Cambridge, MA: Harvard University Press, 1975.

Bateson, Gregory. *Steps to an Ecology of the Mind*. Chicago: University of Chicago Press, 1999.

Baumeister, Roy F. *Escaping the Self: Alcoholism, Spirituality, Masochism, and Other Flights from the Burden of Selfhood*. New York: Basic Books, 1991.

Bernard of Clairvaux. *The Steps of Humility and Pride*. Trappist, KY: Cistercian, 1973.

Bill W. *As Bill Sees It: The A.A. Way of Life, Selected Writings of A.A.'s Co-Founder*. New York: Alcoholics Anonymous World Services, Inc., 1999.

———. *Three Talks to Medical Societies.* New York: Alcoholics Anonymous World Services, Inc., n.d.

Bloom, Alfred, ed. *Living in Amida's Universal Vow: Essays in Shin Buddhism.* Bloomington, IN: World Wisdom, 2004.

Bobzien, Suzanne. *Determinism and Freedom in Stoic Philosophy.* Oxford: Clarendon Press, 1998.

Buber, Martin. *I and Thou.* Translated by Walter Kaufmann. New York: Scribner, 1970.

Cavell, Stanley. *In Quest of the Ordinary: Lines of Skepticism and Romanticism.* Chicago: University of Chicago Press, 1988.

Confucius. *The Essential Analects: Selected Passages with Traditional Commentary.* Translated by Edward Slingerland. Indianapolis: Hackett, 2006.

Connolly, William. "Stoicism." http://ecole.evansville.edu/articles/stoicism.html.

Danner, Jason. *Beyond the Either/Or: The Relation between the Aesthetic and the Ethical in the Philosophy of Emmanuel Lévinas, Søren Kierkegaard, and Jean-Luc Marion.* Ann Arbor, MI: University Microfilms International, 2013.

Dent, N. J. H. *The Moral Psychology of the Virtues.* Cambridge: Cambridge University Press, 1984.

Denzin, Norman. *The Alcoholic Self.* London: Sage, 1987.

———. *The Recovering Alcoholic.* California: Sage, 1987.

———. *Treating Alcoholism: An Alcoholics Anonymous Approach.* Newbury Park: Sage, 1987.

Derrida, Jacques. "Force of Law: The 'Mystical Foundation of Authority.'" Translated by Mary Quaintance. *Cardozo Law Review* 11 (1990): 92–1045.

———. *Rogues: Two Essays on Reason.* Translated by Pascale-Anne Brault and Michael Naas. Stanford, CA: Stanford University Press, 2005.

———. *Writing and Difference.* Translated by Alan Bass. Chicago: University of Chicago Press, 1978.

Dewey, John. *A Common Faith.* New Haven, CT: Yale University Press, 1934.

Diamond, Jonathan. *Narrative Means to Sober Ends: Treating Addiction and Its Aftermath.* New York: Guilford Press, 2002.

Dobbins, James C. *Jōdo Shinshū: Shin Buddhism in Medieval Japan.* Honolulu: University of Hawai'i Press, 2002.

Dunnington, Kent. *Addiction and Virtue: Beyond the Models of Disease and Choice.* Downers Grove, IL: IVP Academic, 2011.

Eliade, Mircea. *The Sacred and the Profane.* New York: Harcourt Brace Jovanovich, 1959.

———, ed. *The Encyclopedia of Religion.* New York: Macmillan, 1987.

Epictetus. *Discourses and Selected Writings.* Translated by Robert Dobbin. London: Penguin Books, 2008.

——. *Moral Discourses of Epictetus*. Translated by Elizabeth Carter. London: J. M. Dent & Sons, 1910.

Fingarette, Herbert. "Alcoholism and Self-Deception." In *Self-Deception and Self-Understanding: New Essays in Philosophy and Psychology,* edited by Mike W. Martin, 52–67. Lawrence: University of Kansas, 1985.

——. *Confucius—the Secular as Sacred*. Torchbook Library Editions. New York: Harper & Row, 1972.

——. *Heavy Drinking: The Myth of Alcoholism as a Disease*. Berkeley: University of California Press, 1988.

Fitzgerald, F. Scott. *The Crack-Up*. New York: New Directions, 2009.

Foucault, Michel. "About the Beginning of the Hermeneutics of the Self: Two Lectures at Dartmouth." *Political Theory* 21, no. 2 (1993): 198–227.

——. *Ethics*. Vol. I of *Essential Works of Foucault*. Edited by Paul Rabinow. New York: New Press, 1997.

——. *The Hermeneutics of the Subject*. Translated by Graeme Burchell. New York: Palgrave MacMillan, 2005.

Frankfurt, Harry. "Freedom of the Will and the Concept of a Person." In *The Importance of What We Care About,* edited by Harry Frankfurt, 11–25. Cambridge: Cambridge University Press, 1988.

——. "On the Freedom and Limits of the Will." In *Necessity, Volition, and Love,* edited by Harry Frankfurt, 71–81. Cambridge: Cambridge University Press, 1999.

——. "On the Necessity of Ideals." In *Necessity, Volition, and Love,* edited by Harry Frankfurt, 108–16. Cambridge: Cambridge University Press, 1999.

Frankl, Viktor E. *Man's Search for Meaning*. Boston: Beacon Press, 2006.

Fromm, Erich. *Psychoanalysis and Religion*. New Haven, CT: Yale University Press, 1978.

Goldberg, Philip. *American Veda: From Emerson and the Beatles to Yoga and Meditation—How Indian Spirituality Changed the West*. New York: Harmony Books, 2010.

Gorham, Geoffrey. *Philosophy of Science: A Beginner's Guide*. Oxford: Oneworld, 2009.

Graham, A. C. *Disputers of the Tao: Philosophical Argument in Ancient China*. La Salle, IL: Open Court, 1989.

Gray, Spalding. *Impossible Vacation*. New York: Knopf, 1992.

Gregory the Great. *Forty Gospel Homilies*. Translated by David Hurst. Kalamazoo, MI: Cistercian, 1990.

Griffin, Kevin. *One Breath at a Time*. N.p.: Rodale Press, 2004.

Guignon, Charles, ed. *The Existentialists*. Lanham, MD: Rowman & Littlefield, 2004.

——. *On Being Authentic*. London: Routledge, 2004.

Hadot, Pierre. *Philosophy as a Way of Life: Spiritual Exercises from Socrates to Foucault*. London: Blackwell, 1995.

———. *The Present Alone Is Our Happiness: Conversations with Jeannie Carlier and Arnold I. Davidson.* 2nd ed. Translated by Marc Djaballah and Michael Chase. Stanford, CA: Stanford University Press, 2011.

Hall, David L., and Roger T. Ames. *Thinking Through Confucius.* Albany: State University of New York Press, 1987.

Hegel, G. W. F. *The Phenomenology of Spirit.* Translated by A. V. Miller. New York: Oxford University Press, 1977.

Heidegger, Martin. *Being and Time.* Translated by John Macquarrie and Edward Robinson. New York: Harper & Row, 1962.

———. *History of the Concept of Time: Prolegomena.* Translated by Theodore Kisiel. Bloomington: Indiana University Press, 1985.

———. *Off the Beaten Track.* Edited and translated by Julian Young and Kenneth Haynes. New York: Cambridge University Press, 2002.

———. *Pathmarks.* Edited and translated by William McNeill. New York: Cambridge University Press, 1998.

———. *The Question concerning Technology and Other Essays.* Translated by William Lovitt. New York: Harper & Row, 1977.

Heller, Joseph. *Catch-22.* New York: Simon & Schuster, 1961.

Hume, David. *An Enquiry concerning the Principles of Morals.* 1751. La Salle, IL: Open Court, 1966.

———. *A Treatise on Human Nature.* New York: Oxford University Press, 2000.

Husserl, Edmund. *Cartesian Meditations: An Introduction to Phenomenology.* Translated by Dorion Cairns. Hague: Martinus Nijhoff, 1960.

———. *The Crisis of European Sciences and Transcendental Phenomenology.* Translated by David Carr. Evanston, IL: Northwestern University Press, 1970.

———. *Zur Phänomenologie der Intersubjektivität.* Edited by Iso Kern. 3 vols. Den Haag: Martinus Nijhoff, 1973.

Huxley, Aldous. *The Human Situation.* New York: Harper & Row, 1977.

Hyde, Lewis. *The Gift: Imagination and the Erotic Life of Property.* New York: Vintage Books, 1983.

Inagaki, Hisao, and Harold Stewart, eds. *The Three Pure Land Sutras.* Revised 2nd ed. Berkeley, CA: Numata Center for Buddhist Translation and Research, 2003.

Irvine, William. *A Guide to the Good Life.* Oxford: Oxford University Press, 2009.

James, William. *The Varieties of Religious Experience.* New York: Penguin American Classics, 2004.

Jennings, James. *The Little Red Book.* Center City, MN: Hazelden, 1986.

Jensen, George. *Storytelling in Alcoholics Anonymous: A Rhetorical Analysis.* Carbondale: Southern Illinois University Press, 2000.

Kierkegaard, Søren. *Concluding Unscientific Postscript.* Translated by David F. Swenson and Walter Lowrie. Princeton, NJ: Princeton University Press, 1968.

———. *Purity of Heart Is to Will One Thing.* Translated by Douglas V. Steere. New York: Harper & Row, 1956.

King, Alice. *High Sobriety: Confessions of a Drinker.* London: Orion, 2008.

Knapp, Caroline. *Drinking: A Love Story.* New York: Delta, 1996.

Kurtz, Ernest. *Not-God: A History of Alcoholics Anonymous.* Center City, MN: Hazelden, 1979.

Kurtz, Ernest, and Katherine Ketcham. *The Spirituality of Imperfection: Storytelling and the Search for Meaning.* New York: Bantam Books, 1994.

Lecky, William Edward. *History of European Morals: From Augustus to Charlemagne.* New York: George Braziller, 1955.

Levin, Jerome D. *Treatment of Alcoholism and Other Addictions: A Self-Psychology Approach.* Northvale, NJ: J. Aronson, 1987.

Levinas, Emmanuel. *The Levinas Reader.* Edited by Sean Hand. Malden, MA: Blackwell, 1997.

———. *Otherwise Than Being or Beyond Essence.* Translated by Alphonso Lingis. Den Haag: Martinus Nijhoff, 1981.

———. *Totality and Infinity: An Essay on Exteriority.* Translated by Alphonso Lingis. Pittsburgh: Duquesne University Press, 1969.

Lewis, C. S. *Surprised by Joy: The Shape of My Early Life.* Rev. ed. New York: Harcourt Brace, 1995.

Lonergan, Bernard. *Method in Theology.* New York: Herder and Herder, 1972.

Long, A. A. *Epictetus: A Stoic and Socratic Guide to Life.* Oxford: Clarendon Press, 2002.

Lusthaus, Dan. *Buddhist Phenomenology: A Philosophical Investigation of Yogācāra Buddhism and the Ch'Eng Wei-Shih Lun.* New York: Routledge Curzon, 2002.

Mackenzie, Catriona, and Natalie Stoljar, eds. *Relational Autonomy: Feminist Perspectives on Autonomy, Agency, and the Social Self.* Oxford: Oxford University Press, 2000.

Mackenzie, Catriona, and Kim Atkins, eds. *Practical Identity and Narrative Agency.* New York: Routledge, 2008.

Marcus Aurelius. *Meditations.* Translated by Martin Hammond. London: Penguin Books, 2006.

Marion, Jean-Luc. *God without Being: Hors-Texte.* Translated by Thomas A. Carlson. Chicago: University of Chicago Press, 1995.

Martin, Mike W., ed. *Self-Deception and Self-Understanding: New Essays in Philosophy and Psychology.* Lawrence: University of Kansas, 1985.

Maslow, Abraham. *Religions, Values, and Peak Experiences.* New York: Penguin Arkana, 1994.

Merleau-Ponty, Maurice. *Phenomenology of Perception.* Translated by Colin Smith. New York: Humanities Press, 1962.

———. *The Visible and the Invisible.* Translated by Alphonso Lingis. Evanston, IL: Northwestern University Press, 1975.

Miller, Jerome. *In the Throe of Wonder: Intimations of the Sacred in a Post-Modern World.* Albany: SUNY Press, 1992.

Miller, William Ian. *The Mystery of Courage.* Cambridge, MA: Harvard University Press, 2002.

Murdoch, Iris. *The Sovereignty of Good.* London: Routledge, 2001.

Narcotics Anonymous. *Narcotics Anonymous Basic Text.* 6th ed. Van Nuys, CA: Narcotics Anonymous World Services, Inc., 2008.

Nietzsche, Friedrich. *Sämtliche Werke: Kritische Studienausgabe.* Edited by Gorgio Colli and Mazzino Montinari. 15 vols. Munich: Walter de Gruyter, 1999.

———. *Sämtliche Werke: Der Will zur Macht.* Stuttgart: Alfred Kröner Verlag, 1996.

———. *The Anti-Christ.* Translated by R. J. Hollingdale. New York: Penguin Books, 1990.

———. *Beyond Good and Evil: Prelude to a Philosophy of the Future.* Translated by Walter Kaufmann. New York: Vintage Books, 1966.

———. *Daybreak.* Translated by R. J. Hollingdale. New York: Cambridge University Press, 1982.

———. *Ecce Homo.* Translated by Walter Kaufmann. New York: Vintage Books, 1989.

———. *The Gay Science.* Translated by Walter Kaufmann. New York: Vintage Books, 1974.

———. *Human, All Too Human.* Translated by R. J. Hollingdale. New York: Cambridge University Press, 1986.

———. "Nietzsche Contra Wagner." In *The Portable Nietzsche,* translated by Walter Kaufmann, 661–83. New York: Modern Library, 1968.

———. *On the Genealogy of Morals.* In *Basic Writings of Nietzsche,* translated by Walter Kaufmann, 437–600. New York: Modern Library, 1968.

———. *Thus Spoke Zarathustra.* Translated by Walter Kaufmann. New York: Viking Penguin, 1966.

———. *Twilight of the Idols.* Translated by R. J. Hollingdale. New York: Penguin Books, 1990.

———. *Untimely Meditations.* Translated by R. J. Hollingdale. New York: Cambridge University Press, 1989.

———. *The Will to Power.* Translated by Walter Kaufmann. New York: Vintage Books, 1968.

Nussbaum, Martha. *The Therapy of Desire: Theory and Practice in Hellenistic Ethics.* Princeton, NJ: Princeton University Press, 1994.

O'Connor, Flannery. *Collected Works.* New York: Library of America, 1988.

Peele, Stanton. *The Diseasing of America: How We Allowed the Recovery Zealots and the Treatment Industry to Convince Us We Are Out of Control.* San Francisco: Jossey-Bass, 1985.

Plato. *Great Dialogues of Plato.* Translated by W. H. D. Rouse. New York: Signet, 2008.

Poland, Jeffrey, and George Graham, eds. *Addiction and Responsibility (Philosophical Psychopathology).* Boston: MIT Press, 2011.

Potter, Andrew. *The Authenticity Hoax.* New York: Harper, 2010.

Putman, Daniel. *Psychological Courage.* Lanham, MD: University Press of America, 2004.

Richards, Norvin. *Humility.* Philadelphia: Temple University Press, 1992.

Ricoeur, Paul. "Life in Quest of Narrative." In *On Paul Ricoeur: Narrative and Interpretation,* edited by David Wood, 20–33. London: Routledge, 1992.

———. "Narrated Time." *Philosophy Today* 29, no. 4 (1985): 259–72.

———. *Oneself as Another.* Translated by Kathleen Blamey. Chicago: University of Chicago Press, 1992.

Robertson, Nan. *Getting Better: Inside Alcoholics Anonymous.* New York: Morrow, 1988.

Rohr, Richard. *Breathing under Water: Spirituality and the Twelve Steps.* Cincinnati: St. Anthony Messenger Press, 2011.

Sartre, Jean-Paul. *Being and Nothingness: A Phenomenological Essay on Ontology.* Translated by Hazel E. Barnes. New York: Pocket Books, 1992.

Schwartz, Benjamin Isadore. *The World of Thought in Ancient China.* Cambridge, MA: Belknap Press of Harvard University Press, 1985.

Seeburger, Francis F. *Addiction and Responsibility: An Inquiry into the Addictive Mind.* New York: Crossroad, 1993.

Sellars, John. *Stoicism.* Berkeley: University of California Press, 2006.

Seneca. *Letters from a Stoic.* Translated by Robin Campbell. London: Penguin Books, 2004.

———. *Moral Essays.* Translated by John W. Basore. Vol. 2. Cambridge, MA: Harvard University Press, 1932.

———. *The Stoic Philosophy of Seneca: Essays and Letters.* Translated by Moses Hadas. New York: W. W. Norton, 1968.

Shinran. *The Collected Works of Shinran.* Translated by Dennis Hirota. Vol. 1. Kyoto: Jōdo Shinshū Hongwangji-ha, 1997.

Smith, Huston. *The World's Religions: Our Great Wisdom Traditions.* San Francisco: Harper, 1991.

Taber, Julian. *Addictions Anonymous.* Bradenton, FL: BookLocker.com, Inc., 2008.

Thune, Carl. "Alcoholism and the Archetypal Past: A Phenomenological Perspective on Alcoholics Anonymous." *Journal of Studies on Alcohol* 38, no. 1 (1977): 75–88.

Tillich, Paul. *Dynamics of Faith.* New York: Harper, 1958.

Travis, Trysh. *The Language of the Heart: A Cultural History of the Recovery Movement from Alcoholics Anonymous to Oprah Winfrey.* Chapel Hill: University of North Carolina Press, 2009.

Van Fraassen, Bas. *The Scientific Image.* New York: Oxford University Press, 1980.

White, William L. *Slaying the Dragon: The History of Addiction Treatment and Recovery in America.* Bloomington, IL: Chestnut Health Systems, 1998.

Wilcox, Danny M. *Alcoholic Thinking: Language, Culture, and Belief in Alcoholics Anonymous.* Westport, CT: Praeger, 1998.

Wilkerson, May. "10 Best Sober Living Cities." *The Fix,* May 12, 2012. http://www.thefix.com/content/10-best-sober-living-cities.

Wilshire, Bruce. *Wild Hunger: The Primal Roots of Modern Addiction.* Lanham, MD: Rowman & Littlefield, 1998.

Wolf, Susan. *Freedom within Reason.* Oxford: Oxford University Press, 1993.

# Contributors

**Russell Anderson** is a doctoral candidate at McMaster University in Hamilton, Ontario, Canada. He works on problems in moral philosophy, specifically moral skepticism, as well as on conceptions of freedom and the place of science in thinking about morality. His research draws from a wide range of traditions and combines a commitment to understanding the genealogy of philosophical concepts with an eye to political and ethical concerns such as empathy, autonomy, and justice.

**Joseph Arel** teaches in the Philosophy Department at Northern Arizona University. He specializes in nineteenth- and twentieth-century Continental philosophy, especially Hegel, and is also interested in the philosophy of religion and aesthetics. He has delivered papers on Hegel's "Unhappy Consciousness" and dialectic of recognition, and his most recent publication is "The Necessity of Recollection in Plato's *Meno* and Derrida's *Memoirs of the Blind,*" which appeared in *Epoché.* He has recently finished co-translating a volume of Heidegger's lectures on Hegel.

**Gerald Cantu** received his PhD in philosophy from the University of California, Irvine, in June 2010. He specializes in ancient Greek philosophy and wrote his dissertation on the relationship between Plato's ethical and political thought in the *Republic.* He has taught courses in general ethics, the philosophy of sex and love, and environmental ethics.

**Corbin Casarez** is engaged in doctoral studies in philosophy at Loyola University Chicago. He taught most recently at the Valencia Campus of the University of New Mexico. He became interested in exploring vulnerability as a positive capacity while living, working, and volunteering in urban communities. He is especially interested in understanding the human capacity to pursue new possibilities despite seemingly insurmountable obstacles and repeated failures. His thinking on these and other matters has been heavily influenced by the work of Jacques Derrida, Emmanuel Levinas, and Giorgio Agamben.

**Jason Danner** received his PhD in religious studies from the University of Virginia. He specializes in phenomenology and Continental religious thought, particularly that of Søren Kierkegaard, Emmanuel Lévinas, and Jean-Luc Marion. His research explores the interaction of aesthetic attention and ethical responsibility in the development of a mature self. He has published and presented papers in a number of venues, including the American Academy of Religion.

**Stuart Grant** earned his doctorate in performance studies from the University of Sydney in Australia. He works in the Centre for Theatre and Performance at Monash University. His research centers on the phenomenology of performance. He is the author of works on place and performance, the audience, performance pedagogy, laughter, rhythm, speaking, and the application of phenomenological methodologies in the study of performance. He is currently working on two major projects: (1) genealogies and methodologies of phenomenology in the study of performance; and (2) the phenomenology of water. He has been in recovery for twenty-five years.

**John Houston** is an Assistant Professor of Philosophy at the College of Saint Benedict and Saint John's University in Collegeville, Minnesota. He specializes in ancient philosophy and ethics and has published work in the philosophy of religion. He earned his PhD at Purdue University, where he was also honored with an award for teaching excellence as an instructor of philosophy. John has presented research at a number of professional venues, including the Indiana Philosophical Association; the Alabama Philosophical Association; the Annual European Studies Conference at the University of Nebraska; and the D. B. Reinhart Institute for Ethics in Leadership at Viterbo University. In addition to his work as a scholar, John is a husband, the father of four children, and a national arm wrestling champion.

**Sean McAleer** (PhD, Syracuse) is Associate Professor of Philosophy at the University of Wisconsin–Eau Claire. He works primarily in moral theory, specializing in virtue ethics and the history of ethics. His work has appeared in the *American Philosophical Quarterly,* the *Pacific Philosophical Quarterly,* the *Journal of Ethics and Social Philosophy, Philosophy and Film,* and other journals.

**Jerome A. Miller** is Professor Emeritus at Salisbury University. He is the author of *The Way of Suffering: A Geography of Crisis* and *In the Throe of Wonder: Intimations of the Sacred in a Post-Modern World.* He has published widely in professional journals and occasionally in periodicals such as *America* and the *Washingtonian.* The issue of vulnerability that he raises in his essay here is one of the principal themes in a manuscript in progress, *In the Throe of the Future: A Traumatological Inquiry into History, Culture, and Normative Order.*

**Wamae Muriuki** taught most recently at the College of William & Mary. He received his PhD in comparative studies at the Ohio State University, with a focus on the religious traditions of Japan. His research interests include the Pure Land, Zen and esoteric traditions of Japanese Buddhism, Japanese religions, phenomenology of religion, and theories of affect. His dissertation addressed the use of affective language in Shinran's True Pure Land (Jōdō Shinshū) school of Japanese Buddhism, and its relationship to Merleau-Ponty's notion of "flesh."

**Matthew Pianalto** is an Associate Professor of Philosophy at Eastern Kentucky University, where he teaches courses in philosophy, applied ethics, and animal studies. His work has been published by *Inquiry,* the *Journal of Applied Philosophy,* the *Journal of Value Inquiry, Philosophical Investigations,* and the magazine *Philosophy Now.* His essay "Moral Courage and Facing Others" was awarded the inaugural Robert Papazian Essay Prize on Themes in Moral and Political Philosophy in 2012 and appears in the *International Journal of Philosophical Studies.* He is currently writing a book about patience.

**Nicholas Plants** is Professor of Philosophy at Prince George's Community College in Maryland. His principal interests are in philosophy of comedy, philosophy and literature, and theories of subjectivity and authenticity as they are developed in existentialism, hermeneutics, and postmodernism. He has presented papers on subjectivity, humor, and philosophical issues in film in a variety of professional venues. His work has been anthologized in *In Deference to the Other.*

**Morgan Rempel** received his PhD from the University of Toronto and is an Associate Professor in the Department of Philosophy and Religion at the University of Southern Mississippi in Hattiesburg. He is the author of *Nietzsche, Psychohistory, and the Birth of Christianity* (Greenwood Press, 2003), as well as articles on nineteenth- and twentieth-century European thought, genocide, ancient philosophy, philosophy and film, and the philosophy of religion.

**Mary K. Riley** is currently studying Chinese and comparative philosophy at the National University of Singapore. She holds an MA in philosophy from Kent State University, where her research focused on the affinities of Confucian and Pragmatic concepts of self. Her current research centers on Daoist ethics. Other interests include the cultural underpinnings of philosophic thought, ancient Greek philosophy, and twentieth-century French and German philosophy. She has presented papers on these topics at numerous conferences.

**Mary Jean Walker** completed her doctoral study in philosophy at Macquarie University, Australia, in 2010, where she is now an honorary associate. Her work on addiction studies to date has focused on moral psychology. Her research interests also include personal identity, narrative theory, and neuro-ethics. She is interested in exploring the links between each of these areas and issues relating to addiction.

**S. E. West** came to philosophy years after earning a bachelor of fine arts degree at Cooper Union. Her doctorate is from the University of Chicago, and she is currently Associate Professor of Philosophy at Delaware State University. West's work addresses the mutual informing of philosophy and psychoanalytic theory, with a particular interest in the relation between self-consciousness and the unconscious, the problem of interpretation, and the nature of human creativity. She is currently working on a new reading of Nietzsche's "perspectivism." She has been sober since February 7, 1998.

**J. Jeremy Wisnewski** is an Associate Professor of Philosophy at Hartwick College. He has written widely on issues in moral philosophy, applied ethics, and phenomenology. His books include *Wittgenstein and Ethical Inquiry, The Politics of Agency,* and *Understanding Torture.* He is the editor of the *Review Journal of Political Philosophy* and *Ethics and Phenomenology,* and he has also edited several books in Blackwell's Philosophy and Pop Culture series.

# Index